JOHN WATTS DE PEYSTER

JOHN WATTS DE PEYSTER
From a Photograph taken in December, 1896

John Watts de Peyster

BY

FRANK ALLABEN

AUTHOR OF "THE ANCESTRY OF LEANDER HOWARD
CRALL," "CONCERNING GENEALOGIES," "THE ARMS
AND PEDIGREE OF KINGDON-GOULD," "THE ARMS AND
PEDIGREE OF SEYMOUR;" EDITOR OF "AMERICAN
GENTRY."

VOLUME I

FRANK ALLABEN GENEALOGICAL COMPANY
Number Three West Forty-Second Street . . . New York

PREFACE

General John Watts de Peyster was one of the unique characters of his generation. He will be known to posterity as the first notable military critic produced by America—the first to treat the battles and campaigns of our great conflicts in the spirit of a true philosophy of the art of war.

He sprang from an old family, of Flemish origin, whose history has recently been traced back for seven hundred years. For centuries it was prominent in the public affairs of mediaeval Ghent. Transplanted to Holland, on account of religious persecution, it thrived in Middlebourg, Haarlem, and Amsterdam, during the brilliant period of Dutch supremacy, and then crossed to the New World. Here it had maintained a conspicuous eminence for seven generations when General de Peyster was born.

He became its most distinguished representative. Effecting widespread reforms in the Militia and in the Fire Departments of the State of New York, he rose to the rank of Brigadier-General, visited Europe as Military Agent of his State, became Adjutant-General, and, by a special act of the Legislature, was created Brevet Major-General for meritorious services before and during the Civil War.

He was a voluminous author. His works include poetry, drama, and innumerable monographs covering an almost incredible range of subjects. The most valuable, of a military or historical character, are notable for their erudition. General de Peyster's peculiar genius found complete expression in military criticism, military history, and military biography. A student of the Thirty Years' War, the wars of Frederick the Great, the campaigns of Napoleon, and those of the great captains of ancient times, the results of his researches on these subjects were published in hundreds of articles and monographs.

To Americans, however, his important contributions to the literature of our Revolutionary and Civil Wars are of paramount interest. We can scarcely find, outside of his writings, any treatment of our battles in the light of scientific military criticism. He was indefatigable in sifting the testimony of authorities, and in collecting and citing historical parallels his industry knew no bounds. Few in Europe, and none in America, have equaled him in the sagacious application of the lessons of the world's military history to elucidate the principles of practical strategy.

General de Peyster left in manuscript an account of his earlier years, and of several episodes of his later life. This autobiographical material has been incorporated in the present volumes. The reader will find in it a vivid and most interesting picture of New York at the beginning of the last century, from the standpoint of a wealthy young aristocrat.

The ideal biography will furnish a complete summary of genealogical antecedents—the many streams of ancestral inheritance, racial traits, tendencies, modes of thought, which, flowing down through multitudinous channels, gradually have converged and, at length, combined and blended their currents in one life history. Yet most "Lives" are unsatisfactory in this respect. A failure to appreciate the importance of ancestry, or the formidable nature of the task of collecting authentic data for the many paternal and maternal lines, induces most biographers to shirk this duty. The genealogical studies of the writer, however, coming to his aid, have enabled him to present a comprehensive outline of the ancestry of General de Peyster.

New York, 29 June, 1908. FRANK ALLABEN.

CONTENTS

VOLUME I

BOOK I

ANCESTRY

BOOK II

EARLY RECOLLECTIONS

CONTENTS

ILLUSTRATIONS

-

CHAPTER I

De Peysters figure notably in the history of mediaeval Ghent. Belonging to one of the old aristocratic families, they were leaders in civic and military affairs, as well as in the industrial activities which raised Ghent to wealth and fame.

In 1322 Heinric de Peyster was a burgher of Ghent; in 1325 was Captain, guarding one of the city gates; and in 1349, 1352 and 1356 was Schepen of the Parchons, a district of the city. Jan de Peyster, son of Captain Heinric, in 1349 was sent by the municipality of Ghent on an important mission to Brabant. The turbulent character of the times in which he lived is reflected in three incidents disclosed by the archives of the city. He fought a duel with Simon de Scoenkere, receiving wounds, and his opponent was compelled by the schepens to defray the cost of medical attendance. His daughter, Anne, was abducted by one Ricquaers, and the offence compounded in 1361, by a payment of five hundred livres. His son, Jan, was assassinated by three men. In 1365 the slayers were condemned to go on a pilgrimage in expiation of their crime.

In 1345 Pierre de Peyster was commissioned Captain of Archers. In 1382 Jan de Peyster was one of five envoys sent to Charles VI of France by the burghers of Ghent after the battle of Roosebeke.

Baudouin de Peyster, son of Jean, grandson of Willem, great-grandson of Jean, great-great-grandson of Baudouin, and great-great-great-grandson of Willem de Peyster, all gentlemen of Ghent, was Schepen of the Parchons in 1476, and in 1477 and 1478 Provost or Dean of the Goldsmiths' Guild. His son, Jean de Peyster was Schepen in 1481, 1489, 1495, 1497, 1500, and

1525, and Provost of the Guild of the Carpenters in 1488-1491, 1494, 1496, 1499, 1504, 1517, and 1521. In 1498 he was Elector of the Prince, the highest office in the city. The granddaughters of Baudouin, Baudouine and Marguerite, were nuns, the former becoming Superior of the Convent of St. Elizabeth at Ghent.

Othon or Oste de Peyster in 1489 was Provost of the Guild of the Carpenters, and in 1546 was Procurator or Solicitor at the Court of Flanders. Maitre Martin de Peyster, son of Maitre Martin de Peyster, grandson of Jean, and great-grandson of Lievin, in 1581 was Professor and Rector Magnificus at the Reformed University of Ghent. His brother, Reynier de Peyster, suffered the confiscation of his property in 1567 for having embraced the "new religion," was imprisoned in 1586, upon the capture of Ghent by the Duke of Parma, escaped and fled to Amsterdam in Holland.

Martin and Gilles de Peyster were engaged in maritime trade. The latter sold a vessel to one Tobast in 1565, and in 1567 obtained a merchant vessel from his brother.

The above are examples of the references to members of this large and flourishing family which abound in the archives of Ghent from 1148 to the Seventeenth Century. In the latter part of this period many of the de Peysters, becoming Protestants, found it expedient to emigrate.

In the Eighteenth Century we find de Peysters in Grammont and Oudenarde, East Flanders, including Sir Henri de Peyster and "Le Seigneur Pierre Franceois de Pester, son of Seigneur Louis, treasurer of the town of Oudenarde," in 1741. We also find de Peysters in Hainault. To this branch of the family belong Jean Baptiste de Pester, Lord of Locquerie, Warin, Maruais, and Ramiquies; Julien Ghislain de Pester, Count of Seneffe and Tournout, Baron de la Ferté de Pestre-en-Sologne, Councillor to the King of France, and Hyacinthe Julien Joseph, Count de Pestre de Bertinchamps.

SEAL OF JAN DE PEYSTER, GHENT, 1517
Drawn by George E. Bissell

Protestant branches of the family became established in Holland, in the cities of Amsterdam, Haarlem, Rotterdam, and Middlebourg, and in England. General de Peyster descended through one of these.

I Hugues de Peyster lived in Ghent in the early part of the Sixteenth Century. His second wife, Antoinette Poelvaech, died 21 March, 1525. From them an unbroken line, down to the de Peysters of New York, has been established by means of documents obtained from Ghent and Holland.

II Josse de Peyster, son of Hugues and Antoinette Poelvaech, appears in the Ghent records as heir to one-third of his mother's estates, 19 December, 1526. He deeded his share to his father, 10 November, 1529. He had issue: (1) Josse; (2) Jacques, mentioned in 1561 and 1563, who married Jeanne Amys; and (3) Jean, who married Jossine van Hecke, and died prior to 23 December, 1578, as we learn from a transaction between two of his sons.

III Josse de Peyster, eldest son of Josse de Peyster, appears in the Ghent records from 1552 to 1585. At one time he was guardian of the children of Othon de Peyster. In the year 1552, with his wife, Elizabeth Danckaert, he was asked to pardon Christian van Hauve, and the latter's wife, for an attempt to steal one of his children. He was married twice. By his first wife, Elizabeth Danckaert, daughter of Thierry Danckaert and Elizabeth van Hiesche, he had issue: (1) Josse; (2) Elizabeth; and (3) Jossine. By his second wife, he had a son, (4) Jacques.

IV Josse de Peyster, eldest son of Josse de Peyster and Elizabeth Danckaerts, on 7 September, 1587, appears in a transaction connected with the estate of his deceased father. On 21 August, 1596, as heir of his mother, he ceded an income to Ferdinand de Salines. The records of Ghent reveal his activity in various other directions. He married Joanne van de Voorde, the daughter of Pierre van de Voorde and Joosyne de Caluwe, and had issue: (1) Josse, of Ghent, Amsterdam, and Middlebourg; (2) Johannes; (3) Jacques; (4) Lievin, of Ghent, Haarlem, and Amsterdam; (5) Jonas, of Ghent and London; and (6) Marie, who married Jacques de Key of Haarlem.

Of these children, both Johannes and Jacques were ancestors of General de Peyster, Johannes forming a link in the direct paternal line, while Jacques was the grandfather of Catharina de Peyster, who married De Heer Abraham de Peyster, of the second generation in America.

This Jacques de Peyster, son of Josse de Peyster and Joanne van de Voorde, was living at Rouen, France, in 1639, and died there in 1676. He married Catharine de Lavoye. They had issue: (1) Sarah, who was born in 1629 and died in 1646; (2) Jacques, born in 1630, who married his cousin, Elizabeth Lequesne, and had a son, Jacques de Peyster, who, in turn, married his cousin, Adrienne Jacqueline, daughter of Pierre de Peyster; (3) Adrien, born in 1631, who was living in 1672, when he was mentioned in letters of his cousin, Isaac, to the latter's brother, Johannes de Peyster, of New York; (4) Samuel, of Rouen, France, born in 1634, died in 1703, who married, first his cousin, Catharine Lequesne, and second, Catharine de Bils, and by the latter marriage had children, Samuel and Catharine, born in Rotterdam; (5) Pierre; (6) William, born in 1638, and living in 1659, when he was mentioned in a letter of his cousin, Isaac de Peyster, to the latter's brother, Johannes de Peyster, of New York; (7) Jan, who was born in 1641; and (8) Catharine, who was born in 1645.

Pierre de Peyster, the son of Jacques de Peyster and Catharine de Lavoye, was born probably about 1636, and in 1660 was a law student at Harderwyk, Holland. He was for a time of Rouen, France, where some of his children were born, but about 1682 he settled at Amsterdam. He married Pietronella Van Kesteren. They had issue: (1) Adrienne Jacqueline, born about 1674, who married, first, her cousin, Jacques de Peyster, of Rouen, and, second, Abraham Van der Hulst, and died at Rouen in 1762, aged eighty-eight, her sole heir being Frederic de Peyster, of New York, grandson of her sister, Catharine, and De Heer Abraham de Peyster, the illustrious New York patriot; (3) Catharina, or Margareta Katrijn; (3) Johannes, who was born in Amsterdam, 30 November, 1685.

Margareta Katrijn de Peyster, as her name appears in her baptismal record, or Catharine, as it was generally written in New York, the second child of Pierre de Peyster and Pietronella Van Kesteren, was born in Amsterdam, Holland, 20 June, 1682. She became the wife of her second cousin, De Heer Abraham de Peyster, of New York.

V Johannes de Peyster, son of Josse de Peyster and Joanne van de Voorde, like his brothers and sister, removed from Ghent, probably on account of his Protestant views. He lived for some time in Amsterdam, where his son, Isaac, was born, and subsequently settled in Haarlem. He was a burgher of the latter city in 1621, and died there in 1648. By his wife, Jossine Martens, he had issue: (1) Johannes; (2) Abraham, who died in England, near London, in 1659; (3) Joanna, who married Bruynsteen; and (4) Isaac, of Amsterdam and Haarlem, whose son, Johan, was a student at Leyden University, and became a Counsellor-at-Law at Rotterdam, of which city he was Schepen in 1705 and 1706. A number of letters from this Johan to his cousins in New Netherland, with two from his father, Isaac, to the latter's brother, Johannes, of New Amsterdam, were long preserved among the de Peyster family papers in America, and certified translations still exist.

VI Johannes de Peyster, son of Johannes de Peyster and Jossine Martens, was born in Haarlem, Holland. He emigrated to New Amsterdam at least as early as 1647, and there married, 17 December, 1651, Cornelia Lubberts, also a native of Haarlem. Johannes de Peyster was a wealthy importing merchant, one of the eminent men of New Netherland. He was Schepen of

2

New Amsterdam under Governor Petrus Stuyvesant;
was Alderman of New York during the first English
administration, under Nicholls; was Burgomaster of
New Orange in 1673, when for a short time the city was
again under Holland; was subsequently Alderman and
Deputy Mayor under the English, and declined to accept
his appointment as Mayor, 15 October, 1677, because of
his imperfect mastery of the English tongue.

He had issue: (1) Abraham; (2) Johannes, baptized
3 August, 1653, who died in infancy; (3) Johannes,
baptized 7 September, 1654, who died young; (4) Maria,
baptized 7 September, 1660, who married, first, Paulus
Schrick, second, John Sprat, and third, David Provoost,
and one of whose daughters became the wife of James
Alexander, and the mother of William Alexander, titular
Earl of Stirling and Major-General in the patriot army
during the Revolutionary War; (5) Isaac, born and
baptized 16 April, 1662, who was Assistant Alderman
of the city of New York, served a number of years as a
member of the Provincial Legislature, and left a numerous progeny; (6) Jacob, baptized 23 December, 1663,
who died without issue; (7) Johannes, born 21
December, 1666, who was Captain in the Militia, Assistant Alderman, Mayor of the city of New York, and a
prominent member of the Provincial Legislature, some
of whose descendants were officers in the Continental
Army during the Revolution; (8) Cornelius, a Captain
in the Militia, Assistant Alderman of New York, and the
first Chamberlain of that city; and (9) Cornelia, baptized 4 December, 1678, who died without issue.

VII De Heer Abraham de Peyster, eldest son of
Johannes de Peyster and Cornelia Lubberts, was born
in New Amsterdam 8 July, 1657, and died in the same
city, then New York, 2 August, 1728. He was the most
illustrious of his race during the colonial period. An
opulent merchant, a civic magnate, and a social grandee,
he became an influential supporter of Leisler and the
intimate and trusted friend of the royal Governor,
Richard, Earl of Bellomont.

DE HEER ABRAHAM DE PEYSTER
From the Original Portrait, 1680

He was Alderman, Mayor, and Colonel in command of the New York County troops. A member of the King's Council, he subsequently became its President. He was Associate Justice of the Supreme Court, and eventually its Supreme Justice. After the death of the Earl of Bellomont, he was for a time Acting Governor of New York, in 1708 became Receiver-General of the Port, and from 1706 to 1721 was Treasurer of the Provinces of New York and New Jersey. An aristocrat of aristocrats, he nevertheless boldly stood for representative government in the Colony, in the days of Leisler. Against William Smith, Peter Schuyler, and Robert Livingston, he maintained that, in the absence of Lieutenant-Governor Nanfan, the members of the Council were equals, and that the Presiding Officer and Acting Governor should be elected by his colleagues of the Council.

He married, during a visit at Amsterdam, Holland, 5 April, 1684, his second cousin, Catharina de Peyster, whose descent has been shown. They had issue: (1) Johannes, who was born 12 July, 1685, and died in infancy; (2) Johannes, born 30 October, 1686, who died young; (3) Catharine, born 7 September, 1688, who married Philip Van Cortlandt, and became the mother of Pierre Van Cortlandt of Croton, Lieutenant-Governor of New York; (4) Abraham, who was born 7 November, 1690, and died young; (5) Johannes, born 3 April, 1692, and died young; (6) Abraham; (7) Elizabeth, twin of Abraham, born 28 August, 1696, who became the wife of the Honorable John Hamilton, Governor of the Province of New Jersey; (8) Mary, born 17 October, 1698, and died without issue; (9) Joanna, who was born 13 July, 1701, and who married her kinsman, Isaac de Peyster, but left no issue; (10) Maria, born 25 August, 1703, who died without issue; (11) Johannes, born 28 February, 1706, and died in infancy; (12) Pierre Guillaume, born 15 January, 1707, who married Catharine Schuyler; and (13) John, born 6 May, 1709, who left no issue.

Pierre Guillaume was the father of Colonel Arent Schuyler de Peyster, Commander of the region from the head of Lake Superior eastward to Lake Ontario, where he exercised over the northwestern Indians an influence only equalled by that of Sir William Johnson over the Six Nations. A grandson of Pierre Guillaume, Captain Arent de Peyster, visited unexplored parts of the Pacific, and was the discoverer of the de Peyster, Ellice, and other islands.

VIII   Abraham de Peyster, eldest surviving son of De Heer Abraham de Peyster and Catharina de Peyster, was born in New York, 28 August, 1696. He was a great merchant, like his father, whom he succeeded in the office of Treasurer of the Province, 2 June, 1721, holding it until his death, 17 September, 1767. He married, 1 July, 1722, Margaret, the eldest daughter of Jacobus Van Cortlandt.

There is extant an old document, containing a "List of Persons invited to, and present at, the Funeral of Abraham de Peyster, Treasurer of the Province of New York, 19th September, 1767," which is practically a register of the great names of the social and official New York of that day. The clergymen in attendance were the Reverend Messrs. Oglevie, Auchmuty, Ingliss, Provoost, Cooper, Ritsmoy, De Runda, and Ladley, while the pall-bearers were Judge Horsmanden, Judge William Smith, Colonel Stuyvesant, John Watts, Philip Livingston, Leonard Lispenard, and William Bayard.

Abraham de Peyster had issue: (1) James; (2) Abraham, born 5 October, 1723, who died young; (3) Catharine, born 3 December, 1724, who became the wife of John Livingston; (4) Eve, twin of Catharine, who died young; (5) Pierre, who was born 19 October, 1727, and who died in infancy; (6) Margaret, born 14 November, 1728, who married the Honorable William Axtell, member of the King's Council; (7) Pierre, born 27 March, 1730, who died in infancy; (8) Frederic, born 8 April, 1731, known as "The Marquis," because of his elegant presence and courtly manners, appointed

RESIDENCE OF DE HEER ABRAHAM DE PEYSTER
Pearl Street, New York

Treasurer of the Province of New York, 18 September, 1767, went to Rouen, France, to inherit an estate bequeathed to him by a kinswoman, and died unmarried in New York, in 1773; (9) Eve, born 2 January, 1733, who died unmarried at an advanced age; (10) Mary, born 26 August, 1735, who was the wife of Doctor John Charlton, an eminent physician; and (11) Elizabeth, born 11 September, 1737, who married Matthew Clarkson, Esquire.

IX James de Peyster, the eldest son of Abraham de Peyster and Margaret Van Cortlandt, was born in New York City, 6 February, 1726, and died at one of his country estates, in Jamaica, Long Island, 27 July, 1799. He was one of the most notable New York merchants of his day, the proprietor of an extensive maritime fleet, which brought rich cargoes into New York from the ports of all the world. A Loyalist during the Revolution, his ships were swept from the seas by American and French privateers, but, in spite of these disastrous inroads upon it, he died in possession of a fortune large for his day.

He married Sarah, the daughter of the Honorable Joseph Reade, a member of the King's Council, and had issue: (1) Margaret, born 18 January, 1749, who married Colonel Thomas James, at one time Commander-in-Chief of the Royal Artillery in North America, and afterwards in command at Gibraltar; (2) Ann Adriana, born 30 April, 1751, who died young; (3) Abraham, born 18 February, 1753, who was a Captain in the British Army during the Revolution, and later became Treasurer of New Brunswick, where he died, leaving descendants, whose male line has become extinct; (4) Joseph Reade, born 8 April, 1754, who left no male descendants; (5) James, born 16 May, 1755, who died 5 June of the same year; (6) Ann, born 24 August, 1756, who died unmarried; (7) James, born 3 December, 1757, who, at the age of twenty, was commissioned Captain-Lieutenant, served under the King during the Revolution, and died unmarried at Lincelles, Flanders,

19 August, 1793, being then First Lieutenant of Artillery; (8) Frederic; (9) Lawrence Reade, born 21 February, 1760, who died 24 June, 1761; (10) Sarah, born 20 September, 1761; (11) Lawrence Reade, born 9 March, 1763, who died 20 January, 1771; (13) Mary Reade, born 18 September, 1765, who married and left issue; and (14) Elizabeth, born 17 January, 1768, who married Doctor William Hamersley, and left issue.

X   Captain Frederic de Peyster, son of James de Peyster and Sarah Reade, and the eldest whose male descendants are living, was born in New York City, 10 December, 1758. Like his brothers, Captain Abraham and Captain James de Peyster, he fought under King George during the Revolution. At the age of eighteen he was commissioned Captain of the Axtell Guards or Nassau Blues, an independent company of Long Island. Later on he became a Captain of the Royal New York Volunteers, and distinguished himself in the Highlands and at Eutaw Springs. After the Revolution he resided for a time in St. John, New Brunswick, subsequently returning to New York. He died in 1834. He became the head of the family by reason of the deaths of his elder brothers without surviving male issue.

His first wife, who died 1 April, 1801, at the age of twenty-eight, was Helen, only daughter of General Samuel Hake, claimant of the title of Lord Hake, and at one time Commissary-General of the British forces in North America. Captain de Peyster's second wife, who died in 1857, was Ann, only daughter of Gerard G. Beekman, Esq., and granddaughter of Lieutenant-Governor Pierre Van Cortlandt.

Captain Frederic de Peyster had issue, six sons by his first marriage, and seven daughters and one son by his second marriage, as follows: (1) Captain James Ferguson, of whom a brief account is given below; (2) Robert Gilbert Livingston, born 27 June, 1795; (3) Frederic; (4) Abraham, born 18 June, 1798, who died unmarried in 1836; (5) Samuel Hake, born about 1800, who died in infancy; (6) Captain Frederic Augustus, who was

BELLOMONT REVIEWING THE NEW YORK CITY TROOPS
FROM THE RESIDENCE OF THEIR COMMANDER,
COLONEL ABRAHAM DE PEYSTER

From a Painting in Oil owned by the late General de Peyster .

Commander of a packet line from New York to Liverpool, was Governor of Sailors' Snug Harbor, Staten Island, and had children, Maria Roosevelt, Richard Varick de Peyster, who was a Union soldier in the Civil War, Justine Watts, wife of Charles Fox Hovey, of Boston, Augustus de Peyster, of Indianapolis, and Robert Gilbert Livingston de Peyster, of Indianapolis; (7) Joanna Cornelia, who was born 7 March, 1804, and who married Robert Whitmarsh; (8) Ann Frederica, who was born 7 June, 1805, and died unmarried; (9) Margaret James, born 9 June, 1806, who died unmarried in 1867; (10) Mary Elizabeth, born 14 April, 1809, who died unmarried in 1892; (11) Pierre Van Cortlandt, born 11 July, 1814, who died unmarried 1 April, 1854; (12) Catharine M. Van Cortlandt, who was born 2 October, 1818, married Benjamin Hazard Field and was the mother of Cortlandt de Peyster Field and Florence Van Cortlandt Field, the latter the wife of David Wolfe Bishop, of New York; (13) a daughter, who died in infancy; and (14)- a daughter, who died in infancy.

Captain James Ferguson de Peyster, eldest son of Captain Frederic de Peyster and Helen Hake, was born 2 February, 1794. Entering the United States Army at the age of nineteen, during the War of 1812, he was made First Lieutenant, 30 March, 1814, and Captain, 14 April of the same year. He was a leader in the social life and public affairs of New York, was a Governor of the New York Hospital, President of the New York Dispensary, for nearly forty years Trustee of the Bank for Savings, Treasurer for nearly sixty years of St. Michael's Church, and Treasurer for fifty years of the Society for Religion and Learning, having succeeded his father in this office. He died in New York, 13 June, 1874. By his first wife, Susan Maria, the daughter of Matthew Clarkson of New York, he had a daughter, Susan Maria Clarkson de Peyster, who married Robert Edward Livingston of Clermont, New York; and by his second marriage, with Frances Goodhue Ashton, he had issue: (1) Frederic James; (2) Jacob Ashton;

(3) Frances Goodhue; (4) Walter, and (5) Helen
Livingston Hake.

XI Frederic de Peyster, son of Captain Frederic de
Peyster and Helen Hake, was born in New York, 11
November, 1796. While a student at Columbia College,
during the War of 1812, he organized and became the
Captain of a company called the "College Greens."
He graduated from Columbia College with the degree
of Bachelor of Arts, and from the Law School with that
of Doctor of Laws. In 1819 he was admitted to the
Bar. He was Master of Chancery in New York City
from 1820 to 1837. He was successively Ensign, Lieu-
tenant, Captain, and Brigade Major of the Tenth
Brigade, New York Militia, was Aide-de-Camp to Major-
General Fleming, and was Volunteer Aide, with the
rank of Colonel, to Governor De Witt Clinton. He was
also Governor Clinton's Military Secretary for the
Southern District of New York.

At the time of his death, 17 August, 1882, it is stated
that he had been connected officially with more clubs and
societies than any other person in New York. He was
Trustee of the Leake and Watts Orphan House, Manager of the New York Bible Society, Director of the
New York Institution for the Instruction of the Deaf
and Dumb, Manager of the Home for Incurables, and
Chairman of its Finance and Building Committee, Vice-
President of the Association of the Alumni of Columbia,
and Chairman of its Standing Committee; was an
original incorporator, a Director, and Vice-President of
the New York Society for the Prevention of Cruelty to
Children; was a founder, Manager, Treasurer, and President of the St. Nicholas Society; was a founder, Trustee,
and President of the St. Nicholas Club; was Corresponding Secretary, Foreign Secretary, Second Vice-
President, and President of the New York Historical
Society; was Chairman of the Board of Trustees and
President of the New York Society Library; was a
Trustee of the Free School Society, an honorary member
of the Mercantile Association of New York, an honorary

Fellow of the Royal Historical Society of Great Britain, a Corresponding Member of the New England Historic Genealogical Society, and an honorary member of the Historical Societies of Massachusetts, Pennsylvania, Maryland, Wisconsin, Florida, Chicago, and Buffalo. He was Senior Officer of the Vestry of the Church of the Ascension, New York.

His published works include Early Political History of New York, 1865; The Moral and Intellectual Influence of Libraries, 1866; The Culture Demanded by the Age, 1869; William the Third as a Reformer, 1874; The Representative Men of the English Revolution, 1876; The Life and Administration of the Earl of Bellomont, 1879; and A Review of the Administration of Governor Colonel Benjamin Fletcher, published posthumously.

He married, 15 May, 1820, in the front parlor of Number Three, Broadway, New York, Mary Justina, the youngest daughter of the Honorable John Watts, by whom he had an only child, General John Watts de Peyster. Mrs. de Peyster died soon after the birth of the latter, and Frederic de Peyster married, second, Mrs. Hone, née Maria Antoinette Kane.

XII John Watts de Peyster, only child of Frederic de Peyster and Mary Justina Watts, was born 9 March, 1821, in the front room on the second story of the house of his maternal grandfather, Number Three, Broadway, New York City—to quote General de Peyster's own words, in the record in one of his Bibles, "on Thursday, at noon, the day being one of the finest it is possible to conceive."

His mother having died, 28 July, 1821, a few months after his birth, he was brought up in the home of his grandfather, John Watts, where his father also resided. During the General's childhood he was in the care of a nurse, Mrs. Frances Trainque.

He was married in New York City, at eleven A. M., 2 March, 1841, by the Rev. Henry Anthon, D. D., to Estelle Livingston, the daughter of John Swift Livings-

ton and Anna Maria Martina Thompson. Mrs. de
Peyster's mother was a native of Savannah, Georgia, the
daughter of Captain William Thompson of the Continental Army. John Swift Livingston was a descendant
of the first Lord of Livingston Manor.

The General and Mrs. de Peyster had the following
children: (1) John Watts; (2) Frederic; (3) Estelle;
(4) Johnston Livingston; and (5) Maria Livingston.

John Watts de Peyster, Junior, the eldest child, was
born at One Hundred and Six, Leonard Street, New
York, 2 December, 1841. He was a Union soldier,
serving as First Volunteer Aide-de-Camp to his cousin,
Major-General Philip Kearney, in the spring campaign
of 1862, afterwards as Second Lieutenant of the Fourth
Regiment of New York Cavalry, and later as Major of
the First Regiment of New York Volunteer Artillery. He
was made Brevet Colonel of the United States Volunteers
for distinguished services at Chancellorsville, and Brevet
Colonel of the New York Volunteers. His father
recorded the following death-notice in one of his Bibles:

"My glorious soldier-son, Major and Brevet Colonel,
John Watts de Peyster, Jr., in my house, 59 East 21st
Street, New York, on the night of the 11th-12th April,
1873, Saturday, April 12th, 4¾ A. M., of atrophy or
consumption, attributable to his services in the field, but
more especially in command of the Artillery of the
Second Division, of the Sixth Corps, Army of the
Potomac, at Fredericksburg, in the campaign of Chancellorsville. He was the first to lie in my new vault in the
rear of St. Paul's Church, Tivoli. Peace to his ashes!
To whomsoever passes over the arch can be addressed
the words first applied to Field Marshal Mercy at Nord-
lingen, 'Sta Viator heroem calces.'"

Frederic de Peyster, second son of the General, was
born at Seventy-three Leonard Street, New York, 13
December, 1842. He was a Union soldier, Assistant
Surgeon to the Eighth New York State Militia in 1861,
being, after his participation in the Battle of Bull Run,
the only surgeon who returned with his regiment to New

York. He was later Second Lieutenant of the Eighth
New York State Militia, assigned to medical duty as
Assistant Surgeon. During the Peninsular Campaign
of 1862 he was assigned as Assistant Surgeon to the
Fifty-third Regiment, "Enfants Perdus." He was made
Brevet Major, United States Army, and Brevet Colonel
of the New York Volunteers, for meritorious and faithful
services at Bull Run, first, 21 July, 1861, and on the
Peninsula in the summer of 1862. He was married 7
September, 1864, to Mary, only daughter of Clermont
Livingston, and great-granddaughter of Chancellor
Robert R. Livingston. He had issue: (1) Mary, who
was born 22 December, 1865, and died 9 September,
1874; (2) Clermont Livingston, born 12 June, 1867,
who studied at Harvard and at Oxford, and who died,
unmarried, 2 December, 1889.

Estelle Livingston de Peyster, third child of General
de Peyster, was born at "the 'Lodge,' at 'Snake Point,'
Red Hook, Duchess County," New York, 7 June, 1844.
She was married, 16 November, 1870, to James Boorman
Toler, and died 12 December, 1889, the death of her
husband following on the morning of the day of her
funeral, 16 December. They had an only child, John
Watts de Peyster Toler, born 17 September, 1871.

Johnston Livingston de Peyster, youngest son of
General de Peyster, was born at the Lodge, Snake Point,
Red Hook, Duchess County, New York, 14 June, 1846.
He was a Union soldier, being commissioned as First
Lieutenant of the New York State Artillery in 1864,
and Captain of the Ninety-sixth New York Volunteer
Infantry in 1865. He was made Brevet Colonel of the New
York Volunteers for hoisting the "first real American
flag" over Richmond, on the morning of Monday, 3 June,
1865. He died in Tivoli, 27 May, 1903. He married 29
November, 1871, Julia Anna Toler, sister of his brother-
in-law, James Boorman Toler, and daughter of William
E. Toler. They had the following children: (1) Esther
Estelle, who married Edward Sturges Hosmer, in 1905;
(2) Mary Justina, who married Howard Townsend

Martin, in 1906; and (3) Carola Anna, who married Garrett Berg Kip, in 1903.

Maria Livingston, the youngest child of General de Peyster, was born in "the main Mansion, Snake Point, Tivoli, Red Hook, Duchess County," 7 July, 1852. She died 24 September, 1857. She was buried in the Watts family vault, Trinity Churchyard, New York. "There," says the record in her father's Bible, "the mortal remains of my angel baby lie on the bosom of the relics of my angel mother. She was a precious child, a peace-maker, the light of our household, the apple of her parents' eyes." Subsequently she was re-buried in General de Peyster's family vault, St. Paul's Church, Tivoli.

Outliving his wife, who died 2 August, 1898, and all his children, General de Peyster died 4 May, 1907, in his eighty-seventh year, at his town-house, Fifty-nine, East Twenty-first Street, New York, on the site of "Rose Hill," the country seat of his great-grandfather, John Watts, Senior.

The de Peyster Arms: Argent, two sheep grazing under a linden tree, proper.

Crest: A linden tree, proper.

Motto: Depasco.

CHAPTER II

I   John Watt, of Edinburgh, Scotland, was Deacon of Deacons, Deacon-Convenor, or Chairman, of the entire allied Trades, Crafts, or "City Corporations," of Edinburgh, from 1584 to 1586. In the old records he is styled "his Majesty's Standard Bearer," and became famous in the religious riot of 17 December, 1596, by his boldness in quelling the mob which was marching upon the Tolbooth, where the King and his Council were sitting. He saved James VI of Scotland,—later James I of England,—from the infuriated populace, and at the head of the Crafts escorted the King to his royal palace at Holyrood. James swore that "had it not been for the loyalty of the Crafts he would have burned the Town of Edinburgh, and salted it with salt," so that Watt may also be regarded as the preserver of the city.

He was elected Collector in 1583-1584, and Burgess, 19 April, 1587. He owned "Rose Hill," formerly a mile or more west of Edinburgh, but brought, by the growth of the city, within its limits, the site of the old house now being occupied by the Morrison Street Mineral Depot of the Caledonian Railway. Watt also owned a place on the Burgh Moor, as is attested by a charter dated 4 August, 1592. Here he was assassinated, 17 April, 1601. One Alexander Slummon was tried for the murder, but was acquitted.

The will of John Watt was recorded 29 July, 1601, having been offered for probate by his widow, Janet Boyd, in behalf of "his lawful bairns," John, Margaret, Janet, and Katherine. It appears, therefore, that she was his second wife. The name of the mother of his children we learn from the reference to her husband's appointment as Burgess, 19 April, 1587, which is as follows: "John Watt was made Burgess of this Burgh by richt of Euphame Porteous his Spouse, lawful daughter to umquihile Patrick Porteous, Merchant of the Burgh."

II John Watt, the son of John Watt and Euphame, or Euphemia, Porteous, is only known to us by the above reference. We do not know whom he married, nor the dates of his marriage and death.

III Adam Watt, of "Rose Hill," must have been born not later than 1620. He was Commissary of Peebles and Writer to the Signet. On 18 December, 1652, a bond for £2735, due him, was executed by Sir James Campbell of Lawers. This bond was registered in Court Books of Justice, 4 March, 1654. It was assigned, 3 December, 1669, to Patrick Watt, one of Adam Watt's sons, and by assignation registered in Books of Council of Session, 11 November, 1680. Adam Watt had two sons: (1) John; and (2) Patrick, whose will, confirmed 23 March, 1698, shows that he died in 1689 or 1690, and was "brother of Mr. John Watt of Rosehill."

IV John Watt, of "Rose Hill," the son of Adam Watt, died in 1679, as we learn from the "Testament of John and Patrick Watt," confirmed 20 August, 1694. Its sole executor was Adam Watt, "lawful son of Mr. J. Watt." The document shows that John Home of Huttonbell owed John and Patrick Watt £751, 3s., 6d., and that Alexander, Earl of Moray, owed £193, 17s., 8d., with £234 of interest, as shown by bond granted by him to Adam Watt, Writer to the Signet, and father of Mr. John Watt. Thus we get three generations: (1) Adam Watt, Writer to the Signet; (2) his son, John Watt, of "Rose Hill"; (3) the latter's son, Adam Watt.

These facts, gathered by means of a research prosecuted at Edinburgh a few years ago, agree perfectly with the account of his ancestry left by the Honorable John Watts, Senior, of New York. From this record we learn that John Watt of "Rose Hill," the father of the Emigrant, had the following issue: (1) Adam, executor of his father's will, who died about 1736, leaving three children, who died unmarried, (i) John, who visited the family of John Watts, Senior, in New York, (ii) Adam, Professor of Humanities in Edinburgh, and (iii) Margaret; (2) Robert; (3) John, who died at Philadelphia, unmarried, about 1707; (4) Margaret, who married Sir Walter Riddell, Bart.; and (5) Alice, who married, first, Mr. Scott, of Fife, and, second, "Mr. Calderwood, Lord Goltown, of the Sessions," as he is called in John Watts' record.

V   Robert Watts, who added a final "s" to his name, was born in 1680 at Edinburgh, or at "Rose Hill," his father's estate, and was the son of John Watt, of Rose Hill.   When about twenty years old he visited New York, and then returned to Scotland.   A little later he returned, and settled in this country, although his son, John Watts, in his family record, stated that it was his father's intention to make his permanent home in Scotland, this intention being relinquished after the death of two of his children, in Edinburgh, soon after the family's arrival there.

He married, in 1706, Mary, the daughter of William Nicoll, Lord of the Nicoll Manor, at Islip, Long Island. They had issue: (1) Ann, born about 1707, who died at Edinburgh about 1724; (2) Margaret, born about 1709, who died at Edinburgh; (3) Mary, born in May, 1713, who married in March, 1732, Captain Richard Riggs, and died in 1736; and (4) John.

Robert Watts died at New York, 21 September, 1750, "about 72 years of age," as his son's record states.

VI   The Honorable John Watts, son of Robert Watts and Mary Nicoll, was born in New York, 5 April, 1715. He was one of the most conspicuous figures in New York life during the decades preceding the War of Independence.   His town-house was on Pearl Street, near Moore, while his country seat, bearing the name, "Rose Hill," in memory of the ancestral estate in Scotland, lay between Broadway, the East River, Twenty-eighth, and Twenty-first Streets.   Lofty elms long stood at the entrance of the estate, at Fourth Avenue and Twenty-eighth Street. The New York home of his great-grand-son, General John Watts de Peyster, was erected on a portion of this estate.

John Watts married, in July, 1742, Ann de Lancey, the daughter of Stephen de Lancey and Anna Van Cortlandt. Mrs. Watts' position in the social affairs of old New York was as brilliant, perhaps, as that of her distinguished husband in public life. He was a Member of the Assembly; served on the commission to settle the question of the boundary between New York and New Hampshire; was one of the Colonial Committee of Correspondence, for many years a Member of the King's Council, and Attorney-General of the Province of New York, 1762-1763. He was one of the founders, and the first President, of the New York Hospital, a founder, in 1752, of the New York Merchants' Exchange, a founder and incorporator of the New York Society Library, and for many years one of its Board of Trustees.

At the outbreak of the Revolution John Watts placed himself on the side of the English government. This, of course, aroused much indignation, and two of his mansions were burned. Much of his property was confiscated, and he sailed for England, 4 May, 1775. He died in Wales in 1789. He and his wife had issue: (1) Robert, born 23 August, 1743, who married the daughter of Major-General William Alexander, titular Earl of Stirling; (2) Ann, born 20 September, 1744, who married the Honorable Archibald Kennedy, and became the Countess of Cassilis; (3) Stephen, born 30 July, 1746, who died in infancy; (4) Susanna, twin of Stephen, who died in childhood; (5) John; (6) Susanna, born 24 February, 1750-1751, who married Philip Kearny, becoming the mother of Major-General Stephen Watts Kearny, and the grandmother of Major-General Philip Kearny; (7) Mary, born 27 October, 1753, who became the wife of Sir John Johnson, Bart.; (8) Stephen, born 24 December, 1754, who was a Major in the British army during the Revolution; (9) Margaret, born 14 December, 1755, who married Major Robert Leake,

JOHN WATTS, SENIOR

and died in 1836; and (10) James, born in 1756, who
died in childhood of the small-pox.

VII The Honorable John Watts, Junior, the son of
John Watts and Ann de Lancey, was born 27 August,
1749. He married his first cousin, Jane de Lancey,
daughter of Peter de Lancey and Elizabeth Colden. He
was a man of great wealth for the period in which he
lived, a great part of the Watts family estates having
escaped confiscation at the Revolution, and was able to
re-purchase part of his father's domain of Rose Hill.
He gave a fortune in the founding and endowment of
the Leake and Watts Orphan House. He was a founder,
and later the President, of the New York City Dispensary.

John Watts, Junior, was the last Royal Recorder of
the City of New York, occupying this office from 1774
to 1777. After the Revolution he held important offices
under the new Government. He was elected for a number
of terms to the State Assembly, of which body he was
Speaker from 1791 to 1794. He was a Member of
Congress from 1793 to 1795. In 1806 he became First
Judge of Westchester County, his country home, "Wood-
lands," being near New Rochelle. He died 3 September,
1836, and was buried in Trinity Church-yard, New York
City.

His issue was as follows: (1) John, born in New
York about 1775, who died unmarried; (2) Henry, born
in New York about 1777, who died unmarried; (3)
Robert, born in New York about 1780, known as the
handsomest man in town, served in the War of 1812 as
Captain of United States Infantry, was on the staff of
General King with the rank of Major, and died unmar-
ried, in 1830, having taken the name of Leake, thereby
securing a fortune left him by John George Leake, an
intimate friend of his father; (4) George, born in New
York about 1783, an officer in the War of 1812, who
distinguished himself especially at the Battle of
Chippewa, 5 July, 1814, as an Aide-de-Camp to General
Winfield Scott, and who died unmarried; (5) Stephen

2

Watts, born in New York about 1785, who died unmarried; (6) Ann, born in New York about 1787, who died unmarried; (7) Jane, born in New York about 1790, who died unmarried; (8) Elizabeth, born in New York about 1793, who married Henry Laight; (9) Susan, born in New York about 1795, who married her cousin, Philip Kearny, and became the mother of Major-General Philip Kearny; and (10) Mary Justina.

VIII Mary Justina Watts, the daughter of the Honorable John Watts and Jane de Lancey, was born in New York, 26 October, 1801. She was married in her father's home, Number Three, Broadway, New York, 15 May, 1820, to Frederic de Peyster. She died 28 July, 1821, leaving one son,

IX John Watts de Peyster.

The Watts Arms: Argent, an oak tree, growing out of a mount in base, vert,—over all, on a bar, azure, a crescent, between two mullets of the first.

Crest: A cubit arm, erect, issuing from a cloud, in the hand a branch of olive, all proper.

Motto: Servire forti non deficit telum.

MRS. FREDERIC DE PEYSTER, NÉE MARY JUSTINA WATTS
From a marble bust executed by George E. Bissell

CHAPTER III

The reputed descent of Étienne de Lancey, the first of the name in America, from the noble French house of de Lancy, as gathered from family tradition and French records, is as follows:

I Guy de Lancy, Vicomte de Laval et de Nouvion, was living about 1432. He married Anne de Marcilly.

II Jean de Lancy, son of Guy de Lancy and Anne de Marcilly, was the second Vicomte, and lived about 1436.

III Jean de Lancy, son of Jean de Lancy, was the third Vicomte, and was living in 1470. In 1484 he was Deputy to the States General at Tours. He fought at the battles of Fournoue and Ravenna.

IV Charles de Lancy, the son of Jean de Lancy, was the fourth Vicomte, and was living in 1525. He married, first, A. Nicole St. Pére, and, second, Marie de Villiers. He had issue: (1) a daughter, by his first marriage, who married Antoine Pioche, of Laon; (2) Charles de Lancy; and (3) Christophe, Seigneur de Raray, who died in 1584.

V Charles de Lancy, the son of Charles de Lancy and Marie de Villiers, was the fifth Vicomte, and was living in 1535. He married, 15 April, 1534, Isabel Branche. They had issue: (1) Charles, the sixth Vicomte, who fought at Ivry, and who married, first, 21 July, 1569, Madeleine Le Brun, and, second, 15 January, 1593, Claude de May; (2) Jacques; (3) Claude; and (4) Barbe.

VI Jacques de Lancy was the second son of Charles de Lancy, the fifth Vicomte de Laval et de Nouvions, and of Isabel Branche.

VII Seigneur Jacques de Lancy was the son of Jacques de Lancy. He married Marguerite, the daughter of Pierre Bertrand, of Caen, and of the latter's first wife, the Demoiselle Firel.

VIII Étienne, or Stephen, de Lancey was the son of Seigneur Jacques de Lancy and Marguerite Bertrand. He was born at Caen, 24 October, 1663. At the Revocation of the Edict of Nantes, in 1685, he fled to Holland, and thence to London. As an English subject he sailed, 20 March, 1686, for New York, where he arrived, 7 June, 1686. Here he became a wealthy merchant, and from the first was prominent in the affairs of the town and the province.

In 1691 he was Alderman of New York. He represented the city and county of New York in the Provincial Assembly from 1702 to 1715, except during the year 1709, and from 1725 to 1737. He was a vestryman of Trinity Church, and, in 1716, contributed £50 to buy a clock for the church. He was also a benefactor of the French Church in New York—"L'Église du Saint-Esprit." One of his most important acts of public benevolence was his introduction, in association with John Moore, of the use of fire-engines in New York. This was in 1731. He died in 1741.

In his will, dated 4 March, 1735, and proved 24 November, he mentions his "mansion house, * * * in the street commonly called the Broadway, in New York, to the northward of Trinity Church," which he bequeathes to his wife during her life-time. This "mansion house" occupied the block between Broadway, Thames, Cedar, and Greenwich Streets. On Stephen de Lancey's marriage, his father-in-law had presented him and his wife with the lot on the corner of Broad and Pearl Streets, the present site of the famous Fraunce's Tavern. In his will Stephen de Lancey states that he has already provided for his son, James, and his daughter, Susanna, and makes bequests to his other children. The legacy to his son, Peter, was "all my mills, mill houses, mill boat, farm and lands situate in Westchester County, upon the Bronx river." He gives Peter also £3000, and to his daughter, Anne, £500, as well as her interest in £12000, invested for his youngest children in the firm of Stephen De Lancey and Company.

Stephen de Lancey had a sister, the wife of John Barberie, of New York. The latter, a Member of the Council of the Province, was a merchant, in partnership with his brother-in-law.

Stephen de Lancey married, 19 January, 1700, Anna, the daughter of De Heer Stephanus Van Cortlandt. They had issue: (1) James, of whom an account is given below; (2) Peter; (3) Oliver, of whom a description follows; (4) Stephen, who died unmarried; (5) John, who died unmarried; (6) Susan, who became the wife of Admiral Sir Peter Warren; and (7) Ann, who married Honorable John Watts, Senior.

James de Lancey, the son of Stephen de Lancey and Anna Van Cortlandt, was born 27 November, 1703. He studied at Corpus Christi College, Cambridge University, and studied law at the Temple, in London. Returning to New York in 1725, he was from 1729 to 1733 a Member of the Provincial Council; in 1733 was appointed Chief Justice of New York, which office he held until his death; in 1753 became Lieutenant Governor,—the same year, by the death of the Governor, Sir Danvers Osborn, becoming Governor until 1755; in 1757 became Acting Governor, remaining such until his death; in 1754 presided over the famous Congress of Albany, composed of delegates from all the Colonies and from the various Indian Tribes; and in the same year, 1754, signed the charter of King's College, now Columbia University. James de Lancey married Anne, the daughter of Caleb Heathcote, Lord of Scarsdale Manor. He died 30 July, 1760.

Oliver de Lancey, the son of Stephen de Lancey and Anna Van Cortlandt, was born in 1717. He served in the French and Indian War; in 1759 was elected to the House of Assembly; and in 1760 became a Member of the Council. At the outbreak of the War for Independence he placed himself on the side of the British, and, in 1776, was made Brigadier General in the Royal Army, being in command of three battalions, known as de Lancey's Battalions. He served until the end of the War, and at its close settled in England, where he died in 1785. General Oliver de Lancey married Phelia Franks, of Philadelphia.

IX   Peter de Lancey, the son of Stephen de Lancey and Anna Van Cortlandt, was born 26 August, 1705. He was a Member of the Assembly from Westchester County for many years, and was High Sheriff of Westchester County. As has been shown, he was a principal legatee in his father's will. He died 17 October, 1770. He married, 7 January, 1737-1738, Elizabeth, the daughter of Governor Cadwallader Colden. Their issue was: (1) Stephen, a lawyer, who was Recorder of Albany, and Clerk of Tyron County; (2) John, a Member of the Assembly from Westchester County, High Sheriff of that County, who married Miss Wickham; (3) Peter, who became a lawyer of Charleston, South Carolina; (4) Anne, who married John Coxe, of Philadelphia; (5) Alice, who married Ralph Izard, of South Carolina, a Delegate to the Continental Congress, 1780-1783, and United States Senator from South Carolina, 1789-1795; (6) Elizabeth, who died unmarried; (7) James, High Sheriff of Westchester County, a Tory during the Revolution, who headed a troop of light-horse, going at the close of the War to Nova Scotia, where he was appointed, in 1794, a Member of the Council, and where he died, in 1800; (8) Oliver, of West Farms, who resigned his Lieutenancy in the British Navy because of his loyalty to the American cause, at the time of the Revolution, and who died at Westchester, 4 September, 1820; (9) Susanna, who married Colonel Thomas Barclay; (10) Warren, who was drowned in childhood; (11) Warren, who ran away from home to join the British forces, was made a Cornet of Horse for his bravery at the Battle of White Plains, and removed to Madison County, New York; and (12) Jane.

X Jane, the daughter of Peter de Lancey and Elizabeth Colden, was born 5 September, 1756, and died 2 March, 1809. She married her cousin, the Honorable John Watts, Junior, son of the Honorable John Watts, Senior, and Ann de Lancey.

XI Mary Justina Watts, wife of Frederic de Peyster.

XII General John Watts de Peyster.

The other line of descent to General de Peyster from Stephen de Lancey and Anna Van Cortlandt is as follows:

IX Ann de Lancey, the daughter of Stephen de Lancey and Anna Van Cortlandt, was born 23 April, 1723. She married the Honorable John Watts, Senior, in July, 1742, and died 3 July, 1775.

X The Honorable John Watts, Junior.

XI Mary Justina Watts, wife of Frederic de Peyster.

XII General John Watts de Peyster.

The de Lancey Arms: Azure, a pennon, or, the flag flying toward dexter, argent, over all, a bar, or.

Crest: A sinister arm, vambraced and embowed, holding the pennon of the shield.

Motto: Certum pete voto finem.

COLDEN

I The Reverend Alexander Colden was a minister of Dunse, Scotland.

II Cadwallader Colden, the son of the Reverend Alexander Colden, was born in Dunse, Scotland, 17 February, 1688, and died at his country seat, at Flushing, Long Island, 28 September, 1776. He completed his collegiate education at the University of Edinburgh in 1705, at the age of seventeen, spent three years in the study of mathematics and medicine, and, coming to America in 1708, practised medicine for five years in Philadelphia. He returned to Great Britain in 1715, and while there married Alice Christie, the daughter of the Reverend Mr. Christie, the minister of Kelso, Scotland.

In 1716 he returned to America, settling in New York City in 1718, at the solicitation of Governor Hunter,

who in 1719 appointed him the first Surveyor-General
of the Province of New York, and Master in Chancery.
He was a member of the King's Council from 1720 to
1760, when he became its President and administered
the Government. Appointed Lieutenant-Governor in
1761, he held this office until his death, and served as
Acting Governor upon the death or during the absence
of several Governors. He was Acting Governor in November, 1765, at the time of the Stamp Act in New
York, at which time the mob burned his carriages and
sleighs on Bowling Green before his eyes, threatening to
hang him. Living until a few months after the Declara-
tion of Independence, he retained his allegiance to the
British Government.

Colden was a leading founder of the American Philo-
sophical Society, and several benevolent organizations
were incorporated under his administration. He was the
intimate friend of Benjamin Franklin, and ranks with
the latter at the head of American scientists and savants
of the Colonial period. He maintained a long correspondence with Franklin, it being the custom of both to
inform each other of their progress in discoveries. He
was also on intimate terms with the astronomer, Halley,
the naturalist, Linnaeus, and other learned men of
Europe. He wrote for Linnaeus a description of some
three or four hundred American plants.

About 1750 Colden obtained the grant of a large tract
of land near Newburgh-on-the-Hudson, and on this
estate, called Coldenham, he carried on his scientific
pursuits much of the time after 1755.

He was the author of a number of learned and valuable
books and pamphlets, among the most important of
which were: Animal Secretions; A History of the
Five Indian Nations Depending upon New York; Cause
of Gravitation; Principles of Action in Matter; An
Essay on the Virtues of the Bortanico or Great Water-
Dock; Observations on Exidemical Sore Throat; Observations on Smith's History of New York. In medical
and sanitary matters he was in advance of many thinkers

of his day. An example of this was his advocacy of the
system now in use, but then regarded as dangerous by
most European physicians, of using cooling methods in
treating fevers. In 1742 he received the thanks of the
Corporation of the City of New York for a pamphlet
showing the danger to public health from unsanitary
conditions which had aggravated an epidemic in New
York at the time.

Governor Colden's wife died in 1762. They had the
following children: (1) Alexander, born about 1716,
died in December, 1774, who succeeded his father as
Surveyor-General, and was also Post Master; (2) Elizabeth; (3) David, born about 1733, died in England 10
July, 1784, having removed from America after the Revolution, who was a physician and man of letters, held
the office of Surveyor-General, and who married Ann,
the daughter of John Willet, of Flushing, Long Island.

III Elizabeth Colden, the daughter of Governor
Cadwallader Colden and Alice Christie, was married 7
January, 1737-1738, to Peter de Lancey.

IV Jane de Lancey, wife of the Honorable John
Watts, Junior.

V Mary Justina Watts, wife of Frederic de Peyster.

VI General John Watts de Peyster.

The Colden Arms: Gules, a chevron, argent, between
three stags' heads and necks, erased and cabossed, or.

Crest: A stag's head, cabossed, or.

Motto: Fais bien, crains rien.

CHAPTER IV

VAN CORTLANDT AND LOOCKERMANS

I   Steven Van Cortlandt was probably a resident of Wyck, in Duurstede, the Netherlands.

II   Captain Olof Stevense Van Cortlandt, born in Wyck, Duurstede, was, as his name indicates, the son of Steven Van Cortlandt. A soldier in the service of the West India Company, he came to New Amsterdam in 1637, on the ship "Haring." At first he acted as bookkeeper, later, under Kieft, as the public storekeeper, afterwards becoming a trader and brewer. These commercial pursuits did not prevent Captain Van Cortlandt from being, from the time of his arrival in the colony, a man of force and natural leadership. The offices of power and dignity held by him show this very plainly. He was Captain of the Train Band, a post, which, in all the colonial settlements, was, from the nature and number of the dangers besetting them, entrusted only to men of tested strength and reliable judgment. In July, 1639, two years after his coming to New Amsterdam, he was appointed Commissary of Cargoes. In 1645 he was elected to the Board of Eight Men, and in 1649 to the Board of Nine Men, of which latter body he became President in 1650. He was Schepen of the town in 1654 and Burgomaster from 1655 to 1659, 1662-1663, and in 1665. In October, 1663, he served as Boundary Commissioner to Hartford, and in 1664 was a Commissioner to treat with Nicolls regarding the surrender of New Amsterdam to the English. He was Alderman in 1666-1667, 1671 and 1673.

Captain Olof Stevense Van Cortlandt married, 26 February, 1642, Anneken Loockermans, from Turnhout, in the Netherlands. She was a sister of Govert Loockermans, at the baptism of whose daughter she was a witness in 1641. Their issue was: (1) Stephanus; (2) Marritie, baptized 23 July, 1645, who married Colonel Jeremiah Van Rensselaer, Patroon of Rensselaerwyck; (3) Johannes, born 11 October, 1648, who died in 1667; (4) Fytie, or Sophia, who was born 31 May, 1651, and married Andrew Teller; (5) Catharina, born 25 October, 1652, who married, first, Colonel Jan der Vall, 3 November, 1675, and, second, Frederick Philipse, 30 November, 1692; (6) Cornelia, who was born 21 November, 1655, and married Barent Schuyler; and (7) Jacobus.

III   Jacobus Van Cortlandt, the third son of Captain Olof Stevense Van Cortlandt and Anneken Loockermans, was born in New York City 7 July, 1658.   He became a New York merchant and a wealthy land proprietor. He owned large estates in the town of Bedford, Westchester, which property descended to the Jay family, and was the proprietor of Old Yonckers, or the Lower Cortlandt Manor, comprising eight hundred and fifty acres on the road to Yonkers, a mile north of King's Bridge. Like his father, he was a man of public spirit, holding high office in the affairs of the Colony.   He was a Member of the New York Assembly from New York City in 1691, represented the Dock Ward in the Common Council, and was Mayor of New York from 1710 to 1719.

Jacobus Van Cortlandt married Eva, the daughter of Pieter Rudolphus De Vries and Margaret Hardenbroeck, and adopted daughter of Frederick Philipse, Lord of the Manor of Philipsburgh.   The date of her marriage license was 7 May, 1691.   Her husband died in 1739. In his will, dated 12 May, 1739, he calls his main estate "The Little or Lower Yonckers," and bequeathes property in New York City to his "eldest daughter, Margaret, wife of Abraham de Peyster."

Jacobus Van Cortlandt and Eva Philipse had issue: (1) Frederick, who married Frances Jay; (2) Margaret; (3) Anne, who married the Honorable John Chambers, Judge of the Supreme Court; (4) Mary, who became the wife of Peter Jay, and the mother of the Honorable John Jay.

IV   Margaret Van Cortlandt, the daughter of Jacobus Van Cortlandt and Eva Philipse, was married, 1 July, 1722, to Abraham de Peyster.

V   James de Peyster.

VI   Captain Frederic de Peyster.

VII   Frederic de Peyster.

VIII   General John Watts de Peyster.

General de Peyster's ancestry also contains two other lines from the first Van Cortlandt, as follows:

I   Steven Van Cortlandt, of Wyck, in Duurstede.

II   Captain Olof Stevense Van Cortlandt, who married Anneken Loockermans.

III   De Heer Stephanus Van Cortlandt, the eldest child of Captain Olof Stevense Van Cortlandt and Anneken Loockermans, was born in 1643. He was the first Lord of Van Cortlandt Manor, having purchased from the Indians in 1683 eighty-three thousand acres of land on the east side of the Hudson, between the mouth of the Croton River and Anthony's Nose, as well as a tract on the west side of the river, which vast estate was in 1697 erected by Governor Fletcher into a Manor.

The first Lord of Cortlandt Manor was essentially an aristocrat. He was of the class of men who, by birth, honored position in the community, and by personal ability, are given, as a matter of course, under a system recognizing these elements of suitability, positions of command and responsibility. He was one of the most brilliant figures of his times, one of the picturesque grandees who add a dignity and grave magnificence to the history of the turbulent little town of New York in the closing decades of the Seventeenth Century.

A typical aristocrat, he naturally distrusted and condemned the popular movement under the leadership of Leisler, and was one of the latter's strongest opponents. Mayor of New York in 1677 and 1686, he also held that office in 1689, when Leisler first assumed command of the city. Leisler's success deprived him for two years

of the membership in the King's Council which, with
the exception of that period, he held from 1680 until
his death.   In 1686 he was Manager of the Revenue; in
1698, Collector of Customs and Receiver-General.   Becoming Ensign in 1668, he rose to the rank of Colonel in
1693, commanding the King's County Militia.   He was
Justice of the Supreme Court in 1693, and was First
Judge of the Common Pleas of King's County.

De Heer Stephanus died 25 November, 1700.   His
will, dated 14 April, 1700, bequeathes a portion of his
Manor to his eldest son, Johannes, and the remainder in
equal parts to his other children.   He married, 10 September, 1671, Gertrude, the daughter of Captain Philip
Pietersen Schuyler, born 4 February, 1654, who died in
1718.   Their issue was: (1) Johannes, who married
Anna Van Schaick; (2) Margrietje, who married, first,
Samuel Bayard, and, second, Peter Kemble; (3) Anna;
(4) Olof, who died unmarried, his will being dated 23
December, 1706; (5) Elizabeth, who was born in 1691;
(6) Maria, who married Kilian Van Rensselaer, Patroon
of Rensselaerwyck; (7) Philip, who married Catharine
de Peyster; (8) Stephen, who married Catalina, the
daughter of Doctor Samuel Staats, one of Leisler's
Council; (9) Gertrude, who married Colonel Henry
Beekman, of Rhinebeck, a grandson of William Beekman, Vice Director of the Colony of Delaware; (10)
Elizabeth, who married the Rev. William Skinner; (11)
Catharine, who married Andrew Johnston, of New York
and New Jersey; (12) Cornelia, who married John
Schuyler.

IV Anna Van Cortlandt, daughter of De Heer
Stephanus Van Cortlandt and Gertrude Schuyler, was
married, 19 January, 1700, to Stephen de Lancey.   General de Peyster descended from two of the children of
Anna Van Cortlandt and Stephen de Lancey.   The first
line of descent is through a daughter.

V Ann de Lancey, daughter of Anna Van Cortlandt
and Stephen de Lancey, and wife of the Honorable John
Watts, Senior.

VI   The Honorable John Watts, Junior.

VII   Mary Justina Watts, wife of Frederic de Peyster.

VIII   General John Watts de Peyster.

The other line of descent is through a son, as follows:

V   Peter de Lancey, son of Anna Van Cortlandt and Stephen de Lancey.

VI   Jane de Lancey, wife of the Honorable John Watts, Junior.

VII   Mary Justina Watts, wife of Frederic de Peyster.

VIII   General John Watts de Peyster.

Through a daughter of the first Van Cortlandt in America, General de Peyster also inherited a fourth strain of the Van Cortlandt blood.

I   Stephen Van Cortlandt, of Wyck, in Duurstede.

II   Captain Olof Stevense Van Cortlandt, who married Anneken Loockermans.

III   Marritie, the daughter of Captain Olof Stevense Van Cortlandt and Anneken Loockermans, was baptized 23 July, 1645. She became the wife of Colonel Jeremiah Van Rensselaer.

IV   Anna Van Rensselaer, daughter of Colonel Jeremiah Van Rensselaer and Marritie Van Cortlandt, and wife of William Nicoll.

V   Mary Nicoll, wife of Robert Watts.

VI   The Honorable John Watts, Senior.

VII   The Honorable John Watts, Junior.

IX   Mary Justina Watts, wife of Frederic de Peyster.

X   General John Watts de Peyster.

Thus General de Peyster was a descendant in four lines from Captain Olof Stevense Van Cortlandt and Anneken Loockermans: (1) through their son, De Heer Stephanus, his daughter, Anna Van Cortlandt, and her daughter, Ann de Lancey; (2) through De Heer Stephanus, his daughter, Anna Van Cortlandt, and her son, Peter de Lancey; (3) through Jacobus, son of Captain Olof Stevense Van Cortlandt; and (4) through Marritie, daughter of Captain Olof Stevense, who became the wife of Colonel Jeremiah Van Rensselaer.

The Van Cortlandt Arms: Argent, the four wings of a wind-mill, conjoined, saltirewise, sable, voided, gules, between five mullets, placed crosswise of the last.

Crest: A star, gules, between two wings displayed, the dexter, argent, the sinister, sable.

Motto: Virtus sibi munus.

LOOCKERMANS

I   Jan Loockermans, probably a resident of Turnhout, the Netherlands, had the following children: (1) Govert; (2) Pieter Janse; (3) Jacob Janse; (4) Anneken.

Govert Loockermans was born at Turnhout, and came to America, first, in 1633.   He returned to Amsterdam, where he married, 26 February, 1641, Ariaentje Jans. Coming again to New Netherland, he was a successful trader and a brewer on a large scale, his brewery being located on Pearl street, New Amsterdam.   A bold, able man, he rose to prominence in the official life of the city, being one of the Board of Nine Men from 1647 to 1650, Schepen in 1657 and 1660, and one of the Orphan Masters in 1663.   In 1670 he was commissioned Lieutenant.   His second marriage, to Marritje Jans, took place 11 July, 1649, in New Amsterdam.   He died probably in 1670.   A step-daughter of Govert Loockermans became the wife of Jacob Leisler.

Pieter Janse Loockermans was in New Amsterdam by 1642.   In 1656 he was a citizen of Beverwyck, and in 1658 was a boatswain in the employ of the West India Company.

Jacob Janse Loockermans was a resident of Beverwyck in 1657.   In 1664 he was one of two commissioners to arrange a treaty of peace between the Mohawks and the Abenaquis Indians.   He was living in 1700.

II   Anneken Loockermans, the daughter of Jan Loockermans, was born in Turnhout, the Netherlands. She came to America probably with her brother, Govert, on the latter's return to New Netherlands, after his first marriage.   The first mention of her found in the records here is on the occasion of the baptism of Govert Loockerman's daughter, Marritje, 1 December, 1641. She was married in the Dutch Church, New Amsterdam, 26 February, 1642, to Captain Olof Stevense Van Cortlandt. She died 14 May, 1684, about a month after her husband's death. Her epitaph was written by Dominie Selyns, and has been mentioned as an example of the poetry of the Dutch Colonial period.   .

General de Peyster had four lines of descent from Anneken Loockermans. These were as follows:

1

III   De Heer Stephanus Van Cortlandt, son of Anneken Loockermans and Captain Olof Stevense Van Cortlandt.

IV   Anna Van Cortlandt, wife of Stephen de Lancey.

V   Ann de Lancey, wife of the Honorable John Watts, Senior.

VI   The Honorable John Watts, Junior.

VII   Mary Justina Watts, wife of Frederic de Peyster.

VIII   General John Watts de Peyster.

2

III   De Heer Stephanus Van Cortlandt, son of Anneken Loockermans and Captain Olof Stevense Van Cortlandt.

IV   Anna Van Cortlandt, wife of Stephen de Lancey.

V   Peter de Lancey.

VI   Jane de Lancey, wife of the Honorable John Watts, Junior.

VII   Mary Justina Watts, wife of Frederic de Peyster.

VIII   General John Watts de Peyster.

3

III   Jacobus Van Cortlandt, son of Anneken Loockermans and Captain Olof Stevense Van Cortlandt.

IV   Margaret Van Cortlandt, wife of Abraham de Peyster.

V   James de Peyster.

VI   Captain Frederic de Peyster.

VII   Frederic de Peyster.

VIII   General John Watts de Peyster.   :

4

III   Marritje, daughter of Anneken Loockermans and Captain Olof Stevense Van Cortlandt, and wife of Colonel Jeremiah Van Rensselaer.

IV   Anna Van Rensselaer, wife of William Nicoll.

V   Mary Nicoll, wife of Robert Watts.

VI   The Honorable John Watts, Senior.

VII   The Honorable John Watts, Junior.

VIII   Mary Justina Watts, wife of Frederic de Peyster.

IX   General John Watts de Peyster.

CHAPTER V

LIVINGSTON AND MAC PHEADRIS

The Livingston family is one of the oldest and noblest in Scotch history. From the time of the traditionary ancestor in the Eleventh Century, who is said to have accompanied Margaret, the future Queen of Scotland, when she entered that country, the Livingstons have been distinguished for their intimate relations of service and their ardent loyalty to the sovereigns of Scotland. Their fidelity to the Stuart cause caused them the loss of their lands, when, in the Eighteenth Century, James, Fifth Earl of Linlithgow, was attainted and deprived of his estates, during one of the Jacobite uprisings.

The ancestor whom legend has assigned as the founder of the great Scotch house was Leving, or Living, a Hungarian noble in the suite of St. Margaret, when she came with her brother, Edgar Aetheling, to the Court of Malcolm Canmore, her future husband. It is said that many of the followers in the train of the Saxon princess remained, after her marriage, in Scotland, where they were granted lands. This may be true; but it is more probable that the head of the Livingston family was a Saxon, since the name "Living" is not an infrequent one among the Saxon chronicles. It was the name of the Archbishop of Canterbury who crowned King Canute, and of other great ecclesiastics of the Saxon times. Perhaps one of the earliest historic references to the family name is in a charter granted to the Canons of Holy Cross Church in Edinburgh. In abstract, this is as follows:

"The Church of Livingston.

Thurstan, the son of Living, * * * greeting: * * * I have granted and by this my charter confirmed to God and to the Church of the Holy Cross of the Castle of the Maidens and to the canons serving God there, the church of Livingston, with half a plough of land and a toft, and with all the rights pertaining thereto, as my father gave them, in free and perpetual alms. * * *."

This Living, the father of Thurstan, held lands during the reign of Alexander I (1107-1124), on the site of the present village of Livingston, in Linlithgowshire.

I The first authentically known ancestor of that branch of the Livingston family from which Robert, the first in America, was descended was Sir Andrew de Livingston, who, before 1295, was Sheriff of Lanach. In 1296 he, with a kinsman, Sir Archibald de Livingston, swore allegiance to Edward I. of England. When that king departed for Flanders, the following year, he called upon a number of the chief men of Scotland to follow him, among these being the two Livingstons. Whether they obeyed Edward's summons is unknown, but the family appears to have been loyal to Bruce, their castle, now in ruins, having been attacked many times during this stormy period, as it was also during the civil wars of Scotland in the reign of Queen Mary Stuart. Sir Andrew de Livingston married Elena, and had a son, William.

II William de Livingston, son of Sir Andrew, in 1328 confirmed to the canons of Holyrood the right of building a mill lade on his property of Gorgyn. He conferred a somewhat similar privilege on the monks of Newbotle, stating that he had done this charitable deed for the good of his own soul, and those of his wife, Margaret, his father, Andrew, his mother, Elena, his children, his predecessors, and his successors. By his wife he had a son, William.

III Sir William Livingston, son of William de Livingston and Margaret, was sent in 1340 with four others to England as hostages for Randolph, Earl of Murray, a prisoner of the English, who was desirous of returning to Scotland to raise a ransom. A year later Sir William returned to Scotland. He was at the siege of Stirling, and was sent on an important mission to France to give information to the Scotch King, David II., of the fact that most of his domain had been freed from the English. When the King came back to his own country he granted to Sir William a charter of the barony of Callendar in Stirlingshire, which had passed to the Crown because of the disloyalty of Sir Patrick Callendar, an adherent of Baliol. Sir Patrick's daughter, Christian, became the wife of Sir William Livingston.

The latter was with his King at the Battle of Neville's Cross in England, 17 October, 1346, and for his valor was made Knight Banneret. With the King he was taken prisoner, but was soon set free. During the period of negotiation for the ransom of King David, Sir William played an important part in the service of his sovereign, being one of the Commissioners to settle this matter and make a treaty between the two countries. He was one of the six Scottish Commissioners who signed the treaty. He died probably some time between 1362 and 1364. Through him the lands of Callendar came into the Livingston family, and also the Kilsyth estates.

By his wife, Christian de Callendar, Sir William Livingston had issue: (1) Patrick; (2) William, who was one of twenty young men of rank named in the above-mentioned treaty between England and Scotland to remain in England as hostages until the King's ransom was paid, in which service his brother, Patrick, became his substitute, the latter probably dying in England; (3) John. That John was the son of Sir William Livingston has been questioned; it has been thought that he was his grandson. It appears probable, however, that Sir William was succeeded by his son, William, and that the latter was, in turn, succeeded by a brother, John.

IV Sir John Livingston of Callendar, the son or grandson of Sir William, married, first, a daughter of Menteith of Carse, and, second, in 1381, Agnes, daughter of Sir James Douglas of Dalkeith. In 1398-9 he was a member of the Council appointed by the King to assist the latter's son, the Duke of Rothsay, in conducting the affairs of the kingdom during the illness of Robert III.

Later Sir John became Auditor, and then Chamberlain, to Robert, Duke of Albany, uncle of King Robert III. He was killed at the battle of Homildon Hill, Northumberland. By his first marriage Sir John had issue: (1) Sir Alexander; (2) Robert; and (3) John. By his second marriage, his children were: (4) Archibald, who was demented; and (5) Sir William Livingston of Kilsyth.

V   Sir Alexander Livingston, of Callendar, the eldest son of Sir John Livingston by his marriage with a daughter of Menteith of Carse, was appointed Justiciary of Scotland. In 1449 he was sent as Ambassador to England. He married a daughter of Dundas of Dundas, and had a son, James.

VI   Sir James Livingston, of Callendar, the son of Sir Alexander Livingston, was the Captain of Stirling Castle. He became tutor to the young King James II. He was created a peer of Scotland, becoming the first Lord Livingston. He died about 1467. By his marriage with Marion, he had issue: (1) James, second Lord Livingston, who was thrice married, but left no issue; (2) Alexander; (3) Elizabeth, who married John, Earl of Ross, Lord of the Isles; (4) Eupheme, who married, first, Malcolm, son and heir of Robert, Lord Fleming, and, second, William Fleming.

VII   Alexander Livingston, the second son of Sir James Livingston and Marion, had a son, John.

VIII   John, third Lord Livingston, the son of Alexander, succeeded his uncle, James, the second Lord Livingston. He married, first, Elizabeth, daughter of Robert, Lord Fleming, and, second, a daughter of Sir John Houston, of Houston. He died before 1510. He had issue: (1) William, son of the first marriage; (2) Alexander, son of the second marriage, whose male line of descendants is now extinct.

IX   William, fourth Lord Livingston, son of John, the third Lord, and Elizabeth Fleming, married a daughter of Hepburn. They had issue: (1) Alexander, the fifth Lord Livingston, and Earl of Linlithgow, whose daughter was the Maid of Honor to Mary, Queen of Scots, one of the four "Queen's Maries;" (2) Margaret, who married John, Lord Hay; (3) Isabel, who married Nicol Ramsay, of Dalhousie; and (4) Robert.

X Robert Livingston, son of William, the fourth Lord Livingston, is the next in the line of descent to Robert Livingston, of the Province of New York, according to a letter which was written to the latter by a brother in Scotland. The following extract from this letter is of much significance.

"I purposed to procure your coat of arms and have prepared it so far that I find you the son of Mr. John, whose father was Mr. Alexander, whose father was Robert, killed at Pinkiefield 1547, and brother german to Alexander, Lord Livingston, their father was William, 4th Lord and 8th of Callendar, who married Hepburn, daughter of Sir Patrick. So your proper coat of arms is this enclosed. Quarterly 1 & 4 argent, 3 gillie flowers gules, slipped propper within a double tressure, umber florescent the name of Livingston, 2nd quartered 1st and last gules, a chiffron argent, a roll between two lions counter rampant of the field, 2nd and 3rd argent 3 martlets gules, the name of Hepburn, 3rd quarter sable a bend between six billets or name of Callendar. Your liveries is green faced with white and red, green and white passiments."

According to the above, Robert Livingston died in 1547, at the Battle of Pinkiefield, when the Scotch army was defeated by the English under Somerset.

XI The Reverend Alexander Livingston, of Monyabroch, the son of Robert Livingston, was presented to his benefice by William, the sixth Lord Livingston.

XII The Reverend John Livingston, son of the Reverend Alexander Livingston, received the degree of Master of Arts from the College of Glasgow, in July, 1621. He was among the most prominent of the ministers of the "Kirk" in Scotland of his time. In 1649 he was sent by the Scottish Parliament as one of the committee to treat with Charles I. at The Hague. It is believed that at two different times he contemplated emigration to America, but in 1662, on being exiled by the Council of Edinburgh, he went to Holland, where he died, at Rotterdam, in 1674. He married, 23 June, 1635, in the West Church at Edinburgh, Barbara, the daughter of Bartholomew Fleming, an Edinburgh merchant. They had a number of children, among them Robert, the Emigrant.

XIII Robert Livingston, the son of the Reverend John Livingston and Barbara Fleming, was born in 1654. In 1673 he emigrated to New York, where he soon became one of the most eminent citizens. On 9 July, 1679, he married Alida, daughter of Captain Philip Pieterse Schuyler, and widow of the Reverend Nicolaus Van Rensselaer.

Governor Dongan granted Livingston, in 1686, a patent for 160,000 acres of land on the Hudson River between New York and Albany. This was the famous Livingston Manor, which, next to that of the Van Rensselaer family, was the greatest of the vast proprietory domains which lay at the foundation of the system of government by aristocracy peculiar to the Province of New York.

Livingston held many civic offices of importance. He was Secretary to the Albany Commissary, Town Clerk, Town Collector, Secretary of Indian Affairs, Member of the Council, Member of the General Assembly from 1709 to 1711, and Speaker of the General Assembly in 1718.

By his wife, Alida Schuyler, he had issue: (1) John, Colonel in the Connecticut Militia, who married, first, a daughter of Governor Winthrop of Connecticut, second, Elizabeth Knight, and died without issue at London in 1717; (2) Philip, born in 1686, who became one of the great merchants of the period, because of his splendid hospitality known as "The Princely Livingston," and was Town Clerk, Secretary of Indian Affairs, and Member of the Council; (3) Robert, who was educated in Scotland, studied law at the Temple in London, practised in Albany, was a Member of the General Assembly from

1711 to 1727, and married Miss Howarden; (4) Gilbert; (5) Margaret, who married Colonel Samuel Vetch, the first English Governor of Annapolis; and (6) Johanna, who married Cornelius Van Horne.

XIV Gilbert Livingston, the fourth son of Robert Livingston and Alida Schuyler, was admitted as a citizen of New York in 1716. He was the County Clerk of Ulster County, and from 1728 to 1737 was a Member of the General Assembly. Gilbert Livingston's share of the Livingston Manor was a large estate near Saratoga. He married at Kingston, 22 December, 1711, Cornelia, the daughter of Colonel Henry Beekman. In his marriage record he is called "of Roelof Janz Kil,"—Roelof Jansen's Kill, in Columbia County, New York.

Their issue was: (1) Robert Gilbert; (2) Cornelia,* who married a member of the Van Rensselaer family; (3) Alida,* who married at Kingston, 24 November, 1737, Jacob Rutsen, Junior; (4) Henry,* who was married; (5) James,* who was married; (6) Gilbert,* who married Joy Donell, of Bermuda; (7) John,* who died without issue; (8) Joanna, baptized at Kingston, 9 September, 1722, who married Pierre Van Cortlandt; (9) William, who was baptized at Kingston, 23 August, 1724, and died at Sparta; (10) Philip, baptized at Kingston, 26 June, 1726, who died, without issue, at Curaçoa; (11) Jacobus, who was baptized at Kingston, 7 April, 1728; (12) Samuel, baptized at Kingston, 1 February, 1730, who died at sea, leaving no issue; (13) Cornelius, baptized at Kingston, 30 April, 1732, who died at sea, leaving no issue; (14) Catharine, who was baptized at Kingston, 21 July, 1734, and who married Jotham Thom; and (15) Margaret, baptized at Kingston, 23 June, 1738, who married Petrus Stuyvesant.

XV Robert Gilbert Livingston, the eldest son of Gilbert Livingston, was baptized at Kingston, 11 January, 1713. He was an officer in the Royal Service during the Revolution. His residence, "Green Hill," at Upper

---

*The dates, and, consequently, the order of births are unknown.

Red Hook, now Tivoli, Dutchess County, New York, later came into the possession of John Swift Livingston, whose daughter became the wife of General de Peyster.

Robert Gilbert Livingston married in New York City, at the old Dutch Church, 3 November, 1740, Catharine, the daughter of John Mac Pheadris. They had issue: (1) Robert, who married Margaret Hude, and had issue; (2) Gilbert, who married Martha Kane, and had issue; (3) Helen; (4) Catharine, who married John Reade, and had issue; and (5) Henry, who married Ann Nutter, and had issue.

XVI Helen Livingston, the daughter of Robert Gilbert Livingston and Catharine Mac Pheadris, was married to Commissary-General Samuel Hake, claimant of the title of Lord Hake, her marriage being celebrated in her father's mansion, "Green Hill."

XVII Helen Hake, wife of Captain Frederic de Peyster.

XVIII Frederic de Peyster.

XIX General John Watts de Peyster.

The Livingston Arms: Quarterly: 1st and 4th, Argent, three gilly-flowers, gules, within a double tressure, flory counter-flory, vert (for Livingston); 2nd, quarterly-quartered, 1st and 4th, Gules, on a chevron, argent, a rose, two lions, passant combattant, of the first (for Hepburn), 2nd and 3rd, Azure, three martlets, or; 3rd, Sable, a bend between six billets, or (for Callendar).

Crest: A demi-Hercules, wreathed about the head and middle, in his dexter hand a club in pale, in the sinister, a snake, all proper.

Motto: Si je puis.

It is said that the Reverend John Livingston, the father of Robert, of New York, quartered only the Arms of Livingston and Callendar, using cinque-foils, instead of gilly-flowers, in the first and fourth quarters. Above the shield he placed Hebrew characters for "Ebenezer." Robert Livingston, the first American ancestor of this distinguished family, had been in a ship-wreck off the

Portuguese coast, and, in commemoration, substituted the figure of a ship in distress for the old crest of a demi-Hercules.

MAC PHEADRIS

Captain William Mac Pheadris resided at Camglass, County Antrim, Ireland, in 1667. One theory of the origin of this family is that the name of Mac Feorais was adopted by the English family of Bermingham, upon the latter's settlement in County Mayo, Ireland.

Early in the Eighteenth Century three brothers and a sister of the name appeared in America. These were, Captain Archibald Mac Pheadris of Portsmouth, New Hampshire, John Mac Pheadris of New York, Gilbert Mac Pheadris, and their sister, who married Read, and had a son, Philip.

Captain Archibald Mac Pheadris settled in Portsmouth as agent of a London iron company. In 1716-1718 he built there the famous brick house, afterwards known as the Warren house. In 1718 he married Sarah, daughter of Lieutenant-Governor Wentworth, and sister of Governor Benning Wentworth. In his will, dated 18 May, 1728, and proved 24 March, 1729, Captain Mac Pheadris made bequests to his children, Gilbert and Mary, to his brother, Gilbert, to the two daughters of his brother, John, and to his sister's son, Philip Read.

Gilbert Mac Pheadris, brother of Captain Archibald, was drowned in 1735 in the West Indies, while en route from the island of St. Kitts to the island of Nevis. He was unmarried, and in his will divided his property between Mary Mac Pheadris, the daughter of his brother Archibald, Susanna Mac Pheadris, "living in New York," and Philip Read. Philip Read was the son of his sister, while Susanna Mac Pheadris was the daughter of his brother, John.

I John Mac Pheadris, brother of the above Archibald and Gilbert Mac Pheadris, and of their sister, who married Read, was married in New York City, 12 December, 1712, to Helen Jansen. She was born in

1693. He died prior to the Revolution, having become a large landed proprietor of Dutchess County. His widow was living in 1776 with her son-in-law, Robert Gilbert Livingston. John Mac Pheadris and his wife had issue: (1) Susanna, born 24 September, 1713, co-heiress of her uncle, Gilbert Mac Pheadris, who, against her mother's will, married a man named Myer, and had three children; and (2) Catharine.

II   Catharine Mac Pheadris, the daughter and co-heiress of John Mac Pheadris and Helen Jansen, was married, 3 November, 1744, to Robert Gilbert Livingston.

III   Helen Livingston, wife of Commissary-General Hake.

IV   Helen Hake, wife of Captain Frederic de Peyster.

V   Frederic de Peyster.

VI   General John Watts de Peyster.

CHAPTER VI

FRENCH AND PHILIPSE

I Philip French was perhaps the son of another Philip
French, since, in the record of the baptism of his son,
Philip, 7 April, 1695, he is called "Philip French,
Junior." He was born in 1667 at Kelshall, County
Suffolk, England, to the poor of which town he bequeathed
five pounds in his will. He was a merchant in England,
and continued this career in America. His brother, John
French, was in command of a merchant vessel, and also
settled in New York.

Here Philip French became an influential and wealthy
man. His residence was on Broad Street, near Exchange
Place, and here he lived in the luxury of the day, seven
slaves being included in his household. He had come to
New York in June, 1689, and soon became involved in
the political turmoil which gathered about Jacob Leisler.
Philip French was an adherent of the anti-Leislerites, and
his opposition to Leisler's administration of the government was so strong that the latter imprisoned him.

On the occasion of a hearing of charges brought
against Governor Fletcher, made before the Lords of
Trade, 28 August, 1695, Philip French, called in his
deposition "Gentleman," made certain statements unfa-
vorable to the Governor. He had charge of the ferry
to Brooklyn before 1699, since in that year it is recorded
as being re-let to him. Speaker of the Assembly in
1698, he was elected to that body for 1703, but did not
take his seat, having in October, 1702, been appointed
Mayor of New York by Lord Cornbury, the Governor.

French was a Member of the Council. He had joined
with Colonel Nicholas Bayard in an address to the English Government in which the Lieutenant-Governor and
the Chief Justice of the Province were accused of bribery.

For this Bayard was tried for high treason, but French had escaped to England. In 1702, the then Governor, Cornbury, having shown himself favorable to the anti-Leislerian party, French had returned, and was, as noted above, appointed Mayor of New York City. In less than a year matters of private business took him again to England, his government and seals as Mayor being left, during his absence, in charge of the Recorder of the City.

He died in 1707. His will, dated 20 May, 1706, and proved 3 June, 1707, gives "to my son, Philip French, all my lands in Suffolk County in England;" "to my three daughters, Elizabeth, Anne, and Margaret, all my lands and estate in East New Jersey, which I lately purchased from Thomas Coddington;" "to the poor of the Parish of Kellshall, in England, £5." It mentions also "children of my brother, John French;" wife, Ann; Lewis Morris; and "my brother-in-law Adolph Phillipse," the last three being named as executors.

Philip French married Anna, daughter of Frederick Philipse, at the Dutch Church in New York, 6 July, 1694. In the record he is styled, "Mr. Philip French, j. m. Van London." They had issue: (1) Philip, who was baptized 7 April, 1695, at the Dutch Church in New York, and who probably died young; (2) Philip, called in the record, "Philippus," who was baptized 17 November, 1697, in the Dutch Church of New York, and was a legatee in his father's will; (3) Elizabeth, who was baptized at the Dutch Church of New York, 14 February, 1700-1701; (4) Margaret, called in the record "Margreta," who was baptized at the Dutch Church of New York, 4 May, 1701; and (5) Anne.

II Anne French, the daughter of Philip French and Anna Philipse, married the Honorable Joseph Reade, Member of the King's Council.

III Sarah Reade, wife of James de Peyster.

IV Captain Frederic de Peyster.

V Frederic de Peyster.

VI General John Watts de Peyster.

I Philip, as his son's name indicates, was the father of the first Lord of Philipse Manor. Of his history there is nothing authentically known. It has been alleged that the family originated in Bohemia, and that, during the religious wars of the sixteenth century, some of its members emigrated to Holland. One tradition states that the mother of Frederick Philipse, the first Lord of the Manor, removed as a widow to Friesland, with her son, Frederick, and other children. Her name is said to have been Eva, and that of one of the other children, Adolphus.

II Frederick Philipse, or "Frederick, the son of Philip," was born in 1626. His birth-place was Bols-waert, a town of Friesland, as appears from his marriage record in the old Dutch Church of New Amsterdam. The exact date of his coming to New York is unknown. Some have thought it was in 1647, and that he came in company with Stuyvesant. He was in New Amsterdam in 1653, when he was appraiser of a house and lot belonging to Augustine Hermans. 9 February, 1658, Stuyvesant granted him land in New Amsterdam, which was confirmed to him 12 April, 1667.

He rose to be the most opulent of the New York grandees of his day. He had learned the trade of carpentry, but soon was absorbed in mercantile pursuits, and presently took rank as the foremost trader of the Colony. He traded with the Indians, with the East and West Indies, and engaged in the slave trade with Africa. His estate in 1674, at the re-conquest of the Province by the Dutch, was assessed at eighty thousand guilders. While that meant a considerable fortune at the time, it was small in comparison with his later wealth. He eventually became the richest man in the Thirteen Colonies.

In 1680 Frederick Philipse commenced to buy from the Indians the vast properties which were to become the Manor of Philipsburgh. His first purchase was ratified and confirmed by Governor Andros 1 April, 1680. Confirmation of all his land holdings was given him 23 December, 1684, by Governor Dongan, and, in 1693, his princely estate in Westchester County, New York, was erected into a Manor, of which he was the first Lord.

He was a Member of the Council under all the English Governors, from Andros to Bellomont,—a period of twenty years,—except during the rule of Leisler. When the latter was chosen by the people and captains of the Train Bands of New York to administer the government, Frederick Philipse and De Heer Stephanus Van Cortlandt, who were Members of the Council, regarded this as an usurpation, holding that the abandonment of the colony by Lieutenant-Governor Nicholson had left them in charge of affairs. Philipse, however, soon accepted the inevitable, and acknowledged the rule of Leisler. In 1698 he resigned his seat in Bellomont's Council, and retired from public life.

He died 6 November, 1702, the record by his wife in the family Bible being as follows: "Anno 1702, the 6th of November, Sunday night at 10 o'clock, my husband, Frederick Philipse died, and lies buried in the church yard in the manor named Philipsburgh."

In his will, made 26 October, 1700, and probated 9 December, 1702, Frederick Philipse mentions "Frederick Flipse, my grandson, born in Barbadoes, ye only son of Philip, my eldest son, late deceased," and "my son, Adolphus Flypse," and says: "I leave to my eldest daughter Eva, wife of Jacobus Van Cortlandt, all that house and ground with the appurtenances in ye city of New York where they at present live, with all rights. Also a lot of ground in ye New street, at the south of the old ware house. And one quarter of all ships, plate goods, etc., to her during her life, and then to her second son. Also a certain mortgage of Dr. Henricus Selinus, upon ye lands of John Richbell, deceased, twenty miles into ye woods, but not to extend over Bronx River into any lands given to my grandson. I give to my daughter Anatje, wife of Phillip French, the house and ground in

New York where they at present live. Also the old
ware house and ground thereto belonging lying in New
Street," etc.

Frederick Philipse married, 28 October, 1662, Margaret
Hardenbroeck, the widow of Pieter Rudolphus de Vries.
The date of her death is unknown, but, 30 November,
1692, he married Catharine Van Cortlandt, the daughter
of Captain Olof Stevense Van Cortlandt, and the widow
of Colonel Jan der Vall.

By his second marriage Frederick Philipse had no
issue. By his marriage with Margaret Hardenbroeck he
had the following issue: (1) Philip, baptized at the
Dutch Church in New Amsterdam, 18 October, 1663,
who resided in the Barbadoes, and who married Maria,
daughter of Governor Sparks, dying before his father;
(2) Adolphus, baptized in the Dutch Church of New
York, 15 November, 1665, who died, unmarried, in 1749;
(3) Annetje; (4) Rombout, baptized 9 January, 1670-
1671, in the Dutch Church of New York, who probably
died young, as he is not mentioned in his father's will.

III   Annetje Philipse, the daughter of Frederick
Philipse and Margaret Hardenbroeck, was baptized in
the Dutch Church of New York, 27 November, 1667.
She was married to Philip French, 6 July, 1694, in
the Dutch Church.

IV Anne French, wife of the Honorable Joseph Reade.
V Sarah Reade, wife of James de Peyster.
VI Captain Frederic de Peyster.
VII Frederic de Peyster.
VIII General John Watts de Peyster.
The Philipse Arms: Azure, a lion rampant, or.
Crest: Out of a ducal coronet, a demi-lion.
Motto: Quod tibi vis fieri facias.

CHAPTER VII

BEEKMAN

I Gerard Beekman was born at Cologne, 17 May, 1558. He studied theology at Frenkendael, near Heidelberg, from 1576 to 1578. He was one of two delegates chosen to visit the Duke of New-Berg, the Elector of Branden-burg, and James I. of England, to solicit aid for German Protestants. He removed from Cologne, to place himself under the protection of the Landgrave of Nassau. Later, he became Auditor and Secretary of the Electoral Chamber at Cleves, in the service of the Elector of Brandenburg. He died at Emeric, 31 January, 1625.

His wife was Agnes Stuning, whom he married at Cleves. She was born 13 January, 1557, and died at Mulheim, 10 March, 1614. They had issue: (1) Hendrick; (2) Harman, second son, who died in London, in 1654, was Secretary to the Prince of Transylvania in Swenbergen, visited Constantinople, and was appointed, in 1634, Lieutenant-Colonel in the army of the Prince of Muscovy; (3) Johan, who died 13 September, 1635, having been a preacher at Mourick and Lower Betowe; (4) Catharine, who died in 1624; and (5) Magaretha, who married Cnoetz, a preacher at Wezel.

II Hendrick Beekman, eldest son of Gerard Beekman and Agnes Stuning, was born at Cologne, 14 September, 1585. He settled at Berge, where he became a land and mill owner. Later he went to Zutphen. He was appointed Secretary of the city of Hasselden, Overyssel. In 1639 the States-General made him Superintendent of the Magazines in the cities of Hasselt and Wezel. He died at Wezel, probably about 1654.

Hendrick Beekman was three times married. His first wife was Geertryd Gomensbagh, whom he married 15 April, 1613. She died 10 September, 1619. He married,

5

second, 24 January, 1621, Mary, the daughter of Wilhelmus Baudertius, a minister at Zutphen, Guelderland,
who made a translation of the Bible into Dutch. She
died at Berge, 17 September, 1630. Hendrick Beekman
married, third, Alida Ottenbeeks, who was born at
Cologne, 8 December, 1605. By his third marriage
he had no children.

His issue by his first and second marriages was: Four
children by the first marriage; (5) Gerard, born in
Zutphen, 20 February, 1622, died in 1678, married
Joanna Plantius, and was a preacher in Grofhuysen and
Avenhoorn in North Holland; (6) William; (7) Martin,
born at Hasselt, Overyssel, 25 August, 1624, married
Maria de Bois at The Hague, 3 August, 1650, was a
Notary and Procureur, and is said to have been Director
of certain branches of Holland's Eastern trade, under
the Dutch Government, and to have served also under
the Dutch West India Company; (8) John, born at
Hasselt, 26 November, 1626, died 15 January, 1684,
married, first, Arnolda Brouwers, and, second, Catharine
Van Rysoort, and was Agent to the Council of Appointment and Supreme Military Council; (9) Andrew, who
died, unmarried, in 1663; (10) Alida, who married
Leonard Ninnix; and (11) Maria, who married, first,
William Harris, and, second, Sas.

III William Beekman, son of Hendrick Beekman and
Mary Baudertius, was born at Statselt, Overyssel, 28
April, 1623. In 1647 he came to New Amsterdam in
company with Stuyvesant, on the ship, "Princess." He
was soon one of the most conspicuous figures in the
Colony. He received by patent, 20 June, 1655, a tract
of land beyond the Kalck Hoek, or Collect. Difficulties
arose about the right of way through this land for cattle
pastured on the Commons. This cattle-path was probably
the origin of Beekman Street, which did not become a
street until 1734. William Street, in New York, also
received its name from William Beekman.

On 28 October, 1658, Beekman was appointed Vice-
Governor of the Dutch Colony on the Delaware. On 5

January, 1663-4 he resigned this post, and, on 4 July, 1664, received the appointment of "Schout," or Sheriff, of Esopus. "Hon. Heer Willem Beeckman, Schout," took the inventory of Jacob Kip in 1665. He became Burgomaster of New York 16 August, 1674, and was Alderman of the city 1678-1682, 1685, 1691-1696. When Andros, the Governor, arrived in 1674, William Beekman was one of a committee of three to go on board "The Diamond," to welcome the Governor, and ask for certain favors for the Dutch in New York.

The following year, 1675, he signed a petition to Andros for exemption from taking the required unconditional oath of allegiance to Charles II., and to be allowed to dispose of estates outside the Province of New York. For this, he with the other signers,—all men of prominence,—was arrested. They were released on bail, and, later, having taken the oath, were acquitted. In 1683, when Thomas Dongan became Governor, Beekman was Mayor of New York, and was one of those appointed to survey Fort James. On 9 November, 1683, he signed a petition to Governor Dongan asking that certain privileges, granted to New York City in 1665, should be confirmed by a charter of the Duke of York. In 1692, when Governor Fletcher arrived in New York, William Beekman was a member of the Common Council. He died in 1707.

He married, 5 September 1649, Catalina de Boots, or de Boogh, the daughter of Captain Frederick de Boogh. They had issue: (1) Marie, who was baptized in the Dutch Church of New Amsterdam, 26 January, 1650-1651; (2) Hendrick; (3) Gerardus, who was baptized in the Dutch Church of New Amsterdam, 17 August, 1653; (4) Cornelia, who was baptized in the Dutch Church of New Amsterdam, 11 April, 1655; (5) Johannes, who was baptized in the Dutch Church of New Amsterdam, 22 November, 1656; (6) Jacobus, who was baptized in the Dutch Church of New Amsterdam, 21 August, 1658; (7) Wilhelmus, who was baptized at Kingston, 20 July, 1664, being then three years old; (8)

Martinus, who was baptized at Kingston, 19 July, 1665;
and (9) Caterina, who was baptized at Kingston, 25
March, 1666.

IV Colonel Hendrick Beekman, eldest son of De
Heer William Beekman and Catalina de Boots, was
baptized in the Dutch Church of New Amsterdam, 3
March, 1652. He held the military rank of Captain 3
March, 1685-6, when he was Justice of the Court of
Sessions for Ulster County. For many years he was a
prominent Magistrate of Ulster County, named as Justice
of the Peace, 30 March, 1692; "Judge of ye Court of
Common Pleas," 26 March, 1696; Judge of Court of
Common Pleas, 20 September, 1703; Judge, 6 March,
1711-12, 12 April, 1712, and 3 September, 1713. He
became a Colonel some time before 7 February, 1695-6,
when, as "Coll Henricus Beekman" he was made a
guardian to the children of Gerritse Cornelis of Hurly.
He was a Member of the Legislature, an extensive land-
owner, and one of the most eminent citizens of Ulster
County.

Colonel Beekman died in 1716. He married, 5 June,
1681, in the Dutch Church of New York, Johanna
Lopers, of New York, the widow of George Davits of
Albany. Her first marriage took place in New York, 13
November, 1674, and by it she had three sons, Jacobus,
Samuel, and Salomon. Shortly before her marriage to
Colonel Beekman she provided for these children's future,
a portion of the document reading as follows: "Johanna,
widow of the deceased George Davits, intends to enter
the married state with Hendricus Beecqman, young man,
therefore the said bride, Johanna Lopers, grants to her
children with said Davits, named Jacobus, Samuel, and
Salomon * * * As guardian over said children she
appoints their uncle, David Davits, and Dirck Jansen
Schepmoes."

Colonel Beekman and Johanna Lopers had issue: (1)
Wilhelmus, who was baptized at Kingston, 9 April, 1682,
and died as a young man in Holland; (2) Catharina,
baptized at Kingston, 16 September, 1683, who married,

first, John Rutsen, and, second, Albert Pawling; (3) Cornelia; and (4) Colonel Henry, who was baptized at Kingston, 8 January, 1688, died 3 January, 1776, married, first, Janet Livingston, second, Gertrude Van Cortlandt, and was a Member of the Assembly and a Judge.

V Cornelia Beekman, daughter of Colonel Hendrick Beekman and Johanna Lopers, was baptized at Kingston, 15 August, 1693. She was married at Kingston, 22 December, 1711, to Gilbert Livingston.

VI Robert Gilbert Livingston.

VII Helen Livingston, wife of Commissary-General Samuel Hake.

VIII Helen Hake, wife of Captain Frederic de Peyster.

IX Frederic de Peyster.

X General John Watts de Peyster.

The Beekman Arms: Azure, a running brook, in bend, wavy, argent, between two roses, or.

Crest: Two wings, addorsed.

Motto: Mens conscia recti.

CHAPTER VIII

NICOLL

I   The first authentically known ancestor of this family is John Nicholls, Gentleman, of Islip, Northamptonshire, England, who was living in 1464. He was buried in the Church of Islip.

II   Henry Nicholls, Gentleman, of Islip, was the son of John Nicholls.

III   John Nicholls, Gentleman, of Islip, was the son of Henry Nicholls.

IV   William Nicholls, Gentleman, the son of John Nicholls, of Islip, was of Willen, in Buckinghamshire. He married, first, Mary, the daughter of Langedeway, and, second, Mary, the daughter of Lawrence Woodhall, Gentleman, of Buckinghamshire. He had issue: (1) Elizabeth, a child of the first marriage, who became the wife of Henry Charge of Wavendon, Buckinghamshire; (2) Roger, a child by the first marriage, who married Susanna, the daughter of George White; and (3) John.

V   John Nicholls, of Clifford's Inn, son of William Nicholls and the latter's second wife, Mary Woodhall, was a resident of the town of Buckingham, in the shire of that name. He was also of Ampthill, in Bedfordshire. He married Jane, the daughter and heiress of John Grafton, Gentleman, of London. They had issue: (1) Matthias; (2) John Nicholls, Gentleman, of Clifford's Inn, London; (3) William; (4) Ferdinand, of Magdalen College, Oxford, in 1619; (5) Elizabeth, who was the wife of Thomas Hall, Bachelor and Professor of Theology; and (6) Catharine.

VI   Matthias Nicholls, or Nicolls, eldest son of John Nicholls and Jane Grafton, was a Bachelor of Law and Theology at New College, Oxford. He was of Ampthill,

Bedfordshire, and was "preacher to the town of Plymouth."

VII Matthias Nicolls, or Nicoll, son of the Reverend Matthias Nicolls, of Ampthill, Bedfordshire, the "preacher to the town of Plymouth," came to this country with Colonel Richard Nicolls, the first English Governor of New York, who is thought to have been his kinsman. Matthias Nicolls served as secretary of the commission appointed to treat with the Dutch at the surrender of New Amsterdam, and Governor Nicolls appointed him Secretary of the Province of New York, and a Member of the Governor's Council. He held the military rank of Captain. By virtue of his office as Provincial Secretary, he was also Clerk of the Court, and his legal career is one of the most important of colonial times. In England he had been a barrister of Lincoln's Inn, and here he was Presiding-Justice of the Court of Assizes, sat in the inferior Courts of Session, was the first Judge of the Court of Common Pleas in New York City, and became Justice of the Supreme Court. In 1672 he was appointed Mayor of New York.

Judge Nicoll was a Deputy to the famous Convention at Hempstead, Long Island, in 1664-65, and is considered the virtual author of the code adopted, known as "The Duke's Laws," which, in spite of many modifications and changes, is the basis of our present law. The absence of the principle of election of officials, for which was substituted that of royal or gubernatorial appointment, should not blind us to the merits of this code, in whose compilation the laws of England, the Dutch law,—derived largely from the Roman codes,—and the various charters of New England were sources.

While we, as Americans, consider that popular election is an essential of political liberty, we should remember that the codes of the very colonies which, better provided for representative government, protested against the Duke's Laws, had no provision for religious toleration. One of the enactments of the Hempstead Convention decreed religious liberty. Matthias Nicoll's influence in

this Convention, if only because of this wise and Christian
law, reflects much honor on his sense of justice as well
as on his legal abilities, as does also his connection
with the General Assembly held under Thomas Dongan's
Governorship, whose first session began 17 October, 1683.
Nicoll, sent as a Representative from New York City,
was elected Speaker, as he was also of the second session
of this Assembly, which began in October, 1684. This
body guaranteed religious freedom to all Christians,—
a measure of civilization then practically unknown in
many of the American Colonies.

Matthias Nicoll was an extensive land-owner, having a
large estate, called "Plandome," consisting of about
two thousand acres, at Little Neck and Great Neck, Long
Island. He died 22 December, 1687. He had married
in England, and had issue: (1) William; and (2)
Margaret, born in 1662, who married Colonel Richard
Floyd, Junior, of Suffolk County, Long Island.

VIII William Nicoll, son of Judge Matthias Nicoll,
was born in England in 1657. He was a lawyer, like
his father, and probably received his legal education
from Judge Nicoll. In 1683 he was appointed Clerk of
Queens County. In 1688, removing to New York City,
he soon rose to eminence as a brilliant lawyer and man
of affairs. He was strongly opposed to Leisler, and
fought against the latter's rise to power. When Leisler
gained possession of the government, in 1688, he sent
Nicoll to prison, where he remained until March, 1691,
when the arrival of Governor Sloughter put an end to
Leisler's authority. The new Governor gave Nicoll a
place in his Council. He retained the office of Councillor
until 1698, when Lord Bellomont suspended him, as he
did a number of the other Councillors, at the time of
the Governor's difficulties with the merchants and traders
over the question of the commerce of New York vessels
with pirates.

Nicoll was a man of great energy, untiring in his
efforts to bring those measures to success which he considered wise or expedient, or to defeat the plans of his

political opponents. He carried this persistency so far as to lend his influence to the execution of Leisler, a measure which was bitterly condemned by the lovers of representative government in that day, as it was by the English Parliament which investigated the Leisler trouble, and as it has been since by nearly all who have carefully studied the historical documents.

In 1695 Nicoll was sent by the Assembly as its sole agent to the King to petition that the other colonies should share in the defence of the borders against the French. In 1701, elected to the Assembly, he was disqualified as a non-resident of Suffolk County, but was re-elected in 1702, and made Speaker. The latter office he held until his resignation in 1718, remaining, however, a Member after that date.

His most important legal suits were as counsel for the defence in the trial of Colonel Nicholas Bayard and Alderman John Hutchins for high treason, in 1702, and at the trial of the Reverend Francis Makemie, a Presbyterian minister of Virginia, whom Lord Cornbury, the Governor, had imprisoned for preaching in New York without securing the latter's permission. The trial of Bayard and Hutchins was in connection with accusations against the administration of Lord Bellomont, made upon news of the appointment of Lord Cornbury as Governor. It was really an outgrowth of the old Leislerian troubles, and Nicoll, with James Emott, his associate in the defence, lost the case. In the charge against Mr. Makemie he was more successful, his efforts resulting in an acquittal for his client.

William Nicoll received in 1697 a royal Patent for an estate which, in 1683, he had bought from the Indians, and which was located on Great South Bay, in Suffolk County, Long Island. Here he built a mansion, which he named Islip Grange, after the home of his ancestors in England. He died in May, 1723. His will was made 17 March, 1718-19, and was proved 27 August, 1723. Therein he is called, "William Nicoll, of Islip, in the County of Suffolk," and mention is made of his

son, Benjamin Nicoll; son, William Nicoll; son, Rensselaer Nicoll; daughter, Mary Platt; daughter, Frances
Nicoll; daughter, Charity Nicoll; son, Edward Nicoll;
and son, John Nicoll. The last two are said to be
minors, and their mother is mentioned as living.

"To my son Rensselaer all my live stock in the Manor
of Rensselaerwyck," runs the will, and to "my son,
Rensselaer Nicoll, all those lands and farms on Shelter
Island, now in occupation of John Shaw * * * But
when my son Benjamin shall assign to his brother
Rensselaer all those lands in the County of Albany which
were his mother's, and which I now possess in her right,
then the above bequest to my son Rensselaer is to deter-
mine and be void, and the said lands on Shelter Island
shall devolve to my son Benjamin." William Nicoll had
married, about 1688, Anna, the daughter of Colonel
Jeremias Van Rensselaer, Director of Rensselaerwyck,
and widow of her cousin, Kiliaen Van Rensselaer, third
Patroon of Rensselaerwyck. She pre-deceased her husband, who married a second time.

He had issue: (1) Mary; (2) Henry, who was
baptized in the Dutch Church at New York, 5 April,
1691, and who probably died young, as he is not
mentioned in his father's will; (3) John, who was
baptized at the Dutch Church, 8 May, 1692, and who
probably died young, as the John mentioned in William
Nicoll's will was a minor in 1718-19; (4) Jeremias, baptized 7 July, 1695, in the Dutch Church, and who
probably died young, as he is not mentioned in his
father's will; (5) Benjamin, named in his father's will,
who married a daughter of Colonel Floyd; (6) William,
born in 1702, died in 1768, unmarried, a successful
lawyer, who was a Member of the Assembly for twenty-
nine years, from 1739 until his death, for the last nine
years of his life being Speaker; (7) Rensselaer, who,
mentioned in the will of his uncle, Kiliaen Van Rensselaer, in 1718, as "the youngest son of my sister Anne
Nicoll," was a legatee of that uncle and of his father,
as shown above, married, and left issue; (8) Catharine,

or Charity, as she is called in the abstract we have given from the will of her father, who married a Mr. Havans, of Shelter Island, and left issue; (9) Frances, who married Edward Holland; (10) Edward, a child by William Nicoll's second marriage, mentioned as under age in the latter's will; and (11) John, a child by the second marriage, and also a minor at the date of his father's will.

IX Mary Nicoll, daughter of William Nicoll and Anna Van Rensselaer, was baptized in the Dutch Church of New York, 6 October, 1689. In 1706 she was married to Robert Watts. It is evident that the "daughter, Mary Platt," mentioned in William Nicoll's will, is so-called through error either of the transcriber or printer of this abstract, for Mary Nicoll, at the time this will was made, had been for many years the wife of Robert Watts, and the latter lived until 1750.

X The Honorable John Watts, Senior.

XI The Honorable John Watts, Junior.

XII Mary Justina Watts, wife of Frederic de Peyster.

XIII General John Watts de Peyster.

The Nicoll Arms: Argent, six cross crosslets, fitché, or, on a bend, engrailed, cotised, or, three eaglets, argent.

Crest: A falcon, wings displayed, or, supporting in her right foot a cross crosslet, patée, fitché, sable.

Motto: Fide sed cui vide.

These Arms, designated as those of Nicholls, of Ampthill, were confirmed by William Saeger, Norroy King of Arms, in 1602.

CHAPTER IX

VAN RENSSELAER

The Van Rensselaer family, whose stately history is one of the most interesting of the Dutch colonial period, derived its name from a manor in its possession, near Nykerk, in Gelderland, the Netherlands. This estate was originally one of those whose ownership conferred nobility, but in modern times has become a farm. It has been said that not many years ago its peasant owner destroyed the ancient gables and weather-vanes, which bore the Van Rensselaer arms. The family owned also an estate near Naarden, on the Zuyder Zee, a short distance from Amsterdam. The Van Rensselaer arms, sometimes quartered with others, remain on numerous old houses and tombstones in the neighborhood of the localities where the family lived.

I   Wolter Van Rensselaer is the first known ancestor.

II   Hendrick Wolters Van Rensselaer, son of Wolter Van Rensselaer, as is shown by his name, married Swene Van Imyck, of Hemegseet. They had issue: (1) Johannes Hendrick; (2) Geesje, who married the Advocate Swaaskens; (3) Walter Hendrick, who died without issue; (4) Anna, who married Bygriup; and (5) Betje, who married Noggyen.

III   Johannes Hendrick Van Rensselaer, son of Hendrick Wolters Van Rensselaer and Swene Van Imyck, married Derykebia Van Lupoel. They had issue: (1) Kiliaen; and (2) Walter Yans.

IV   Kiliaen Van Rensselaer, son of Johannes Van Rensselaer and Derykebia Van Lupoel, married Nelle Van Vrenokum, and had issue: (1) Hendrick; (2) Engel, who married Lieutenant Gerrit William Van Patten; (3) Claes, who married Jacobina Schrassens; and (4) Johannes, who married Sandrina Van Erp, styled Waerdenburgh.

V Hendrick Van Rensselaer, son of Kiliaen Van Rensselaer and Nelle Van Vrenokum, married Maria Pasraat, and had issue: (1) Kiliaen; (2) Maria, who married Rykert Van Twiller.

VI Kiliaen Van Rensselaer, son of Hendrick Van Rensselaer and Maria Pasraat, was the first Patroon of Rensselaerwyck. One of the great merchant princes of Holland, dealing in precious stones and other wares, and a banker, from its inception he was one of the Lord-Directors of the all-powerful West India Company. Through his connection with that organization he acquired his vast estates in the New Netherlands, which really constituted a principality, owing fealty only to the States-General of Holland and the West India Company, and thus similar in character to the princely fiefs of the Middle Ages.

In 1629 the charter for Patroons, called "Freedoms and Exemptions," was adopted. Acting under this, in April, 1630, Van Rensselaer's agents purchased for him from the Indians a tract of land west of the Hudson River and south of the mouth of the Mohawk, twenty-four miles by twenty-four miles, and one on the east side of the Hudson, twenty-four miles in length. A patent for this territory was issued 13 August, 1630. Another tract, purchased in 1637, made the entire estate forty-eight by twenty-four miles, including seven hundred thousand acres of tillable land. More land, however, was added from time to time, as is shown by Indian deeds dating from 1630 to 1727.

Kiliaen Van Rensselaer had a map made in 1630, in which the northern and southern boundaries are exhibited practically as they were defined in more recent documents, with the river and an indefinite strip of land on each side. This curious map, made on parchment, is one of the most ancient documents regarding Rensselaerwyck. There is in the New York Historical Society a printed grant, made in 1630, in which certain privileges were conveyed by the West India Company to Rensselaerwyck.

The first colonists arrived in May, 1630. They built a settlement near Fort Orange, and named it Beverwyck. This is the site of the present Albany. Van Rensselaer had entered into a partnership with certain other Directors of the West India Company, in relation to his colony, but this did not affect his rights and powers as Patroon. These were essentially those of a great feudal baron of the Middle Ages. Rensselaerwyck had its own court, and was exempt from the jurisdiction of the government at New Amsterdam, though this freedom was, of course, frequently disputed by the authorities there.

Each year the first Patroon sent out new colonists since, according to his charter, his right to acquire new lands depended upon his energy in populating them. Careful, well-planned organization marked the colony. The colonists, even before leaving Holland, were assigned to definite lands and offices in the new settlement. On their arrival they were enabled, without delay, to take up their places and their work, thus fitting, without friction and confusion, into an orderly system of colonial life.

Kiliaen Van Rensselaer married twice. His first wife was Hildegonda Van Byler; his second, whom he married in 1627, was Anna Van Wely, of Amsterdam. She was the daughter of Jan Van Wely, the younger, of Barneveldt, who was a resident of The Hague, and of Leonora Haukens, of Antwerp. Jan Van Wely was a jewel merchant, and it is possible that Kiliaen Van Rensselaer was associated in business with his father-in-law.

The first Patroon of Rensselaerwyck never visited his American possessions. He died in 1646. He had issue: (1) Johannes, of whom an account follows; (2) Maria, who died without issue in Holland; (3) Hillegonda, who died without issue in Holland; (4) Eleonora; (5) Susanna, who married Jan de la Court, in Holland; (6) Jan Baptist, Director of Rensselaerwyck, who married in Holland Susanna Van Wely, and had issue: (7) Reverend Nicolaus, who married Alida Schuyler; (8) Rikert, Treasurer and Stadtholder of the Estates on the north of Vianen, who married Anna Van Beaumont, in Holland; and (9) Jeremias.

Johannes, son of the first Patroon of Rensselaerwyck by the latter's first marriage, was invested with the title and rights of Patroon, as his father's successor, by Act of the States-General in 1650. He never, however, visited his domain. He married Elizabeth Van Twiller, and had a daughter, and a son, Kiliaen Van Rensselaer, the third Patroon, whose history appears below.

VII   Colonel Jeremias Van Rensselaer, son of Kiliaen Van Rensselaer, first Patroon of Rensselaerwyck, and Anna Van Wely, was born in Amsterdam. He came from Holland to New Netherland in 1658, to succeed his brother, Jan Baptist, as Director-General of Rensselaerwyck, and remained in control of the barony until his death. When the English threatened New Amsterdam, Stuyvesant invited him to preside over the Convention for providing means of defence. An able, moderate, and popular executive of Rensselaerwyck, he was completely successful in winning and holding the friendship of the Indians. He married, 27 April, 1662, Marritje, the daughter of Captain Olof Stevense Van Cortlandt, the record on the book of the old Dutch church of New Amsterdam reading: "Jeremias Van Rensselaer, j. m. Van Amsterdam, en Marritje Cortlant, j. d. Van Amsterdam."

Colonel Van Rensselaer's will was made 10 October, 1674, and he died on the fourteenth of that month. His widow was appointed, in 1675, Treasurer of Rensselaerwyck, her brother, De Heer Stephanus Van Cortlandt, being Bookkeeper, and her brother-in-law, the Reverend Nicolaus Van Rensselaer, the Director. The latter's death, in November, 1678, left Lady Van Rensselaer in charge of the barony, a responsibility which indicates her possession of unusual powers of administration. She died 24 January, 1688-9.

Colonel Jeremias Van Rensselaer and Marritje Van Cortlandt had issue: (1) Kiliaen, born 24 August, 1663, in whose will, dated 11 June, 1718, with a codicil made 4 September, 1719, and proved 10 May, 1720, wherein he is called "Killian Van Rensselaer, of the manor of Rensselaerwyck, Gentleman," is the following, "I leave to Rensselaer Nicoll, the youngest son of my sister, Anne Nicoll, all that farm at Bethlehem;" (2) Anna; (3) Hendrick, born 23 October, 1667, a resident of Greenbush, New York, who married, in 1689, Catharine Van Bruggen, who was baptized 19 April, 1665; (4) Johannes, who was born in 1670; and (5) Maria, born 25 October, 1672, who married Peter Schuyler.

VIII Anna Van Rensselaer, daughter of Colonel Jeremias Van Rensselaer and Marritje Van Cortlandt, was born 1 August, 1665. She married, first, her cousin, Kiliaen Van Rensselaer, the son and heir of Johannes, second Patroon, and, therefore, the third Patroon of Rensselaerwyck.

He had come to New York from the Netherlands, and had been naturalized under the English government. He and his cousin, Kiliaen, the son of Colonel Jeremias Van Rensselaer, were jointly constituted the two first Lords of the Manor of Rensselaerwyck, when, by the Patent of Governor Thomas Dongan, 4 November, 1685, the Colony of Rensselaerwyck was converted into a Manor, the town and fort of Albany being omitted from the grant.

At the time of the English conquest of New Netherland, Governor Richard Nichols had granted to Jeremias Van Rensselaer, 18 October, 1664, "all the privileges and authority * * * * he did enjoy and execute before the surrender of New York." On 8 May, 1666, King Charles II. directed Governor Nichols to grant a Patent to Jeremias Van Rensselaer to confirm him in "the privileges and authority," as they had been granted him two years before. In Governor Dongan's Patent of 1685 "the Lordship and Manor of Rensselaerwyck" was granted to "Killian Van Rensselaer, the son of Johannes Van Rensselaer and Killian Van Rensselaer, the son of Jeremias Van Rensselaer, their heirs and assigns forever," as "one Lordship and Mannour."

Kiliaen Van Rensselaer, the son of Johannes, died 22 February, 1687, leaving no issue, his wife, Anna. Van Rensselaer, being the sole executrix of his estate. His will, made on the day of his death, and proved 7 June, 1687, in which he is styled "of Watervliet, Patroon of the Lordship and Manor of Rensselaerwyck," mentions his wife, Anna; cousins, Hendrick, son of his uncle, Jeremiah Van Rensselaer, the children of Jeremy, son of John Baptist Van Rensselaer, and of Dominie Johannes Carlinnias; sister, Nelle Maria; and aunt, Petronella Van Twiller. It refers to the Manor, to land in Gelderland and at Clein, Overhoorst, District of Barnvelt, in the Hospell van Voorthuysen, and to a house and lot at Newkerk.

Up to 1695 the estate was not divided among the Van Rensselaer heirs. In that year Kiliaen, the son of Jan Baptist Van Rensselaer, came over from Holland to effect a settlement with the New York heirs, the children of Jeremias Van Rensselaer. On 1 November, 1695, a document was signed by which the heirs in Holland released to those in the Province of New York their rights in the Manor of Rensselaerwyck, in exchange for a release of all rights in the family properties in Holland. Rensselaerwyck thus passed to the children of Jeremias Van Rensselaer. Besides the Manor they owned sixty-two thousand acres, known as the Claverack, or Lower, Manor. On 20 May, 1704, Kiliaen, the eldest son of Jeremias Van Rensselaer, obtained a Patent for all this land. His brother, Johannes, had died without issue. To his brother, Hendrick, he conveyed the Claverack Manor, 1 June, 1704, with fifteen hundred acres known as Greenbush. To his sister, Maria, he deeded another tract, and to his sister, Anne, wife of William Nicoll, he deeded a tract in the town of Bethlehem, west of the Hudson.

Anne Van Rensselaer, daughter of Jeremias and widow of Kiliaen Van Rensselaer, married, second, William Nicoll. This marriage took place probably in 1688.

IX   Mary Nicoll, wife of Robert Watts.

6

X The Honorable John Watts, Senior.

XI The Honorable John Watts, Junior.

XII Mary Justina Watts, wife of Frederic de Peyster.

XIII General John Watts de Peyster.

The Van Rensselaer Arms: Gules, a cross moline, argent.

Crest: A high basket, from which issue flames, all proper.

Motto: Niemond zonder.

CHAPTER X

The records of Amsterdam show that a Pieter Schuyler, or Schuylert, born in Cologne, appeared before the Burgomasters of Amsterdam, with his wife. The latter was Catharina, the daughter of Cors Jansen Buyck, of a well-known Amsterdam family. She was married to Pieter Schuyler prior to 1639. It is probable that this Pieter Schuyler was the father of Captain Philip Pieterse Schuyler, the first of the name in America.

I Pieter Schuyler was probably a resident of Amsterdam, Holland.

II Captain Philip Pieterse Schuyler, shown by his name to have been a son of Pieter Schuyler, came to this country from Amsterdam. On 12 May, 1650, he married, at "Beverwyck"—the old name of Albany—Margareta Van Slichtenhorst. He became a wealthy trader, and was Commissary or Magistrate at Fort Orange from 1655 almost continuously, under Stuyvesant and Nicolls, until his death, 9 May, 1683. His rank of Captain was gained at Albany, 1 November, 1667. Captain Schuyler was eminent in military, political and social life. His coat of arms was one of those painted upon the windows of the old Dutch Church at Albany. In his will, which he made jointly with his wife, 1 May, 1683, and which was proved 4 March, 1683-4, he mentions eight children, "Gertruyd, the wife of Stephanus Van Cortlandt; Alida, the wife of Robert Livingston; Petr, Brant, Phillip, Arent, Johannes, and Margaret Schuyler."

Captain Schuyler and Margareta Van Slichtenhorst had issue: (1) Gysbert, who was born 2 July, 1652, and died young; (2) Gertrude; (3) Alida; (4) Peter, who was born 17 September, 1657; (5) Brant, who was

born 18 December, 1659; (6) Arent, who was born 25
June, 1662; (7) Sybilla, who was born 12 November,
1664, and died young; (8) Philip, who was born 8
February, 1666; (9) Johannes, who was born 5 April,
1668; and (10) Margaret, born 2 January, who married, first, Jacobus Verplanck, and, second, John Collins.

III Gertrude Schuyler, daughter of Captain Philip
Pieterse Schuyler and Margareta Van Slichtenhorst, was
born 4 February, 1654. She married, 10 September,
1671, De Heer Stephanus Van Cortlandt, and died in
1718. Through her daughter, Anna Van Cortlandt,
who married Stephen de Lancey, two lines of Schuyler
descent can be traced to General de Peyster.

1

IV Anna Van Cortlandt, wife of Stephen de Lancey.
V Ann de Lancey, wife of the Honorable John
Watts, Senior.
VI The Honorable John Watts, Junior.
VII Mary Justina Watts, wife of Frederic de
Peyster.
VIII General John Watts de Peyster.

2

IV Anna Van Cortlandt, wife of Stephen de Lancey.
V Peter de Lancey.
VI Jane de Lancey, wife of the Honorable John
Watts, Junior.
VII Mary Justina Watts, wife of Frederic de
Peyster.
VIII General John Watts de Peyster.

3

III Alida Schuyler, another daughter of Captain
Philip Pieterse Schuyler and Margareta Van Slichtenhorst, was born 28 February, 1656. She married, first,
10 February, 1675, the Rev. Nicolaus Van Rensselaer.
Her second marriage took place in 1679, when she
became the wife of Robert Livingston. Through her a
third Schuyler line appears in the ancestry of General
de Peyster.

IV   Gilbert Livingston, son of Alida Schuyler and Robert Livingston.

V   Robert Gilbert Livingston.

VI   Helen Livingston, wife of Samuel Hake.

VII   Helen Hake, wife of Captain Frederic de Peyster.

VIII   Frederic de Peyster.

IX   General John Watts de Peyster.

The Schuyler Arms: Vert, issuing from a cloud, proper, a cubit arm, in fess, vested, azure, holding on the hand a falcon, close, all proper.

Crest: A hawk, close, proper.

VAN SLICHTENHORST

I   Arent Van Slichtenhorst was probably a resident of Nykerk, Gelderland. He had issue: (1) Arent Van Slichtenhorst, who was a celebrated poet and historian; and (2) Brant.

II   Brant Arentse Van Slichtenhorst was, as his name indicates, a son of Arent Van Slichtenhorst. In 1648 he came to "Beverwyck," afterwards Albany, as Resident-Director of the Colony of Rensselaerwyck. This chief magistrate and superintendent of the colony was a man of education.   Becoming involved in conflicts with Stuyvesant over questions of authority and jurisdiction affecting the rights of the Patroon of Rensselaerwyck, he was arrested, escaped from prison, was re-arrested, and finally released. Later on he resigned his office to Jan Baptist Van Rensselaer, and, in 1660, returned to Holland. He was a man of justice and liberty, always maintaining the rights of the colony as guaranteed under the charter of Freedoms and Exemptions of 1629. His wife having died in Holland, he brought to America with him his two children: (1) Gerrit, who became a Magistrate of Albany and Schenectady, and was later a resident of Esopus; and (2) Margareta.

III   Margareta, daughter of Brant Arentse Van Slichtenhorst, was born in Nykerk. She was married at the age of twenty-two, according to the old family record written by her husband, to Captain Philip Pieterse Schuyler. She survived her husband twenty-eight years, dying in 1711. Robert Livingston, her son-in-law, was one of the executors of her estate.

General de Peyster inherited three strains of Van Slichtenhorst blood, being descended from two children of Margareta Van Slichtenhorst and Captain Philip Pieterse Schuyler, through one of whom a double line comes down.

1

IV Gertrude Schuyler, daughter of Margareta Van Slichtenhorst and Philip Pieterse Schuyler, and wife of De Heer Stephanus Van Cortlandt.

V Anna Van Cortlandt, wife of Stephen de Lancey.

VI Peter de Lancey.

VII Jane de Lancey, wife of the Honorable John Watts, Junior.

VIII Mary Justina Watts, wife of Frederic de Peyster.

IX General John Watts de Peyster.

2

IV Gertrude Schuyler, daughter of Margareta Van Slichtenhorst and Philip Pieterse Schuyler, and wife of De Heer Stephanus Van Cortlandt.

V Anna Van Cortlandt, wife of Stephen de Lancey.

VI Ann de Lancey, wife of the Honorable John Watts, Senior.

VII The Honorable John Watts, Junior.

VIII Mary Justina Watts, wife of Frederic de Peyster.

IX General John Watts de Peyster.

3

IV Alida Schuyler, daughter of Margareta Van Slichtenhorst and Philip Pieterse Schuyler, and wife of Robert Livingston.

V Gilbert Livingston.

VI Robert Gilbert Livingston.

VII Helen Livingston, wife of Samuel Hake.

VIII   Helen Hake, wife of Captain Frederic de
Peyster

IX   Frederic de Peyster.

X   General John Watts de Peyster.

By blood and inheritance General de Peyster was a
typical New York aristocrat.   The roll-call of his ancestry assembles the chief of the famous ruling families of
colonial New York—de Peyster, Livingston, Van Cortlandt, Van Rensselaer, de Lancey, Schuyler, Beekman,
Philipse, Watts, Nicoll, French and Colden.   Four of
these, Van Rensselaer, Livingston, Van Cortlandt, and
Philipse, were the great manorial grandees of the
Province.   A martial spirit stirred the blood of the de
Lanceys and the Schuylers; the Nicolls and the Livingstons were lawyers, jurists, politicians and statesmen;
Colden was a philosopher.

General de Peyster inherited a double strain from the
de Peysters and the de Lanceys, a triple strain from the
Van Slichtenhorsts and Schuylers, and a quadruple
strain from the Loockermans and Van Cortlandts.   By
blood, therefore, if not in name, he was more of a de
Lancey than the de Lanceys themselves, more of a
Schuyler than the Schuylers, more of a Van Cortlandt
than the Van Cortlandts.

The racial ingredients in General de Peyster's ancestry
make it strikingly typical of New York.   The de Peysters were Flemish, as were the Haukens, and perhaps
the de Vries and de Booghs; Nicoll, Reade, French,
Woodhall, and Grafton are English stocks; de Lancey is
French; Mac Pheadris, Irish; Watts, Colden, Christie
and Livingston, Scotch; Schuyler, Beekman and Hardenbroeck, probably German; Van Cortlandt, Van Rensselaer, Philipse, Loper, Huygens, Van Slichtenhorst, Van
Wely, Jansen and Loockermans, Dutch.   At least seven
races, of those whose blended blood and genius laid the
foundations of New York, compounded their influences
at the birth of General de Peyster.

BOOK II

EARLY RECOLLECTIONS

CHAPTER XI

For the early period of General de Peyster's life we are fortunate in having his personal reminiscences, dictated to an amanuensis in 1876, at the age of fifty-five. These possess a peculiar interest. Presenting the New York of his youth from the view-point of a young aristocrat of an intensely vivid temperament, their freshness and originality invest them with the charm and manner of one of the great creations, in the form of autobiography, of our masters of fiction. The General criticizes persons and things with a freedom which, throughout his life, won him the respect of great minds, and the petty enmity of the mean. The reader may not always agree with him, but he will be interested in the early impressions of so extraordinary a personality, and in this picture of social life in the early part of the Nineteenth Century.

These reminiscences, hitherto unpublished, are given in General de Peyster's own words, in this and the following chapters.

My first recollection, if it is an exertion of individual memory, is of two children that were brought to play with me, when I was about two years old. This was at a house, which I have often since recognized, about the junction of the Eighth avenue with the Bloomingdale road, whither we had moved to get rid of the yellow fever—or that is the reason which has been given me for our being there.

Between this period and four or five years of age my recollections are vague: pictures present themselves to me, but I cannot assign the dates, although they are

perfectly vivid. I see faces, I hear voices, I recognize
localities. One thing I do recall, and with disgust—the
manner in which I was crammed with food. The way
arrow-root was forced down my throat, while I lay prone
and helpless across Mammie Trainque's knees, has made
me hate that nourishing article, and the silver vessel
from which it was administered, ever since. If any
escaped, she used to hoe it up with her forefinger, and
then shove it into my mouth, wiping that finger between
my open lips, so that I am often nearly sea-sick at the
thought.

My dress was nothing like the dresses of children at
this day. I wore ample frills, almost ruffs, around my
neck, and long aprons, almost to the ankles; but underneath were very respectable imitations of trousers and
jackets. I slept in the same bed with Mammie, on
feathers, in a room heated with sea-coal, which I consider injured my health; and I was pampered in every
way. I had heavy plum cake, *ad libitum*, and mince
pies, in season, at all hours. Beppy, my foster sister,
was as admirable a cook as she was an excellent woman.
How Mammie bullied her, and her tyranny wrecked her
life. Beppy was fidelity itself, and to the last moment
as true as steel. I do not believe that a better woman
ever lived on the face of this earth. I have never seen
one like her. Both she and Mammie died while I was
watching them, of disease of the heart. When she was
so weak that she could scarcely walk, while she was in
charge of my place, because she deemed it her duty
to protect things during my absence, she would climb a
hill nearly an eighth of a mile long, away back in the
field, to drive out from a field of oats the turkeys of
thieving neighbors.

One thing I recollect with horror. Mammie and her
cronies used to delight in stories of ghosts and similar
subjects, and I used to get down in the bed, to the very
foot, under the covering, with every fiber quivering, and
then have such dreams that the recalling of them excites
horror at this day.

And yet Mammie was an excellent woman; but she had no judgment. She would have saved my life with her heart's blood. Nevertheless, I believe that her want of common sense laid the basis of all the misery of my life. She ruined my stomach with dainties, and she spoiled me in every way that a poor little chap could be spoiled. With all this, she would have risked her life for me, and afterwards for my son, Watts, at any moment, as was proved.

Besides the servants, there was in the house where I was born, No. 3 Broadway, my dear old grandfather, Honorable John Watts. I suppose he was what the world, in its worthless judgment, styles a stern man. To me, he was ever the gentlest and best. What should I have been without him? He realized what has been said of St. Paul: "Defective health, united with a vitality like iron, and a will of steel." He was seventy-three as he first lives in my memory, and just so he continues until within a few weeks before his death. He was as straight as an arrow, about five feet ten, with the springy step of an Indian. He was the handsomest old gentleman I ever saw. He had bright, dark-blue eyes, like sapphires—I have no recollection of another pair of such colored eyes—and the most exquisite, silky, silver, curly or wavy hair. He could ride like a guacho, walk like a hunter, and the Honorable Samuel B. Ruggles has often told me that, so concisely did he think and express himself, he could say more on a page of note paper than most men on a sheet of foolscap.

Two of his sons, my mother's brothers, were living in the house. Besides my aunt Elizabeth, these were all that were left of a family of ten. Robert, as conceded by every one, was the handsomest man in New York, and so I remember him. Every one of his associates told me, when I had grown up, that he was as glorious in his disposition as he was in his appearance. He led a very gay life, exposed himself without a care for his health, and was bled to death by his cousin, Dr. John Watts, a perfect sangrado, although a most eminent physician. It was the fashion of the day to phlebotomize. This bleeding converted an inflammation of the lungs into consumption, and he lingered, to die on the threshhold of golden fortune. I was held up in my father's arms for him to smile good-bye to me. My dear, kind, generous, universally-beloved uncle, "Bob" Watts!

Uncle Stephen differed from him as much as day does from night. Uncle Robert was magnificent in his proportions. Stevie was small, but beautifully made. Nevertheless, he had the courage of a lion, and the will of my grandfather. That expresses all that need be said. This will was the cause of his death. He was very ill, but said he would get up and walk around the Battery, in November. The famous Dr. Post answered, "Stephen, if you do so, it will be the last walk you will ever take on earth." He got up, dressed himself, and took the walk, came home, went to his bed, and died. "Mrs. Trainque," said he to my nurse—it was a brutal November day—"I felt the wind go through me like gimlets of ice."

Stephen was a great sportsman. What hampers of game of forest, field and stream I have seen him bring home! He was a great driver, too; drove a tilbury and tandem; had beautiful dogs. Barstow, his favorite setter, died of grief when his master was dead.

My grandfather, as stated, was a wonderful rider. Strange to say, neither of my two uncles could or would make a show on horseback.

To demonstrate Stephen's coolness: one day Stephen, when out shooting, came upon an enormous "copperhead." The snake struck at him, but, quicker than the snake, Steve dropped his gun, and blew his head off.

Robert was a great tease. He used to torment Stevie's life out of him; but, with all the difference of size, he never dared to let Stevie come to close quarters, for Stevie was a perfect tiger when his blood was up.

What an irregular house was that dear old home, No. 3 Broadway! Grandfather used to breakfast in every kind of style, anywhere from 4 A. M. to noon. I got my breakfast between 7 A. M. and 9. Robert breakfasted in his apartments somewhere—well, in the course of the day. I remember he used to drink green tea, strong enough to blow the top of your head off. Stevie occupied a part of the third story. I know he was almost as bad as Bob, but then he was less at home. He used to be off shooting and fishing for days and weeks.

Three o'clock was the nominal dinner hour, but I seldom remember more than two at table. As for tea, that was taken promiscously as to time and place. After tea, how often grandfather and I went to the theatre! What time Uncle Bob used to come home nobody ever would have known, had it not been that we sometimes heard a cheery voice caroling a stave or whistling a tune in the room under the nursery. He idolized me, teased me, and appeased me with magnificent presents. I have never seen such toys from that day to this. How often Mammie has taken me out of my crib and carried me down to his room to finish my sleep by his side!

The reception of Lafayette took place in 1824. I have impressions of what occurred. Once I believed I remembered everything distinctly. Now it is impossible to decide if it is only the memory of the individual facts, or of what I was told and saw. Uncle Bob was bosom friend of Sam Gouverneur, who married a daughter of President Monroe. The latter lived with "Sam" in Houston street, near Broadway, and there Lafayette was a constant guest. I perfectly remember the aged President, in his satin knee breeches, hovering over a grate in the dingy parlor—for dingy it was to me, accustomed to grand, bright rooms.

The first indelible impression on my young mind, and it is as vivid as if it had occurred yesterday, was the celebration of the completion of the Erie Canal. The top of No. 3 Broadway was comparatively flat, and there was a railing around it. Southwards a sort of bridge projected to an enormous chimney, next to No. 1, built by my great uncle, Hon. Archibald Kennedy, afterwards

eleventh Earl of Cassilis. From this bridge and the
roof there was an unobstructed view up Broadway and
down State street, as well as of Greenwich street in the
rear, through the open space, about fifty feet. The
demonstrations of respect were on the 26th of October,
1825. I was then four and a half years old. The
procession (or part of it) formed on the west side of
Greenwich street, with its right on Marketfield street;
it then wheeled or countermarched, passed up Greenwich
street to Canal street, thence to Broadway, up Broadway
to Broome street, by the latter across to the Bowery,
down the latter to Pearl street, and through this around
to the Battery.

On the Battery the display by land united with the
aquatic party, and thence the whole, united, marched
up Broadway to the City Hall. The city by day was
wild with enthusiasm, and ablaze with illuminations at
night. I know this: that I have witnessed other cele-
brations on which a vast deal more money had been
expended, but none which were anything like as effective.

Little shaver as I was, I was peculiarly struck with
the Faculty and Students of Columbia College, in their
silk gowns. That they were dressed in this style, like
parsons equipped for the pulpit, and why, I remember,
bothered me considerably.

The butchers made a magnificent display. They had
three or four cars, each followed by detachments of
butchers, mounted on horses of the same color, bay for
one, black for another; and they *were* horses, and their
riders knew how to manage them. The saddlers and
harness-makers were likewise admirably represented.
Uncle Bob had given me a large, exquisite, toy horse,
which we named "White Surrey." Just such a real
horse, led by two black grooms in Moorish dress, headed
their Society.

In their part of the line, the Boat-Builders' Association displayed the Whitehall boat that won the great
race, 20th May, 1825, a triumph which was then the
boast of every class in the city, and continued to be long

THE COUNTESS OF CASSILIS, NÉE ANN WATTS
From a Painting

afterwards. I think this boat was afterwards exhibited at "Scudders" or the "American Museum."

The Fourth Division comprised the Fire Department, and it never appeared as it did on this occasion. People worked for love in those days; there was no blackmailing, nor dirty tricks. A little money went a great way, because it was expended faithfully, and those who could assist with their professional or mechanical aid accomplished all that man could, gratuitously.

Colden's Memoir of the Grand Canal Celebration, royal octavo, over 400 pages, was "presented by the City of New York to the Honorable John Watts, Recorder of the City of New York in 1774, and First Judge of West Chester County in 1803." My grandfather was legally Recorder until he was succeeded by Richard Varick, in 1783. He held a number of other important public offices, but he was not a loquacious man, or else I would know a great deal more about my native city. One thing impresses itself: he remembered New York when, as to the compact portion, it was within Wall street.

No one ever saw a procession to better advantage than I did this. I saw the start from my grandfather's, No. 3 Broadway, which, as I said, ran through to Greenwich street, and the close from my Aunt Laight's room, southeast corner of Broadway and Flat and Barrack Hill, now Exchange Place. As for the illuminations in the evening, people said they were very fine. I must have seen them, for everybody was devoted to me, and took me everywhere; but, poor little shaver, I must have been too tired out when night came to remember anything.

People may laugh at this relation of my experience, and say that it is the result of subsequent conversations. What, then, will be the judgment when I put down that I remember the reception of Lafayette in the previous year, 1824? (He landed in New York 15th August, 1824.) It was not dwelt upon because it is simply a dim impression, whereas the panorama of the canal celebration absolutely passes before my eyes as a reality every time that I think about it.

7

Lafayette is associated in my mind with many years of happiness, for I had a pet dog called the "Marquis de Lafayette." It was brought to me by my Uncle Robert, but I cannot say whether it came direct from Lafayette himself, or from him through ex-President Monroe. This dog was unlike any one I have since seen. No tiny black and tan terrier was more exquisitely formed; but it was a French dog, some relation to a French pug. It lies buried under a sand-stone slab in the yard of No. 3 Broadway, inscribed "Mark," his pet name; but, as the remains of men are not respected in Gotham, it is not to be supposed that those of dogs are. Like many a noble knight, sung of in poetry,

"His bones are dust,"

and most like his memorial has been built into the foundations of the warehouse on the site of our stable on Greenwich street. Uncle Robert Watts was very intimate with Sam Gouverneur, son-in-law of President James Monroe, and it was through his connection we got the dog.

I must have seen Lafayette and have been presented to him, but for some reason or other he could have made no impression on me. Perhaps a good reason for this arises from the fact that I never took stock in him, considering him a very much overrated character. My father, Frederic de Peyster, Jr., was military secretary to the justly celebrated Governor De Witt Clinton, who was Executive of the State in 1825, and as everybody made a great deal of me on account of my connections, I was taken everywhere and permitted to put my tiny hand in the big hands of the greatest people. Moreover, my grandfather, Frederic de Peyster, Esq., was an intimate friend of Governor Clinton, and had been closely associated with him in the establishment of our common school system. Whether I was presented to Lafayette or not, my memory would not be worth a copper, if it did not retain the fuss made over him.

New York rang with "Hurrah for Lafayette!" as it never rang with any other name except "Jackson." No man in the United States, in my lifetime, had the individual popularity of "Old Hickory." Even I, as a boy, was a Democrat when he ran, but I never belonged to that party after I came to comprehend matters and had a vote.

Before quitting this subject, a few words about President Monroe. When I was about nine he came to New York to live permanently with his son-in-law, Sam Gouverneur. "Sam" was a real genial man—no saint. He resided in Prince street, just east of Broadway. Mr. Monroe looked just like the usual pictures of him. He was very kind to me; I recall him in his black velvet or satin knee breeches, sitting close in by the side of the front parlor fireplace. He did not strike me as a man who should be or who had been President of these United States. My uncle, Robert Gilbert Livingston de Peyster, who helped Jacob Barker to save the picture of Washington when the English burnt the National Capitol, 24th August, 1814, knew him well.

When I was five years old I was first sent to day school, Mr. Preswick's. He was a gentle pedagogue, and helped to spoil me, took interest in my fishing tackle, and gave me many a certificate entitling me to a penny, for merit in scholarship, which were good for dollars at home.

Before I went to him, my dear old Aunt Laight had coached me through the rudiments. I could spell Abecedinarian, and words of that calibre; yes, hard words, which if I could spell as well now, would give me the prize at every "spelling bee."

Poor Mr. Preswick! He had a little boy on whom he doted; he wandered down on the dock, fell in, and was drowned. They got him out very quickly, and I remember they rolled him on a barrel—the worst thing they could have done—but he was gone. Even the holidays which resulted could not brighten the gloom cast over us little ones by this sad event. If it were yesterday, instead of fifty years ago, my sad walk home on that occasion could not be more present to my mind.

I was seven years old when the political contest between John Quincy Adams and Andrew Jackson occurred. This campaign was one to be remembered. Money was not squandered in the prodigal manner of the present day, but what was lacking in expensive humbuggery was more than made up in bitterness and enthusiasm. My instincts were all in favor of Adams, but they were swept away by the electrifying influences which emanated from the victory of Jackson over the British at New Orleans. This, too, despite the hand-bills with the six coffins of the Kentuckians he shot for want of discipline!

As soon as I could read, my wise father had given me books, *ad libitum*, and, if I never was good at anything else, I was excellent at reading, and the amount of it that I had done, when most boys really begin to read, is something almost incredible. What is still more remarkable, I have forgotten very little of the gist of what I read at that time.

As soon as the Harpers began to publish their Family Library, it was bought for me, and for many years I read every volume as it came out. The result of my reading had made me acquainted with Jackson's career. With him I had fought his duels; the Creeks, the Seminoles, the British; had hung Arbuthnot in Florida, and handled the Spanish Governor of that Territory in the only way that can bring such hidalgos to their senses.

Here let me slip in a remark. Jackson is said to have really saved New Orleans by his night attack of December 23d, 1814, because this daring slap in the face made the British over cautious afterwards. Hereby time was gained, and in war, time is often of inestimable value. Human life, property, money, are often of no account, even if expended with the utmost prodigality, provided they gain the necessary time. My mother's cousin, Captain John Watts, of the British Army, afterwards Deputy Warden of Walmer Castle, under Wellington, corroborated the view above taken of this night attack. He was at the capture of Washington, and in the attempt on New Orleans. He described how he was awakened by the unexpected fire of the Americans, a ball going through his camp-kettle, which hung over his head. If he did not use the very words, he said as much, I think. At all events, he admitted it was a very spirited affair on the part of the Americans.

By the way, this Captain Watts, B. A., who had seen a great deal of service, related an anecdote of what occurred to him in Washington, when his troops entered, which is worth repeating. He said that he had been hard put to it, and sadly needed a change of linen. Stepping into a store, he offered to exchange his dirty shirt, which, however, was of the finest linen, and beautifully frilled, for a clean one, however coarse the material. The American agreed, and the swap was made on the spot. As Captain Watts turned to go out, the American said to him, "Look here, mister, I have let you have a clean shirt, but let me tell you, if I get a chance, I sha'n't hesitate to dirty it by putting a ball through the body inside of it."

At this time I was seven years old, as I said. I was already quite a good horseman. A pony, almost a horse, was either hired for me, or bought for me. I guess he was only on trial, for soon afterwards there was no horse around that I did not use, under the saddle or in harness.

About this time Uncle Stevie died. For a few days I had been sent around to the town house of my grand-father de Peyster, on the west side of Broad, just above Garden street. I was taken home to see Stevie in his coffin. Dear old grandfather, himself, led me up into the death room. So strong was the impression left upon my mind by the sight of that marble face, that, thirty years afterwards, when I repaired the old Family Vault in Trinity churchyard, and reboxed the coffins, the lid of his came off, and I recognized the remains by the hair and the contour of the skull. While I stood, awe-struck, beside my deceased uncle, grandfather walked up and down the room, stately as ever, murmuring, "Poor Stevie! poor Stevie!"

My cousin, Philip Kearny, Jr., afterwards the famous Union General of the Rebellion, subsequently had this room. He often reminded me of our Uncle Stephen, with his extreme nicety of dress and precision of habits. When he came, our military studies commenced, to which I have alluded in my Life of the General.

[While General Kearny and the writer lived together in the house of their grandfather, from 1829 to 1834, almost all the leisure time of both was spent in mimic campaigns, with armies composed of from four to six thousand leaden soldiers, with perfect trains of artillery, and even other adjuncts of a well-provided host. Battles were fought according to a digested system, which even regulated what proportion of those knocked down, by the mimic fire of musketry or artillery, should be considered as dead, or too severely wounded to take part in the rest of the campaign, and how many as slightly wounded, and how long the latter should be looked upon as remaining in the hospital before they were again available.

The firing was done with small spring-guns, one shot for each cannon, one for each regiment or separate detachment of infantry, and so many for each line of sharp-shooters. When the firing, alternating, had gone through both lines of battle, the different bodies were moved a shorter or longer determined distance, according as they belonged to the different arms, over spaces dictated by the real relative speed of the different services, whether light or heavy cavalry, light or line infantry, field or reserve artillery. This was not left to hazard, but according to a written or stipulated code.

Field works and permanent fortifications were constructed of pasteboard, and the irregularities of ground represented by piles of books and similar objects, built up in accordance with agreement, before operations commenced. One siege lasted a number of weeks, and the tidy, dearly-beloved, and respected old housekeeper, wife of a former sword-master at West Point, was driven almost wild by the accumulation of dust, and the appropriation of huge dining-tables, of solid mahogany, the pride of her heart, whose oiling and polishing absorbed the greater part of her time. Every other kind of table, or flat piece of furniture, was impressed, which could be dragged out of its place and made available to eke out the theatre of action. She could scarcely be pacified at the subsequent disorder of the spacious rooms, and the prohibition, strictly enforced, against sweeping and dusting, lest the bustle should knock down or disarrange the soldiers.

Fleets of paste-board were even attempted, but maritime operations could not be made to work, since many a pellet which hit the sides of a vessel would level all on board, and then a quarrel would ensue, as to how many were killed and how many wounded, which often ended in a fight, and put an end to mimic hostilities, until the actual hostilities, between the leaders, were settled, and the wounded honor of either or both was appeased. A very forcible shot from one of the spring-guns, close at hand, against a paste-board ship, had the same effect· as the impact of one of Farragut's vessels, when they butted the iron-clad "Tennessee" in the Bay of Mobile. All the poor little leaden soldiers were knocked off their feet, and a number overboard.

As the question of how many knew how to swim, and how many ought to be drowned, was never taken into consideration when the code of procedure was drawn up, it led to so much argument that the belligerents came to the conclusion of Napoleon; that it was as useless for them, as for him, to attempt the empire of the sea.

Kearny continued to enjoy this amusement even while he was in college, and perhaps still longer. When he began to go into society, he took so much pains with his dress, and spent so much of his time out of the house, that he gradually relinquished a game which had given him such great delight and occupation for years.*]

*The paragraphs within brackets, inserted here, are from General de Peyster's "Personal and Military History of Philip Kearny."—F. A.

There was a perfect menagerie in the yard of No. 3 Broadway. Deer gazed upon strangers with their soft black eyes, and died suddenly. Dissection by our butcher revealed the cause in over affection for each other, or the rabbits testified by licking them, since he found large and hard balls of hair in their stomachs. Rabbits, flop-eared, straight-eared, and all kinds of eared, burrowed under the ground, and rats countermined them from the stable and ate their young in their burrows. Opossums hung by their tails from the trees, and sometimes got into the neighbors' houses and made themselves disagreeable. Peccaries gnashed their tusks; and dogs flashed their teeth, sometimes in each other, sometimes in my guilty legs, and oftener in the innocent legs of visitors. It was a pandemonium when something started a chorus.

As for birds, they were innumerable. Pigeons of all kinds spoiled the rain water of our neighbors, to the ruin of their tempers, and our own to the injury of our stomachs, for drinking water was bad in New York in those days, and was peddled around by the pail, from a cask on wheels. The Manhattan water was scarcely drink-able, spoiled by a long passage through pipes bored out of logs of wood. To afford some idea of the number of birds, there was one cage about six feet square, and ten feet high, filled with the most beautiful and vocal varieties. One night the rats made an inroad and left it like a Bulgarian village sacked by a horde of Bashi-Bazouks. It is said that the English drum ushers in the sun, from a chain of posts encircling the globe. On our premises the sun was welcomed, from a chain of coops encircling the extensive yard, with the note of every bird which, at that time, commerce had brought to New York.

CHAPTER XII

A NEW YORK BOARDING-SCHOOL

Next year, when I was eight, the "Sorrows of Werther" began. I had become a thoroughly spoiled chap, allowed to do pretty much as I chose, and a great many things that I chose were very naughty.

My grandfather was a very large landowner. He owned land in thirty-two counties. Besides, he was proprietor or patroon of the Lower Claverack Manor, a tract ten miles square around the City of Hudson, in Columbia County. Hundreds of tenants used to come to see him, and, as I was looked upon as his heir, they used to bow to me as the young Patroon, and if I had been a prince I could not have been more pampered. My nurse was also housekeeper; consequently royalty did not fare better. Her daughter, Beppy, presided over the dainties, and you may be sure I did not lack.

Her son, Peter, was my henchman. The whole family were musical; he was a sweet singer indeed. Between them they taught me over two hundred songs, and I could sing them until I got the bronchitis, in 1851. Since then, comparatively speaking, I can scarcely turn a tune.

Black Tom, the coachman, most faithful, even to the death, of a class now extinct, but "most dissipated and careless of niggers," was my bond-slave. He developed my equestrian qualifications. He once saved my grandfather from a terrible accident with a vicious horse, which shied with the gig into a ditch, and did everything bad a horse could do. Tom clung to that animal's head, at the risk of his life, until grandfather could be extricated.

Fate took me in hand about this time and packed me off to boarding-school. I believe even Mammie was willing to let me go, however sorry, very soon afterwards. Mammie's system of spoiling me followed me thither, and at that boarding-school, while I gained an immense deal, I met with an accident which, developing seeds planted at home by many things intended as kindnesses, ruined my health for the rest of my life.

The boarding-school was the Washington Institute. It is said that Lafayette paid it a visit, and, on being requested to name it, gave it this title, which it always afterwards bore.

When I first became a pupil we were all compelled to wear the uniform which, it is said, Lafayette selected when he gave it its title. When I left, I do not think a single scholar continued to wear it. It made perfect guys of us. Imagine a lot of little shavers in Continental uniform—blue coats, faced, turned up, and lined with buff, and big brass buttons; buff vests, with moderate flaps. Strange to say, I never have been able to recall what I wore on my head or my legs, nor can Major-General Charles K. Graham, U. S. V., who was a fellow-pupil. I think we wore beavers, with a cockade in the side; blue pantaloons in winter, with a buff stripe or cord down the leg, like the present police, white cloth ones in the spring, and linen in summer. I know, in the rural district, they used to take me for a little sucking midshipman, for the uniforms were not unlike. Those who did so were civil, but those who did not were extremely unpleasant in their remarks, and poked fun at me until I abhorred my livery.

The school structure was a very large square building, fronting north, standing on an elevation on the south side of Thirteenth Street, which had been dug down some twelve feet or more. There was quite a large garden attached, to the east, and this, together with the yard play-grounds, occupied, I should think, fully one-half the central area of the block between Twelfth and Thirteenth streets, the Bowery, and Third Avenue. The east and south sides were bounded by enormous sheds, for the boys to play under in rainy weather. One end, at

first of the west, and then of the south shed, was fitted
up as a theatre, and before I left I became a very prominent comic performer. Twice the theatre was broken
up because the faculty thought that it drew our minds
away from our studies. In fact, they several times
traversed really extensive preparations for display. Once
we got up races, some boys playing horses and some boys
playing charioteers. The harness was elaborate, and the
jockey costumes very handsome. Why this was knocked
in the head I never could imagine; that it was a punishment for some violation of the rules is pretty certain.
Still, considering the outlay, preparation, including an
immense amount of practice, and the hopes lavished upon
it, it deserved a less stern fate. Nevertheless, the school
was the most liberally managed educational institution
to which I ever belonged, or with which I was ever
acquainted.

Taking schoolmasters as a class, Dr. Wickham, the
principal, was a notable exception for benignity and
excellence. He did try to make us happy, and he was
not mean in furnishing us with amusement. While I
am writing, grateful recollections are swelling up in my
bosom. I did not, could not, perhaps, appreciate him at
his full value then.

He was a tall, not ill-formed man, with a dark,
pleasant face, and a very large nose. An Irish laborer
once wantonly split it in two with a spade, and it was
"an object" ever after. I am happy to say that my
father was the means of capturing that Irishman. The
arrest was made at the risk of the parties' lives, and this
wicked Paddy was sent to State Prison for a term of
years, for resisting a police officer, but nothing was done
to him for his injury to Dr. Wickham. To prove the
Doctor's gentle disposition, he not only forgave the man
who marred him for life, but carried comforts to him
in the prison.

Think of this—and he had terribly disfigured the
Doctor, with a broad, raised, indigo welt, diagonally
across the whole length of his nose, from eyebrow, on

one side, to lip, on the other! The Doctor was not a handsome man afterwards, but that did not stop him from getting a second wife.

His first wife, the one we knew, was a gentle little woman, and a great invalid; she died while I was there, of protracted liver complaint, and I believe even we rude boys were sadly affected, although it brought us a holiday.

During the first part of my sojourn, Dr. Wickham had a partner, Mons. Arnoux or Arnaud. He was a nice man, also. The dormitory, in which I first slept, was separated from his bedroom by folding-doors. How often after "taps" he had occasion to separate those folding doors with his "Silence-la, He!" Like most Frenchmen that I have met, he did not get along pleasantly in his own family. A curious circumstance which, with all my intention to be frank, is best left unsaid, preceded Mr. Arnoux's leaving. We never had a good successor. Arnoux certainly was sufficiently French to give the right accent to our conversation, if not the right accent to our morals.

Arnoux was very kind to me; he was the means of my learning to skate, hiring from a loafer boy the first pair of skates that were ever buckled on my little feet. We had some wonderful skaters at this school. One, the son of the then proprietor or landlord of the great Ballston Spa Hotel, besides doing a number of extraordinary feats, could leap an ordinary rail fence, if memory serves, on rockers. Boys are not as manly now as they were then, neither are men, say what you please.

Although Arnoux was nominally second in command, a German named Lutz exercised the prerogatives. He was a wonderful, certainly the most learned man, in mathematics and natural philosophy, that I have ever encountered. What is more, he could make a practical use of everything that he knew, and impart information in a way that was perfectly marvelous. He was a peculiar man, but a good one; he had favorites, pets, curiously selected. One painful benefit of being a

protégé was the inevitable necessity of working harder
than anybody else. He crammed his chosen few to the
extent of their powers of receptiveness. For instance,
by the time I was nine I had been through the first five
books of Euclid. He so grounded me in geometry that
I never afterwards went to a school where I did not
take the prize in this branch without much further labor.
He taught me—oh, how it racked my little head—to
multiply nine figures by nine figures, setting down the
result in a single row.

Do not let anyone imagine he was perfect. He was
very quick-tempered, and then, as is the rule, unjust.
The great punishment of this school was the "bread-and-
water table." At this the delinquent fasted on bread
and water, while the rest feasted at the long tables, on
three sides. It was a humiliation worse, to a spirited
boy, than a really painful punishment. The only time
that I was disgraced, during my whole stay, was by being
jerked out from my seat at table and placed in this sort
of pillory by Professor Lutz. Doubtless I had deserved
punishment a thousand times, for I was a mischievous
boy, naturally, and utterly spoiled, but on this occasion
I was innocent. There was some disturbance at meal-
time, Lutz presiding, because Wickham was absent.
Lutz got angry, made a dab in the direction, lit on me,
and I was disgraced. What is more, he never would
listen to reason, nor acknowledge that he was wrong.
We had an explanation, and I was restored to favor,
but I do not think we were ever as good friends as before.
Fortunately this occurred a short time before I left. It
rankled. I felt like a good soldier who, near the close
of his term of enlistment, loses a chevron through the
fault of another.

Nevertheless, Lutz was an excellent man. I owe an
immense deal to him; he made a little man of me. He
had cultivated my memory. I had not a forgetting
disposition then, and in that respect I have not changed.
He led us in gymnastics, he led us in our marches,
which were very long and laborious, often at a double-

quick; he mingled with our games, rewarding manliness, and exciting it. I believe he singled me out for favor on account of the tearless manner in which I stood pain, like an Indian. He shared our little feasts, simple but appetizing, and did not spare his money to procure apparatus for the finest experiments in natural philosophy and astronomy.

I forgot to mention that he taught us surveying also, and, before I was ten, I could survey a piece of land as well as one-half of the civil engineers who make a living by it.

Forty years after I had lost sight of him, I heard of him in Indiana. His name had been changed to that of John Lutz Mansfield. He had been professor in Transylvania University, Lexington, Kentucky, then acting President, had married, changed his name, moved to Indiana, become Major-General in the militia, and had a son, a Colonel in the Union Army during the Rebellion; and there I lost sight of him. I repeat, again, he was a wonderful man.

Next to him came Mr. Sayres. I never liked him, but he was a good man, brave as a lion, and he and Lutz were always rivals in gymnastics and gymnastic experiments. It appears to me that he was our head English teacher, but I do not think he had an agreeable disposition, and I do not believe that I owe much to him, except the respect due to true manhood.

Besides these, there was a succession of teachers of Spanish, French, Writing, Speaking, and even Singing. One queer old gentleman, who taught us Elocution, I encountered, still at it, within a very short time. If all the successive classes he has taught tormented him as much as we did, and profited as little by his lessons, he has not had an agreeable life.

CHAPTER XIII

The summer holidays of my first year at Washington Institute, if I am not mistaken as to the year, constitute a marked epoch in my life. I have said that my grandfather owned lands in a great many counties of this State, but, for some one reason or another, he seemed to regard those in Chenango County as most worthy of his personal attention. His headquarters were at a cottage or farmhouse which he owned, about one mile north of Sherburne. It had no pretensions, but was very comfortable, standing on an elevation overlooking a very pretty stream worthy its title, "Handsome Brook," and a flat valley, about a mile broad, bounded by hills grown with primeval woods. The enormous hemlocks have chiefly impressed themselves.

From the front stoop the lawn sloped rapidly to a ha-ha surmounted by a low picket fence. The latter could not be forgotten, because a fine sorrel colt, belonging to my father, attempted to jump it, missed his leap, fell on it, and ran one of the small square pickets deep into his chest. The wound was ugly, but the animal subsequently recovered and brought a good price. This ha-ha bounded a road to the west; on the other side was a zig-zag rail fence. Thence the bank plunged down into "Handsome Brook."

I could never forget the lay of this ground. Shortly after our arrival (the journey thither will be next described) a craft was constructed for me, the first which had ever broken the virgin surface of Handsome Brook. It was the supreme effort of the combined genius of a native carpenter, my excellent father, and a vast council of people who had seen boats of all kinds, as well as canoes and other floating barbarous constructions. It

111

in this case, it seemed to me as if my whole thoughts
were bent on getting help from that boat. I have no
recollection of counting on my father. A third time I
went down, and, when I came up again, I have always
said I was astraddle of the log which knocked me out of
the boat, which thus kept my head above water. At all
events as soon as my head showed itself, my father
threw himself into the water, and, in less time than
you could say Jack Robinson, had me ashore. He always
claimed the whole credit of my preservation. I concede
it, because he deserves it, but always used to think that
that log had something to do with it. This I know,
however, that, having had a chilling at the hands of
Handsome Brook, I next came near having a warming
at those of my father. He was clad in some kind of
fashionable blue-striped Chinese gossamer silk, and his
bath made it fit so tight to him that he looked in this
suit as if it constituted a sort of blistered skin. The
effect was so ludicrous, I burst out laughing, and he
wanted to thrash me for my want of gratitude for my
preservation.

Here an observation occurs to me which I must jot
down before I forget it, namely, the difference in deport-
ment between the rich and poor towards each other in
those days and these present. Then, mechanics and
farmers had an independent manner which, while it
asserted their own manhood and self-recognition, nevertheless exhibited a respect for class position, especially
if united with acknowledged family preëminence. If
the last was accompanied by wealth and intellect, the
respect was more strongly manifested. Still, let demagogues say what they will, fifty years ago social position
from birth was admitted.

I repeat, to emphasize, there was more manliness among
the people at large, more honest independence. Men
would not cringe for money as they do now, and then
spit, so to speak, on the hand of the benefactor. The
debtor did not look upon his creditor as a blood-thirsty
tyrant, nor the creditor on the debtor as a victim.

There was still a strong tie of good will between land-
lords and tenants in the rural districts, for the cursed
foreigner had not come in with his leveling and com-
munistic ideas, and as yet the money-idolizing, mischief-
making New Englanders had not acquired their present
general ascendency.

I speak of New York, whose political institutions,
before the Revolution, formed a comparative feudal
aristocracy, and this never entirely disappeared until our
legislators and executives were debauched into legal confis-
cators through the influence of what is known as anti-
rentism. A patroon, or great landholder, still retained
a great deal of his power and influence, if not his actual
original power, when I accompanied my grandfather in
his visits to his estates, that is, down to about 1833. It
was not until my grandfather died, in 1836, and a new
generation came in, that anti-rentism burst its shell and
became the deadly poisonous reptile it has proved to be.
Then it was that officers became more and more generally
elected, and emigrants flooded in; that judges and
lawyers, and all who sought popularity, prostituted their
honor and banded with the many to deprive the few
of their rights and the respect due to them.

One of our next-door neighbors was a well-to-do
farmer, named Hatch, who owned a first-rate grist-mill
and a rather primitive saw-mill, supplied by the pond
in which twice I came near being drowned. Hatch was
a specimen American, tall and well made, with a handsome face; intelligent, self-reliant, respecting himself,
winning and compelling respect, honest and ready to
work. He would do a "whopping" day's work for an
average day's wages.

His ox-team was as fine as I have ever seen, deep
blood bays, without a speck of white. How they would
"yank" out an old root or stump, and "snag" out
a half-decayed log, for one of the enormous bonfires
they used to build for my amusement! I have seen
these oxen settle down on their knees with a fair, strong,
even pull, to start a reluctant piece of timber.

The miller proper was a regular little nut of an Englishman, of the name of Proper. He had been a British soldier, perhaps a deserter, but he gloried in having fought us at Chippewa, Lundy's Lane, and the other stoutly contested battles of the War of 1812-15, along the Canadian frontier. He looked every inch a soldier and could drill elegantly. How many wordy contests and arguments I had with him about these engagements! I was pretty well posted, because my uncle George Watts had been prominent in them; likewise Major-General Izard, my grandfather's near connection, and Colonel, afterwards Major-General, Stephen Watts Kearny. Although several of my blood relations had taken part upon the other side, I was thoroughly patriotic, and oftentimes our bitter talks were as indecisive as several of the battles, which both sides claimed as glorious victories.

Halt! I have got far ahead of my story.

The question in order is, How did we get to Sherburne? The party went three or four successive summers, and each time we took a different road. Once by the way of Kattskill, once by the way of Albany, and once partly by way of the Erie Canal. One year we went up the river in the *Lady Clinton* safety barge; she was towed by a steamer, and took a night and a day to go to Albany, or else two days and a night. Either way, we slept on board. I find all these routes marked on an old map, on which I used to record my journeys.

The most interesting road was partly or altogether along the old Ithaca turnpike, and, young as I was, the beauty of the ride struck me forcibly. Grandfather and nigger Tom rode in one gig, behind old "Spunk," a famous bay horse, who died a glorious death on one of these journeys, winning a race of sixteen miles, from Cherry Valley to Cooperstown. Father followed in another gig with your humble servant. Once or twice the cavalcade was augmented by a couple of saddle horses, which were ridden in succession by different members of the party. Once or twice, also, we landed at

Kattakill, then a small, quaint, dead old Dutch village.
Thence, turning the northern spurs of the Kattakill
Mountains, we drove to Cairo.

All along the scenery was glorious, especially in the
end of September, or beginning of October, when the
leaves had begun to turn. From Cairo, the county seat
of Greene County, we made a sweep through the southern
point of Schoharie into the northern angle of Delaware.
I remember my attention being called to the fact that
we were crossing the head waters of the Delaware, a few
miles below the source of its longest, the west, or
Mohawk's branch, in Lake Utsayanthe. Otherwise,
pretty much all that I saw has passed from my memory,
unless I can refresh it from some old letters. I do
remember crossing the Susquehanna, and then the Una-
dilla, just above their junction, and, slip as I was,
admiring the scenery. On this line, we struck the
Chenango River at Oxford, and thence proceeded due
north, about fifteen miles, to Shelburne. The Chenango
is a very tame stream, and we did not hold it in honor,
because its principal fish were "suckers," which are mean
to catch and meaner to eat.

The second route was west from Albany, through
Duanesberg, Schoharie, Cobbleskill, Cherry Valley,
Cooperstown, Otsego, Burlington, Garratville, Columbus,
and then came Sherburne. Somehow or other, we must
have traveled this road more than once, for the names
of several of these places are perfect "household words"
to me. At Schoharie I was astonished to see an elegant
city carriage, with a complete appropriate turn-out, in
this then comparatively wild region. Both grandfather
and father shook their heads, and would not explain its
appearance there, but I wormed out of some one, perhaps
out of the gossipy Tom, that it belonged to a New
Yorker who had been caught cheating at cards, and had
to go into exile in this out-of-the-way place, where he
owned some property. Morals were different in those
days, and if a man was guilty of a dirty trick, even if
he made money by it, he was sent to Coventry.

No one will ever forget old (Fred?) Story, the noted tavern-keeper, stage proprietor, and horse dealer at Cherry Valley. One year he was boasting of a famous gray horse that he had, and challenged grandfather to a race across the mountain to Cooperstown. I think the gray fell dead on the road, but he died in consequence of this day's work. It cost grandfather "Spunk," who had been Uncle Stevie's horse, and deserved more mercy. "Spunk" died, or was left behind to die. Grandfather thus lost his valuable horse by this "hell of a drive," and nearly lost his more precious life. The horse he hired to take "Spunk's" place ran away with him, and pitched into a ditch.

Cooperstown, on Otsego Lake, is a vivid picture in my mind, as I then saw it. I remember it well, for four reasons.

First, because it was the home of the celebrated American novelist, Cooper, who married a kinswoman, a near relative of my grandfather, and a nearer of my grandmother, Jane de Lancey.

Second, because on seeing Governor Clarke's enormous mansion, near the head of the lake, I wondered how any one who had money enough to build such a house, and could keep it up in such style as he did, could have been insane enough to plant himself in such a region. I afterwards was very intimate with his son, at present one of the largest landholders and hop growers in the State of New York. Grandfather told me a great deal about this country, and I used to make notes which must be somewhere among my papers, if not destroyed. I remember less, because I trusted more to notes than to memory, and I have found this to be invariably the case, through life, whenever I have done so.

Third, I once walked the streets with a remarkably tame raccoon on my shoulders, and a still more remarkable horsehair cap on my head. Father and I had two, just alike, and they astonished the country people, whose old-fashioned beavers were just as astonishing to me. This raccoon was a very wonderful animal. He lived

with us for a long while as one of the family, played
and slept with the dogs on the parlor rug, and was a
charming pet. We had him a long while and he was a
universal favorite from kitchen to parlor.

One night he got loose, killed a chicken, and tasted
fresh blood, the first in his life, for I got him, a sucking
baby. From that moment his whole nature changed. He
became perfectly savage, and my "parients" parted with
him, to save me from the fate of the chicken. By this
time he had grown to be an enormous size for his species,
almost as big as a sprightly cub bear. Throughout life
I have respected raccoons for his sake.

Speaking of pets, I must make a confession, not in
the style of Rousseau's, but equally wicked. During my
first visit to Sherburne somebody gave me a black squirrel.
It was the tamest, loveliest, most beautiful pet that a
little boy ever had, and I was very cruel to it. One day
it wanted to come out of my pocket, and I pinched its
poor little nose to make it stay in. When I wanted it
to come out it was dead, smothered. It was too gentle
to have said, with the ghosts, which, according to Shakespeare, made his last night and its dreams so terrible to
Richard III.,

"Let me sit heavy on·thy soul to-morrow."

But my treatment of that squirrel has sat heavy on my
soul for forty-eight years.

Fourth, in Cooperstown I saw an extensive general
training of the old-fashioned "uninformed" militia, as
some people, ignorantly transposing syllables, used to
call them, but not altogether without justice. The con-
cluding evolution was intricate, and on that account
imposing, but not calculated to inspire respect for the
warriors who executed it. It was called "hunting the
fox." A distinguished officer, all lace and buttons, with
a very tall feather, led off a vast array of armed and
patriotic citizens, with gleaming bayonets, in single or
Indian file, to the sound of martial music. This brave
leader seemed to constitute himself the spindle of a spiral
aggregation, until the warriors who had previously been

formed around the open square were wound up tight around him, like a watch-spring wound up tight.

I was wondering how they could ever untwist themselves, when this Saul-like commander, with the magnificent plume, gave an order, in a voice like Ajax defying the thunderbolt, and———they all sat down in each other's laps. The effect was startling. I looked up to my father with inquiring eyes. He had been a valiant commander likewise, but even he was impressed. He made a gesture of silence and attention. The music had ceased. Then I saw that magnificent plume rise, like the head of a "Jack in a box" when the spring is touched. He gave another order, and around him rose that coil of armed men; and as they rose, music's voluptuous swell,—or rather voluminous swell, for the majority of instruments were drums,—filled the whole air with sonorous sounds, and I saw that magnificent plume unwinding that coil with the same majesty with which it wound it up.

I looked at my father again. The veteran smiled. I say "veteran," because he had sprained his wrist carrying dirt to help build the defences of the hills overlooking Harlem Plains, in 1812. He smiled, because, like myself, he had been engaged in a mental calculation of how that multitude of armed men, squatting in each other's laps, like niggers in the hold of a slave ship, could ever be disentangled again. He smiled, because the mystery was solved, and his mind was at ease.

I followed that magnificent feather home to its quarters, with the raccoon, on my shoulders, more astonished than I was, if such a thing could be. These quarters were a jeweler's shop, with the ceiling too low for the feather. Through the window, aglow with a lamp, for it was before the time of gas, I saw the hero of the plume return his sword to its scabbard, with a snap that proclaimed to the world that duty had been performed and completely. Then, filled with wonder at this remarkable display of tactics, which I could never find in a book, I returned to the tavern to fill the stomach of myself and my raccoon with whatever we could find palatable.

More than three decades elapsed between my last visit to Cooperstown with my grandfather, and my next visit with my dear Aunt Laight, my mother's sister, and only survivor of a generation of ten. Methought, never had a place so little changed in such a length of time. I recognized many of the spots which had interested me in my boyhood, while at Sherburne. But I was as much a stranger as Rip Van Winkle when he returned to Kattskill after his sleep of twenty years.

At Columbus, our last halt before reaching our destination, I saw an "officers' training." It was such a perfect contrast to the one I have previously described that it made me believe that something might be made out of the militia. The cavalry uniforms present were really beautiful, and, from what I have learned since, must have been imitated from the English service. Scarlet coats, faced with black velvet, richly trimmed with lace, white pantaloons(?), with heavy leather helmets, trimmed and crested with bearskin, tall white feathers tipped with red, and an abundance of horsehair down the back.

If the cavalry were strikingly elegant, the riflemen were equally jaunty.

I forget the rural artillery, but it seems to me the uniform of this arm was like that of the infantry, except that the former was trimmed with red and gold, and the latter with white and silver. I wore the infantry uniform for several years. Many people thought it was very tasty, but I thought it was damnably ugly, and cursed Macomb, Mapes & Company for its concoction. All the foot, then, wore those fearfully heavy and ugly bell-crowned leather hats, which were not as yet styled Shakos. I think the infantry sported black feathers tipped with red, and the artillery red feathers tipped with black, but I won't be sure.

I afterwards saw a general training at Sherburne. It was an event for such a village. The crowd was enormous. The cavalry, as ever, were splendid, wherever I saw them in the rural districts; well mounted, good riders, elegantly dressed, and performing whatever they undertook with a precision of which the New York City horse was incapable. Then the riflemen—were they not called Bucktails in Western New York, as a rule wearing them instead of feathers?—were appropriately dressed in dark green (?); well drilled, and capital marksmen.

I can always call up before my vision the cavalry with admiration, and the riflemen with solid pleasure; whereas the infantry and artillery in the country are always blurred in my memory. Those in New York City I saw so often that each arm, and each variety of uniform, is as present to my recollection as if I were inspecting them now.

A great many things of interest occurred to me at Sherburne. The first year the horses in general were at my command. The next year I had a horse of my own, and I had a gun. I was told that originally it had been in the wars. The barrel was beautifully inlaid with silver, and it had been shortened to transmute it from an instrument of war into a "birding piece." It had a flint lock, and many a flash in the pan developed in my little mind a custom of objurgation which, then, I reserved for private opportunities, but indulged in publicly at a riper age.

A local gunsmith had introduced a percussion lock, with a fulminating pea instead of a cap, something like the principle adopted in the Austrian army upon the suppression of the flint-lock. This did not answer my expectations, and it was again changed for the regular percussion hammer and cap. Restocked, but with the old lock, barrel, and mountings, this gun stands within grasp while I write, and it carries a great deal better and farther than many modern and more pretentious pieces.

Some of the happiest hours of my life were passed at Sherburne. I had a horse and rode and drove where I chose. I was trusted. I had some narrow escapes, but they taught me how to take care of my self. I had a gun, and a companion, generally a good deal older than myself, and I roamed through the primeval forests, filling my game bag with a variety of birds which were then common, but now so uncommon as to be rare visitors to the same region. Partridges were plenty, and almost every kind of feathered game abounded; and, as for wild pigeons, they came in flocks sufficiently large to remind a reader of the description of them in Cooper's "Leather-Stocking."

Although the forests were still spacious, wild, and almost as desert as at the end of the previous century, deer no longer harbored in them. I was told that there were deer still to be found off to the northwest, towards Chitteningo Point. Nearly fifty years afterwards I went up to Chittenango Falls, and they laughed at me for my pronunciation, when an old settler remarked that I was the one who had a right to laugh, for many years ago everybody said Chitteningo. What place was designated as the Point, I do not know. I went a-fishing, and was rewarded with full creels. Boys are not usually choice in their "catch," but often, while our party was angling for common prey, we caught magnificent trout with worm bait and primitive apparatus, in the most unexpected places.

One of my constant comrades was a youth or young man who could cut off a partridge's head with a single ball, and bring down a squirrel without breaking the skin, except sometimes that of the head. He had a tame crow, which was so much attached to him that he had to lock him up whenever he went out, to prevent the crow's accompanying him, perched on his shoulder.

As stated, my grandfather's cottage was on a hill, and the owner of the crow lived on the opposite side of the valley or plain. One day, when he was over at our house, my father asked him what was the reason he kept all the time in the shadow of a tree. "To keep out of sight of that darned crow," he replied. "I thought I had locked him up securely, but there he is on the

fence looking out for me, and if he gets sight of me he'll
be over here in less than no time. While I keep behind
this tree he can't see me, although I see him."

Boy like, I insisted on the experiment being tried.
The young man stepped out into clear view, and, in
almost as short a time as it has taken to pen this story,
the crow was perched upon his shoulder, evincing every
possible manifestation of delight at having found his
master again. I do not recollect if this crow could talk,
but there were some pet crows around that could talk,
for tame crows were quite a feature in the region.

Let me reflect, how much soever I will, the occurrences
of three summer visits to Sherburne are commingled in
the picture of the happiest memories passing through
my mind as I write.

One of our pets was a bald-headed eagle. Captured
when just beginning to fly, he soon grew into one of
the noblest specimens. With one wing cut, he used to
remain around the house and carry on a truceless row
of screams and barks with my French poodle. Sometimes
he would get across the brook, and then I used to go
to drive him home, for I soon learned to manage him by
means of a long pole with broad prongs at the end. I
would set "Fanny" at him. This would attract his
attention. Then I would get the prong, from behind,
under his wings and force him homewards by a series of
hops or bounds. Once in a while he would take to the
water and flop or flap himself across quicker than Flora,
a woolly Leander, could swim in pursuit.

We brought him to New York, sent him out to Bloomingdale, and there he stayed till the patience of my
grandfather de Peyster, equal to that of Job, could stand
the destruction of his poultry no longer. The eagle's
favorite perch was the top of the pump. I used to
make long trains of corn from different points thither.
Hissing the geese, quacking the ducks, and clucking the
chickens, they would stream hitherward, gladly picking
up the scattered golden grains, until a dense multitude
of poultry would encompass the pump.

Aloft Aquila would sit, as if carved out of wood, with his head turned directly sternwards, as only eagles can, resting on his back and almost hidden in the tufts of feathers at the base of his wings. Bald-head was not asleep; he was only playing 'possum. Suddenly, with a scream, such as only eagles can give, he would drop into that mass of poultry, strike down a gander lifeless with one blow of his beak, and walk off with a rooster in one, and a drake in another claw, as if he was shod with the living boots children read of in Fairy Tales, that uttered voices as they went.

One day he got tired of poultry. The nigger washer-woman had a little nigger boy. This nigger boy had been warned against the eagle, but upon him, like all boys, especially nigger boys, instruction had been wasted. Perhaps he had a boat, and wanted to sail it in the horse-trough, but, whatever he desired to do, he wished to go to the pump, and there he got what he certainly did not desire to have. Bald-head saw him coming and sat as still as one of the sculptured eagles over my ancestral gate-posts, and, when nigger boy stooped to the trough, he swooped upon him with a scream which was fortunately echoed by the child, for it roused the people.

Poor children's clothes are seldom made to fit, for they generally inherit the garments of their elders. Happily it was the case in this instance. The eagle's talons, instead of gathering up little darkey's sable hide, only took up a handful of the slack of his trousers. More happily it was a nigger, and not a white boy. His head was hard. The eagle had only ploughed two or three channels through his wool, with the aid of his beak, when down charged the infuriated mother with a clothes pole. Bald-head was always ready for a fight, and her skirts were in ribbons, and her swarthy limbs shone, streaked with red, like a fashionable stocking pattern, when the men arrived.

This decided the eagle's fate. The wails of orphaned and widowed poultry had been uplifted in vain, but the rails of this exasperated colored lady aroused the neigh-

borhood. The eagle was given to Uncle Gus. Uncle Gus
was the commander of a Havre packet. He took the
eagle to France and presented it to Louis Phillippe.
The Citizen-King gave him a silver medal, as large as a
dessert plate, magnificently embossed with the likenesses
of himself and family, and bestowed the eagle on the
Jardin des Plantes. As eagles are said to live a hundred
years, he may have been eaten during the siege of Paris;
but as birds grow tough with age, it must have required
all the skill of an artistic cook to convert him into a dish
which was not as heavy and painful to digest as a
German missile. So ends the story of our eagle.

One of our journeys to Sherburne, I think the last,
was partly or altogether by the Ithaca mail stage. Stage-
coaching in those days was quite an institution. The
drivers took a pride in their work. They drove with a
dexterity to which Colonel de Lancey Kane's is mere
child's play. I have seen them jerk their loads through
roads that would have made the valiant Colonel's hair
stand on end, and this, too, not on a decorously managed
hand gallop, but full tilt, full gallop, a half run down
hill, then swaying, pitching, tumbling the passengers
around inside like peas in a rattle, and keeping on the
same gait all along the flat, to win with the impetus half
the ensuing hill. Many of the horses were worthy of
places in city harness, and the drivers looked after their
condition with as much pride as the proprietors, from
interested motives.

How they deteriorated before they entirely went out
of fashion no one knows better than I, for I had to travel
a route, for over a hundred miles, which was entirely
dependent on stage lines as long as the river was frozen.
Out west, forty-five years ago, I have seen a six-in-hand
team, worth a pile of money, before a stage-coach loaded
down like Noah's Ark, and "yanking" it along "smart."
This, too, over soft roads. And twenty years afterwards
I saw the mail line, from New York to Albany, drawn
through the Highlands by such a set of scarecrows that
they could scarcely drag the mail up the stony pitch

rising northwards from Annsville Creek, just above
Peekskill. I often wondered that an old-fashioned driver,
who "knew what was what," could ever have brought his
mind to handle the reins over such contrasts to the
pets of his early Jehuism.

Finally, what music those drivers would get out of
their long, simple, tin horns! They would have flayed
Colonel Kane's guard, as Apollo did Marcyas, if he had
come tooting around with his primitive tones.   The
stage driver's horn made everything positively cheerful,
as its music came nearer and nearer, now softened by a
dip into a hollow, now ringing out as it crested a hill-top,
until the steaming four-in-hand stopped before the
welcoming tavern, amid a flourish that made the village
echo.

Nor did the driver take two hands to his toot. He
would jam his whip into the left hand, already crammed
with reins, jerk his tin horn out of a rough loop by the
side of his box, and sound a fanfare which would have
put to the blush the very French clarions which blared
out victory on the heights of the Alma. At the first note,
how the horses would prick up their ears, lay them back,
straighten their tails, lay into the harness, and jerk off
on full trot, or break into a spanking gallop! Hurrah!
Hurrah! Hurrah! I see them now! I can feel it now;
my pulses beat responsive to the very thought, quickened
as if, at this moment, I was perched on the box and
whisking down the hill into the valley of the Chenango!

One of the new structures in Sherburne was an Episcopal church, and while we were there Bishop Hobart
came on a visitation. He was very intimate with my
grandfather de Peyster, and, consequently, I had heard
a great deal about him, but no acquaintance with him in
New York could afford an idea of his popularity in the
country. He possessed a great many of those qualities
which a bishop should have to win success among a
primitive population. He took with the people in as
great a degree as he won the partiality of the more
cultivated classes. It seems to me that he was the most

popular Episcopal bishop I have ever known, and I have known none, intimately, of any other sect.

Bishop Wainwright was a cultivated man, but unjust and partial in clerical matters, a sensuous man, and, to me, mildly repulsive. Bishop Potter, of Pennsylvania, was an active, able, well-bred, useful supervisor. Bishop Cleveland Coxe was charming as a simple clergyman, and highly accomplished and capable in literature. Either he or his brother was a school-fellow of mine at the Washington Institute. Whoever it was, he was author of Saul, and he is an exception to a remark I make further on, that this school produced no pupil afterwards successful in the world, for characteristics that win their way in the world are equally valuable for getting ahead in the Church. Bishop Whittingham stands highest in my opinion, and that in the capacity which gains ground through sheer manhood. In the proper time, with Romanist belief, he possessed the qualities which might have developed into a Hildebrand.

One more story about Sherburne, and we will have to leave the subject with as much regret as I left the place.

My grandfather, as I said, possessed enormous vitality, but no health. He was accustomed to sudden, violent attacks, which often seemed to be mortal. He had one of these at Sherburne. The village practitioner, in despair, summoned all the fraternity within reasonable driving circuit, to hold a consultation over the case of "the Judge."

Where the carcass is, there the eagles, vultures, or crows will be gathered together. They came from every quarter of the heavens, or the other place, to be able to say that they helped to kill or save the rich New Yorker. The row of gigs or sulkies, fastened to the low picket fence, was appalling. I know it was so to me and to Tom. We held consultations together, watched the solemn faces of the medicos, and if they smiled, took hope. If they looked solemn, Tom's heart and mine went down into our boots.

Thus these ravens came and went for several days. One day they came stringing out with their saddle-bags over their arms, and filed off towards Sherburne, about a mile distant, to get their dinner. They left behind an afflicted household, for they had said "the Judge must die." They implied that human skill was exhausted, and as they were its exponents, the decree was irreversible.

It is said that the Ethiopian cannot change his skin, but Tom sat on the front steps looking blue indeed. I was awe-struck.

All at once I heard my grandfather's voice. My father came out, and gave an order to Tom. Tom's unearthly blue darkened into healthy black, and I rushed in to my dear old grandfather, to see him actually taking what the country people would persist in calling a "dish of tea." As in several previous and subsequent cases, Nature had slipped in at the last moment to relieve a digestive crisis, and "Richard was himself again."

Towards sunset the flight of Æsculapian crows returned. They first cawed aloud in chorus, and then they stuck their bills together and cawed in whispers. If a younger brother crow did not look solemn enough, the elder brethren rebuked him with an increased solemnity of demeanor.

Little boy as I was, I watched them with a juvenile feeling which, with years, has solidified into a masculine certainty. I have a weak dependence on the opinion of doctors when those that I love are in peril. When I am sick myself, doubt overrides faith. Gay wrote his own epitaph,

> "Life's a jest, and all things show it,
>   I thought so once, and now I know it."

Just so of medicine.

Alluding to Gay's epitaph: after I read it, in Westminster Abbey, while traveling in search of a cure for a terrible and protracted pain in the head, resulting from a fall which broke my nose, I went home, and, influenced, doubtless, by my painful experience of life, wrote down these lines of the English poet, and beneath them added that life was

"A bitter practical joke."

For this my father, who was strictly orthodox, was angry enough to cane me. It was not wise, perhaps, to be so heterodox on paper, but in after years I found that some of the best and wisest men entertained very much the same opinions. Fenelon, the celebrated and gentle bishop of Cambrae, wrote very analogous ideas in his old age—if Voltaire's quotation of the bishop's six lines is reliable. The great Frenchman had no reason to misquote; and a number of philosophers have set down very much the same deductions.

Montaigne pronounced "the whole world nothing but an endless farce." The author of "Shadows in Outline" remarked, "Depend upon it, life is a grim joke;" and Wellington, the most practical man that ever lived, on more than one occasion expressed his opinion that, although he had been one of the most prosperous of men, "there is nothing or little in this life worth living for."

As for poor Solomon, if he did write Ecclesiastes,—for many modern commentators wish to deprive him of the credit of the authorship,—he summed it up as "vanity and vexation of spirit." The Germans translate this "alles Eitel und Jammer," whose literal interpretation is, utter emptiness and wretchedness. Old Campe, in his exhaustive dictionary, says that a Jammer look is one awakened by the highest grade of suffering; which is just the old sardonic laugh, the offspring of a poisonous herb in Sardinia, which, under the veil of a facial expression resembling laughter, expresses an inward crisis of agony which terminates in death.

But let us look up our crows, for this is a tremendous digression. Having cawed in common salutation, and having cawed in consultation, the flock encountered Tom, another sort of crow, and cawed in simulation. I use this word because they veiled the assurance of receiving an answer in accordance with their croaking predictions under the semblance of a desire for good tidings. Tom's black face glowed like an ebony image freshly polished. "Yah! Yah! Yah! The Judge am in de barn-yard, looking at him pigs." And Jim Crow's bad grammar scattered the medical crows.

I was going to leave Sherburne without mentioning my grandfather's farmer. He was a character; if Tom had a black skin, old Mr. ———— had a black heart, judged from the standpoint of orthodox religious sentiment. St. James says, "The devils believe and tremble." I will not record my impressions of this gentleman's orthodoxy from the basis of St. James. He did believe and tremble, but it was at the devil. He had implicit faith in a personal, frequent, bodily manifestation of Satan. He had a book, or books, or pamphlets, detailing the same; and he did a great deal to cap the climax of misery in my juvenile soul, already accumulated therein through the unfortunate babblings of my dear old Mammie.

The kitchen had one of those enormous wood fire-places which swallowed up a cart-load of wood, nine-tenths of the heat of which went up the chimney. Before this, when ablaze, the face was roasted, while the back froze. When the wood had burned down and become a bed of cinders, tempered with ashes, Mr. ———— would light a clay pipe and crowd in on one side; Tom, with another pipe, on the other side; while I, on a low stool, and no pipe, sat drinking in their horrible stories, as they sucked in the blessings of the tobacco. The hard-featured white man had enough of the devil in him to feel a grim defiance of the devil while his health and strength endured.

Tom was a timorous nigger, and he used to sit with eyes starting out of his head, and big as saucers, venturing timid corroborations of his white brother's horrible lies; meanwhile I used to drink in all this nonsense, until, if it had not been for sheer pride of superior intellect, position, and white blood, before that unmanned nigger, my knees would have knocked audibly together as I

stole away to bed. After one of these séances I believe
Tom did not go to bed at all, but, as the ashes grew
cold, shivered in his corner, fearful of leaving the protection of the household fairies, or penates, which even a
nigger's mythology recognized as protecting and presiding
over the household hearth.

Besides diabolical stories, this horrible old man
was as great on the subject of ghosts. I would have
felt much more comfortable at night, and around
churchyards, if I had known Infantry General W. P.
Wainwright then. He says that he used to believe in
ghosts in his younger days, but was cured by Jeremy
Bentham's logic, viz.: "There might be ghosts of bodies,
but how about the ghosts of breeches and garments in
general?"

If I had told my father one-hundredth part of what
occurred in that kitchen, I believe he would have broken
old ———'s skeleton into as many pieces as the fragments of a clay pipe under an infuriated heel. As for
Tom, I wouldn't have given much for his carcass after
a revelation. I never peached, but I declare that the
superstitious nonsense instilled into my boyish mind cast
long attenuated shadows over my whole life, and, despite
the critical acuteness of my strong intellect, their poison
is not entirely neutralized, under peculiar circumstances,
even now that my hair is gray. As an illustration, ———
had a pamphlet with a frontispiece depicting the devil—
horns, hoof and tail—as he appeared to a lot of gamblers
on Sunday, and, according to text, twisted their necks.
I think Tom's feelings were hurt by this representation,
for the printer's ink, and dirt, made him and the devil
one color.

Strange to say, I remember no other figure in this
kitchen distinctly, and yet it seems to me that the farmer
had a wife, who stole around with bated breath, and
was completely "under his 'cow.'" Some one made
first-rate griddle cakes, for those I do remember. How
my father could have been blind, through all the perverse
influences acting upon me, I cannot now conceive. If

ever there was a brave, manly man created, it was he, and yet he allowed me to remain in such a mire until it required an immense amount of moral washing to get off the stains.

Some natures are inaccessible to such villainous nonsense. It sheds from their common sense as water from a duck's back. Others take it in as the shower is absorbed by a sandy soil, and hold it in everlasting suspense, like such a soil, with a strata of hard pan below.   For instance, my foster sister, Beppy, was no more affected, to appearance, by Mammie's ridiculous tales and traditions, than an apostle by the superstitious doctrines of the worshippers of Obi or Bogi that he has set out to convert. Life is a mystery; the human mind a greater. Acute intellects develop in the same atmosphere in which mediocrity also flourishes, in the same way that grand oaks grow luxuriantly in swamp land congenial to the brashiest wood.

CHAPTER XIV

MORE SCHOOL DAYS

After every glorious summer trip to Chenango County I returned in the late fall to the "Washington Institute," and oh, with what intense regret I chafed under its mild but healthy discipline, while fresh from the utter freedom of the field, forest, and stream!

Endowed with an active, inquiring, grasping, in some respects devouring, omniverous mind, I learned a great deal, but I am sorry to say I was neither taught by wise method, nor did I hive my store methodically. I rushed into Latin from pride; was admitted at my own request, and, too young to appreciate what I learned, took a disgust to it.

And yet, strange to say, although subsequently I liked my Greek lessons best, Greek, like Spanish, which I afterwards studied, has almost become as if it had never been; whereas, at early middle age, my Latin came back sufficiently to be eminently useful. Here let me say, of all the dead and living languages, of which I know more or less, Greek has my appreciation for its superior beauty, but I fairly love the German, and deem it more expressive than the ordinary diluted English of to-day.

One of the faculty of this Institute was Mr. Theodore A. Fay, afterwards a noted writer, Secretary of Legation at Berlin in 1851-2, and Minister to Switzerland at a much later date. Strange to say, I never came personally in contact with him, then or since, although I have worn his military hat on our little theatrical stage, and played Rolla or Pizarro in it. I say "military hat," because he belonged to some military organization in the city, and we rummaged out part of his uniform, and "conveyed them," to use Shakespeare's word. Afterwards, when, as Military Agent, I was in Europe, in search of useful information to embody in my report, I had a corre-

spondence with him, and am indebted to him for some .
exquisite drawings, for the elucidation of that portion of
my report relative to the Berlin Fire Department.

This allusion revives the consideration of our theatre.
We did some plays remarkably well, despite incongruous
habiliments and wooden scabbardless swords. Sometimes
ludicrous incidents occurred; and once a dramatic
struggle nearly degenerated into a fisticuff set-to. Tom
Hughes had borrowed a pair of white gloves from one
of our chambermaids. He was a gawky fellow, much
bigger than myself, and had had difficulty in getting his
bulky paws into the kids. In fulfilling my part I had to
tear off his gloves to disclose a wound or mark on which
the plot hinged.

Carried away by the scene, I acted the part to the life,
and the entity of the glove became a non-entity. Thereupon, Tom, who was a bully, interpolated language which
was not in the play, and informed me, so that the
audience heard it, that as a set-off to the torn glove, I
should go to bed with a pair of black eyes, because he
would have to pay the girl for her kids.

My temper was never very patient, and swords of lath
would have represented deadly rapiers, on the spot, but
for intervention, which sadly disarranged the progress of
the piece. The theatre company and the audience left
the house to form a ring, but I believe that Lutz, to
whom Hughes referred the affair with a blubbering voice,
decided that, as my grandfather was rich, I ought to
pay for the gloves, and, as I regarded the word of Lutz
as law, the affair was settled as he decided.

I learned to draw, and I learned to paint, and could
do both quite well for a boy, but everything taught at
this school was taught without method. I picked up an
immense amount of information—truly a vast amount—
but I verily think that the loose way in which it was
imparted made its acquisition a simple cultivation of
the memory.

My friend of subsequent days, Brigadier-General Israel
Vodges, U. S. A., a marvellous professor, for some time

at West Point, says, "Memory is Attention;" and Dr. Maudley, in his "Body and Mind," enunciates opinions which amount to pretty much the same thing. Dr. Scudder, East Indian Missionary, used to say that "Memory was a great box; that everything we ever learned went into this box, but that in it some people kept things in order so that they could lay hold of what they wanted at a minute's notice, while others mixed them up higgledy-piggledy, and could hardly ever find what was required. Nevertheless, nothing perished; everything was there."

I believe that all we learn is photographed, so to speak, in such minute characters, on the tablets of our memory, that an ordinary brain is capacious enough to contain the negatives accumulated through the longest life. An effort of memory is the extrication of one of these negatives, and the application of a microscope of superhuman power. So that memory is not only an effort of attention, to acquire, but of will, to profit by the acquisition.

We certainly were not looked after at this school as little boys ought to have been. I could publish revelations that would make moral parents' hair stand on end, even if as crisp as a negro's. What is more, the exposure that I went through doubtless hardened my constitution, for I must have had a constitution of iron to outlive all I underwent, with a stomach ruined at an early age by pampering. How often have I gone with wet and half-frozen feet, day after day; and with wet clothes, too. We were inspected, it is true, but the inspections were purely superficial.

Dr. Wickham, Prof. Lutz, and others, our chiefest chiefs, knew nothing of the naughtiness that was going on. This makes me say there was a want of method in the school, and want of method has been the worm in the flower and in the fruit of my whole life.

One of my dearest friends,* the most eminent chief

---

*Major-General Andrew Atkinson Humphreys.

of the highest scientific department in this country, and, taking him all in all, except George H. Thomas, the ablest soldier and general of our war, has always said that I was one of the most remarkable men, naturally, that he ever met; that I had a perfect geometrical mind; but that, in the same way that the wicked fairy neutralized the numberless good gifts of the favoring fairies, by one little defect, imparted through her ill will, even so I had failed, through want of early discipline.

I myself can see that this is the principal cause, and its effects were magnified by bad health, untrammeled freedom as to myself, and an independence of thought and will which, in a great measure, like all virtues and vices, is hereditary. Or, perhaps, to speak more properly, my independence is the result of an amalgam of various inherited qualities.

People say I am conceited, but they are jackasses. One of my best friends, Infantry General Wainwright, who has been most intimate with me for over forty years, has always said, "John is not conceited, but he knows what he knows." People who do not know what *they* know, call this conceit. Our Rector says I am a man who thinks aloud. Let this all go, however.

There was no salutary method at the Washington Institute. At the next school I went to, there was too much false method.

Neither turned out a pupil who ever attained a high position, according to the estimate of competent judges. To my knowledge, they turned out two wonderful original thinkers. "Two of the only twelve I ever met," said one of the most remarkable of our successful editors, John Swinton, himself an original, if one ever existed.

A celebrated French author remarks that, out of the thirteen hundred millions of men on this planet, there are not ten thousand who think for themselves; the rest either need, or desire, their thinking to be done for them. I belong to the small class, and the results that I have worked out for myself, gazing into the vast wood fire of my library, I have found scattered through the works of the philosophers of all ages.

We had a manuscript newspaper at the Washington Institute, and I always think it was a great honor that my poetical contributions were accepted with avidity. I wrote anything but bad rhythm before I was nine, and I contributed one or two articles to the "Parlor Magazine" before I was eleven. I have copies somewhere among my papers. Moreover, I inspired some exquisite poetry, and one or more of these effusions are to be found in the works of Thomas Pickering, one of our sweetest native poets, highly celebrated in his day as the author of the "Buckwheat Cake."

While I was at the Washington Institute I witnessed a spectacle which scarcely any one will believe could have occurred, without interruption by the police, in a city so moral as New York was at the time, some forty-five years ago. This was a regular old-fashioned English "bull-bait." It took place in what was then wide, open grounds, having their centre where the granite German Savings Bank now stands, at the corner of Fourteenth Street and Union Square.

I have witnessed scenes since, in the rural districts, which were simply preludes, and concluded with orgies, which I did not witness, in which human beings of both sexes participated, which as far transcended this "bull-bait" as the tallest oak the pigmy mushroom. Nothing could exceed in ferocity the New York exhibition.

A number of us boys were up on the west sheds, which overlooked the present Union Square, when a tremendous concourse of human animals came up the Bowery, dragging along a frantic ox or bull, by means of ropes extending about a hundred feet out from each horn, held by hundreds of hands. On the sidewalks were scores of men, leading bull-dogs. A stake, or swivel-topped iron pin, was driven securely into the ground, then one rope was cast loose, and the ox or bull left to plunge and tear in the centre of a circle a little larger than that of which the rope, still attached, constituted the radius.

People may ask, how could you see all this so distinctly? The roof of the shed was ten or twelve feet higher than the playground; the playground itself, ten to twenty feet higher than the street, so that we looked down into the ring, as it were, from the top of a tree. Our stable roof was at least one-half higher, and I do not know but we were on that.

We saw a number of dogs gored and tossed, but the poor bull got no resting spell. No sooner was one dog disposed of than another was let loose, until almost worn out, with his tongue lolling out of his mouth, a heavy dog was set at him, caught him by the tongue, and either tore it to pieces, or tore it out altogether. I was fascinated with horror. This last occurrence made me deathly sick, and all that followed is a blank. This torture must have lasted for a good deal more than an hour, for the days were long, and we got out of school early; and it lasted, without interruption, until evening closed over the horrid scene.

I was taken away from the Washington Institute on account of my health. They said I got the fever and ague there. Now, I don't believe it; but I was very glad to make others believe it at the time, because I wanted to get away from boarding-school.

My conscience pricks me, when I think of it, because, by tacitly following the deceit, I injured Dr. Wickham's interests. I remember that he looked very reproachfully on me as I left, and dropped some remark, intimating that my leaving, as I did, was a poor return for the kindness shown me.

I wish I had left otherwise; but I had some justification. I was homesick. I was the caged bird, pining for freedom; I was the pampered pet, longing to get rid of the Spartan diet and return to the flesh-pots of Egypt. This admission is honest and manly; but where was the excuse for the doctors, who played into the hands of a little boy, to his detriment, for the benefit of their pockets? Mammie Trainque commenced the ruin of my health, and doctors completed it.

I believe that if I had remained in the hands of the doctor, I would not have lived to get married; and if I had continued to put implicit faith in any one who succeeded him, I would never have overcome a single one of the maladies which have afflicted me.

Let the doctors go for the present. Some have made me love them, and one or two have inspired the highest respect, but, looking back, I do not think that a single, solitary one of them has understood my case. Whereas, if they had, I am certain that I should not drag through so many miserable hours as I have done and do.

The famous, fortunate Caliph of Cordova, Abb der Rhaman III., after a glorious reign of fifty years, could only enumerate fourteen· days of unalloyed happiness. I have lived over fifty-five years, and, since I left the Washington Institute, I do not remember a single day of complete health. I have had three-quarter days, half days, quarter days, and hours when I shook off disease and felt that I could move Olympus, and have actually shouted for joy at the unusual relief.

Health excites me into a condition like intoxication, and, if possible, I get into the woods and yell it out. As a rule the "black dog," as my ancestral Scotch say, is always perched on my shoulders, and his food is black bile. I am satisfied that if I could get my liver straight, throw aside tobacco, and not take up some stimulant as a substitute—as is ordinarily the case—I might enjoy a long, green old age.

In explanation of what I mean, my mother's cousin, Anthony Barclay, formerly British Consul, was a great wine drinker. He made a trip across the prairies for his health, where he could not get wine. He took to snuff as a substitute. As soon as he got back, he threw away the snuff and resumed his wine. Just so, the moment I quit tobacco, I have a terrible craving for stimulants and coffee.

I said I left the Washington Institute on account of a slight attack of fever and ague, a molehill, which Dr. G——— S——— converted into a mountain.

There was better reason, but it did not develop itself until a year or_two afterwards.

I have said that Professor Lutz used to lead us out on what the French style "military promenades." On one occasion we came across a tremendous tree, whose roots had developed to an almost incredible extent in a sandy soil. This tree had blown down, and, falling, had left behind a deep pit in the sand, so that from the top of the roots, in air, to the bottom of the excavation, the distance was very great. I have always told the story, making it twenty feet, but, looking up as I write to the lofty ceiling of my office, I think I must have added five, or else I would not be here to tell the story.

Some of the big boys crawled up on top of these roots and stumped the smaller boys to "follow your leader." I think I jumped once or twice safely, but, emboldened by impunity, I became careless. My pantaloons caught in a little dry root, and, instead of landing on my feet, I pitched into the soft sand below, and my nose, always a prominent feature, lit on a solitary pebble, placed there by Fate to receive it. I was picked up, set on my legs, and got back to the school—how, I cannot imagine. My nose, they say, was broken.

Big as it was, it disappeared in the swelling of my face. The result was continuous headache. Years afterwards it broke me down; I was ordered to Europe. Dr. Roux butchered me in Paris. To create a seton in my left arm, he cut a gash which sent the blood out in a fountain. I have got a scar which looks like the vestige of a grape-shot. The seton, or vigorous youth, or the sea voyage and a European trip, relieved me of the headaches, but I have never had a healthy nose since.

Roux was a famous surgeon, but he was a French brute, and a French brute transcends all other brutes, just as French nature differs from human nature. Dr. Hosack, a friend of mine, asked him about a patient on whom he had operated. The poor devil died a short time after his removal from the operating table. "Oh," said Roux, "he took to religion, and died."

Removed from the Washington Institute, I was placed at the fashionable school of the Rev. Mr. Huddart, then in full blast in Beaver street. At the Washington Institute there was too little method, but human nature. Here, there was too much method, and no humanity.

Mr. Wickham, the principal of Washington Institute, was a very good man. In contrast to Mr. Huddart, he was an angel. Both were clergymen. Wickham was an American, Huddart an Englishman, and the one had all the virtues of his race, and the other all the disagreeableness of a Britisher. I cannot recall the Church or sect to which the former belonged, but he did not make religion repulsive. The latter was a thoroughbred Episcopalian, and such brutality and partiality as he sometimes evinced, and such temper as he always gave way to on slight occasions, would have set any one against the religion under which he developed.

I shall return to this again, but it is impossible to refrain from mentioning that he once flogged a boy so severely that, by the force of the blows, the works of the victim's watch were driven through the outer casing. I verily believe he did this for nothing else but to show off his authority before a strange teacher. It is a wonder the boy did not try to kill him.

Huddart was a brute. He once locked me up in his study to await an interview. I had a many-bladed penknife. I broke every blade, but I cut out the lock, got out of a window, and safe off home; nor would I return until immunity from punishment was perfectly secured. He flourished for a time "like a green bay tree," but afterwards came to grief. Let me record my opinion of him: he was a bully, a tyrant, and a brute, but a very able man, as regards education.

How different are my recollections of the faculty of Washington Institute! I must say this much for Huddart: if he was a tiger among sheep, and the inquisitor among victims, he was a perfect British bull-dog among the gray-hounds, poodles, and spaniels, which constitute the bulk of the

world. I did learn a great deal in this school; but, if
I had not broken loose, he would have made me what
the Jesuits make of their docile pupils—*"perinde ac
cadaver."*

What I had learned at the Washington Institute, he
fixed, as certain chemicals precipitate and crystallize
matters susceptible to their influence. I look back to
my probation with Huddart as a painful apprenticeship
under a meanly despotic master; and I record it here, as
the result of manhood's endorsement of youthful experience, that the Rev. Mr. Huddart ought to have had just
such a flogging, repeated periodically, as I saw him once,
without provocation, inflict on Gore Callender, who was
big enough, if he had had a soul, to have smashed his
infernal clerical nose.

I forgot to say that the double brick dwelling on the
north side of Beaver street, near Broadway, was occupied
or owned by my grandfather prior to his purchase of, or
moving into, No. 3 Broadway. This was afterwards
Huddart's boarding-school. The carriage entrance and
way, to the west of it, was the playground, and the
recitation rooms were either within the walls of the old
stables and carriage house, or else upon their site.

Huddart's second in command, and classical professor,
was the famous William Henry Herbert, another
Englishman; a bad tempered man, bad husband, bad in
every way; but as full of ability as an egg is of meat.
After a career which has rendered his name celebrated
for his literary publications, on sporting subjects particularly, he committed suicide; and, strange to say, his
intimate, the brother of one of my dearest friends,
terminated his life in the same manner. Herbert's wife
was a pretty, meek, attractive woman, as much of the
lady in appearance as Herbert was the gentleman. I
have heard it stated he was one of those
          "Who, be it understood,
    Had left their country for their country's good."
He had done something which he ought not to have
done; whether absolutely criminal, or profligate, I do

not recollect. He was one of the most talented men I ever met. A ripe scholar, an elegant draughtsman, an accomplished writer, a complete sportsman, a pleasant companion; and, with all this, he had a streak of meanness in him. Boys see deeper into men, and farther through them, than the world thinks. He was implicated in the famous Washington Hotel rumpus, which eventuated in a challenge from ————— to Sam Neal; and people, at the time, said that he did not evince the pluck on this occasion which might have been expected from such a self-announced, fire-eating Don.

It is curious, but my stay at Huddart's has a sort of dreamy appearance about it, when I look back upon it. I do not remember it with pleasure, and very few of those with whom I was even slightly intimate survive.

My health broke down entirely at Huddart's, in consequence of that thump on my nose. The doctors ordered me to Europe; and, in charge of my father, and in company with my cousin, Phil Kearny, afterwards the famous "one-armed devil," and "chilled iron" Union Major-General, I sailed for Havre in the French packet-ship, "Utica," commanded by my uncle, Gus de Peyster, about the 1st of May, 1834.

CHAPTER XV

If ever a boy felt promoted to manhood by a single step, I did when I went aboard ship. I was just thirteen, very large for my age—in fact, I got my growth at fifteen, and I have never spread, developed, or increased in weight since then. I have been a little more or less fleshy at different periods, temporarily, but whenever I have risen or fallen above or below the mean line, I always found myself back to it by some concatination of circumstances.

Our passage in the "Utica" was a tedious one. A more curious lot of passengers was scarcely ever gathered together in one cabin. Among these was a young Mexican lieutenant of artillery, who drew very cleverly. Among my papers I have some beautiful drawings of Mexican artillery, executed by him. Mexico then had an army, fine in uniform and equipment, if in nothing else.

I kept a detailed journal of this journey which is stowed away somewhere among my multifarious manuscripts. That portion which related to Lombard happened to relate to a season of inundations so exactly resembling the summer of 1859, that I was enabled to explain the mysterious movements of the French and Austrian armies, in consequence of tremendous rains, such as we had experienced there twenty-four years previous. I published a long series of articles on the subject in the New York *Express*, preserved in one of my numerous scrap books.

Another passenger was the eccentric Dr. J. C. Nott, of Mobile, Alabama, who made a great reputation as an ethnologist and craniologist. He was a "janius," as poor Power, the comedian, used to pronounce it. By the

way, I knew Power slightly. He was a big-headed,
rollicking Irishman, but a pleasant-mannered man. He
looked to me as if he had had the small-pox bad, but
the meeting, photographed on my memory, was after a
dinner with a convivial "brother Pat."

Dr. Nott was a queer little man, and if he was really
bright, he did not show it in our company. He stag-
gered people in Europe with his actions and questions.
At Marseilles he said he was going to the East, that he
would assume the Turkish dress and habits, and pass
himself off for a Mohammedan. Dear father innocently
asked him if he could speak Turkish or Arabic; Nott
as naively answered, "Not a word." He would have
been a Yankee jay in Turkish peacock feathers—in both
cases, the voice revealing the deception.

On another occasion we found Mr. Hamet, U. S.
Consul at Naples, who was still there when I went back
in '52—"the same old veritable Jacobs"—in a perfect
state of disgust. "I have had a queer fellow country-
man here this morning," he said, "one Dr. Nott, of
Mobile." Nott had been playing the part of the Queen
of Sheba, and trying him "with hard questions."
Unfortunately, Hamet was no Solomon. "What do you
think he asked me?" said Hamet. "Mr. Hamet," said
Nott, "how many olives will an olive tree bear?" "Just
think, sir, and he never even mentioned the size of the
tree!"

Dr. Nott's son, who was with him, was a regular
specimen of a Southwestern man of the day. One day
the ship gave a lurch, threw him across the "poop-deck,"
and when he fetched up, suddenly, the shock jerked a
tremendous "bowie knife" out of his bosom. It made
a good deal of talk among our peaceful congregation,
and we wondered if he thought that in Europe he was
about to encounter a civilization like that in which he
had been reared.

Another queer customer was a schoolmaster, who had
come out to the United States to teach French, and was
going back disheartened and disgusted. He spoke some
10

patois French, and was one of those noodles who thought
it would go down among the savages, with which most
Europeans believed that the United States was peopled.
A highly educated lady on board exclaimed, "Heaven
help the children that creature undertakes to teach!"

Uncle Gus took him out, about free, from pity, and
gave him a short berth, at the extreme stern. He was
gotten up on the Don Quixote pattern, and if he did not
pay for his passage in money, he did in suffering. When
he undoubled out of his "bunk," it was very much like
unfolding a ruler with a multitude of joints. He said
he was very grateful to the good captain, but it required
all his geometry to get into his berth and keep there.

One day he was unwell and we visited him. His
enormous long head was braced perpendicularly against
one end, which his shoulders also touched; his tremendous long feet were planted flat against the other; his
knee-pans touched the bottom of the upper berth, and
the rest of his body was disposed zig-zag. A berth in
the stern is lively, even in a calm. He said it was
unpleasant, that it abraded his sharp angles. The
expression of his face did not belie his words, and
certainly his visitors could not dispute with him as to
the correctness of his remarks. Their truth was too
apparent. How he stood it was a marvel.

Here let me remark that Europeans, at this time,
held the almost universal opinion that the people of the
United States were black, and many looked upon me as
an Albino; nor is this error entirely dispelled, even
to-day, in many localities.

We landed in Havre on one of the last days of the
"merrie month of May," or first of "leafy June." What
a contrast between republican simplicity and royal fuss
and feathers! We were boarded by a lot of officials in
lace and cocked hats, grand enough for field marshals,
by whom "the smallest favors were gratefully received
and thankfully acknowledged."

I have often thought what fools the wisest people are.
Every traveler knows that all the Continental channel

ports are tide harbors. We arrived about half ebb, and so had to wait for a number of hours, not only for the turn of the flood, but until very near high water, before we could get into the basin. Meanwhile our consignee came off with fruits, delicacies, and fresh butter. The butter in France is made without salt, and when good, has always been delicious to me.

Notwithstanding this attention to our creature comforts, and the luxurious living on board, we were so mad to get ashore that we crowded into some small luggers, at the risk of our lives, were stopped by the port authorities, on account of some absurd French harbor ordinances, and were hardly landed when the dear old "Utica" came gliding in, towed by hundreds of old women and girls, whose privilege it is, each receiving a sou or a double-sou for the service.

A great many things struck me, as a boy, that I used to miss at riper years. As I have often quoted, "humans" belong to two classes, "Eyes," and "No-eyes." I always ranked with the "Eyes." While I was young, I saw farther and more, because my mind was fresh. When I grew older, I was too much occupied with things, which I deemed of more importance to mark many interesting incidents, because they did not affect my interests.

While lying in dock, years afterwards (1852), Captain Wotton, of the "Franklin," U. S. steamer, which was navigated in a silence, broken only by the short necessary orders, called my attention to a French war steamer, warping into the basin. "Now watch that craft," said Wotton, "and you will find that everyone is bawling at once. That is the reason why the Celt or Frenchman is unfit for a sailor."

He spoke the truth. A listener would have supposed this French vessel was manned by a multitude of chattering baboons. Her decks were a pandemonium of voices.

Mr. James Hamilton, who went out to deliver the "Kamschatka," built by his son-in-law, George Schuyler, for the Emperor of Russia, told me that this steamer received more damage, hauling into dock in Cronstadt, than she had during the whole tempestuous voyage. He said the detachment of Russian sailors, sent on board, were just as stupid as brutes, and were treated as such by their officers; who atoned for their own ignorance by knocking their men about and down with handspikes. He said that their inexpertness and barbarism was horrible to witness.

The fact is there has never been but one breed fit for sailors on the face of the earth, and that is the conglomerate Theotiscan, styled by the Celt Saxons. This embraces the inhabitants of the Scandinavian and Cimbric peninsulas; of the coast thence, westward, around to Dunkirk, and England proper. What is more, strange to say, this race furnishes the best soldiers, and the most solid infantry, "the sinews of an army."

I ought to have included the Americans, and while America was still America, our sailors were the kidney of the wheat. Now our ships, like our streets and our polling places, are filled with the offscourings of creation —many creatures so vile that an Armada might go down, and, if the officers were saved, the world would experience a relief.

I will simply, at first, block out my journey, for the details are in all my journals.

From Havre, by diligence, we went to Paris. There I took medical advice, and was ordered to the baths of Cauterets, in the Pyrenees. One route, thither, by diligence again, lay through some of the most interesting portions of France. It ran through Orleans, familiar to me through my reading about Jeanne d'Arc; Blois, for the murder of the Duke of Guise by Henry III.; Chambord, noted for giving his title to the real Bourbon, the Pretender, Henry V.; Amboise, notorious for its massacre of French Protestants by the Guises, the prelude to St. Bartholomew; Tours, in a great measure ruined by the revocation of the Edict of Nantes; Chattellerault, famous for giving a French title to the Scotch Regent, James

JOHN WATTS DE PEYSTER AT THE AGE OF THIRTEEN
From a Silhouette taken in Paris in 1834

Hamilton, second Earl of Arran, and for its cutlery (I bought a knife here, with multitudinous blades, which gave me a marvellous delight, only equalled by the pain of losing it from a steamboat on the Rhine); Poictiers, most famous for witnessing one of the greatest defeats ever inflicted on the French by the English; Bordeaux, the second seaport town of France; Tarbes, Wellington's hardest fight, as he stated, where the British again whipped the French.

Finally we reached Cauterets, a neat little mountain town in an elevated valley, surrounded by colossal peaks. The baths are sulphurous, and I went there to profit by them. Although it was the middle of summer, it was very cold. The reader will be surprised when I tell him that, of all I saw while I was in this savage region, nothing struck me so as a gigantic dog, a monster of the mighty breed on which the shepherds rely for the defence of their flocks against wolves and bears. He was the largest canine I ever set my eyes on, far bigger than "Sultan," my own St. Bernard, bought in Switzerland, who grew to be over forty inches in height. We found him near the Lac de Gaube.

If ever I set foot on Spanish soil, it was this day, for the Pont d'Espagne is only six miles from Cauterets, and is on the frontier. Here also I saw one of those Spanish mules, considered superior to horses, and large as any but equine monstrosities. It was a magnificent jet-black animal, gaily and richly caparisoned, and ridden by a rider worthy his mount. Both seemed out of place in this savage mountain solitude, to which the dog and his master were congenial—the former watching the burrow, in which the latter harbored like a native marmot, or an American woodchuck. The only other time that I nearly got into Spain was when I was driven, in December, 1851, by the tempest, into the Port of Palamos, where the absurd Spanish quarantine laws would not allow me to go ashore.

From Cauterets we went (always by diligence) to Toulouse; Carcassonne, one of the most curious old places I ever saw; Narbonne, another of the same style; Montpelier; Nismes, where I had a severe fit of sickness, and dictated my journal to my father, as an amanuensis, from my bed; Avignon, a lovely spot, whither I have three times returned with pleasure; Aix-in-Provence, and Marseilles. Here we took the steamer, "Henry IV.," landed at Genoa, Leghorn, Civita Vecchia, and entered Naples early in the morning.

I was much disappointed in my first sight of Naples, its bay, and Mt. Vesuvius, and honestly think that New York harbor was as handsome, while it was yet clear of all the utilitarian abominations which now disfigure it. Then it was very dear to me. Now, if I outlive my friends and relatives, New York would be hateful to me, for it is a commingling of Dublin, Hamburg, and Inferno. We went up Vesuvius, visited Pompeii and Herculaneum, exhausted the Neapolitan curiosities, took a vetturino, and following the beaten track through Capua and Terracina, and the Pontine Marshes, reached Rome in the most unhealthy season of the year.

I enjoyed good health in this old centre, but Phil Kearny got, and nearly died of, the Roman fever. I was disappointed in Rome, as I was disappointed in Pompeii; and although I had unusual advantages, through Jesuit influence, neither then nor afterwards, strange to say, did I ever enjoy Rome as some people say that they do.

Florence is charming. A man must see Vesuvius, but really I have been struck with a great many places more than Naples or Rome.

Kearny's illness traversed our plans and changed our route. We took a vetturino to Civita Vecchia, and steamer, back to Leghorn and Genoa.

At Genoa we hired a vetturino, and after climbing the Maritime Alps, and getting down upon the plain of the Po, we encountered the most tremendous rains and inundations. These changed our route several times.

We were the last carriage allowed to cross the Serivia at Tortona. The bridge was already awash, and the approaches under water so deep that I have still prints and papers, stained with the muddy flood which got into our trunks, in the rack on the rear of our carriage. We had to dismount, and I had difficulty in making my way through the water, which rushed furiously across the road.

On the —th day of November, 1834, aged thirteen years and about eight months, I landed from the Liverpool packet, "Virginian," Captain Harris, after a pleasant but by no means speedy voyage of about four weeks (twenty-seven days).

Several incidents occurred on this voyage which were curious. Among these, a whale took a fancy to our ship, and kept such close company with us that I wanted to be allowed to fire a shot at it. To this the captain objected, because he said that he was afraid that if the monster got riled, he might, to use the language of the old sea song, "cut a flourish with his tail," and smash things up generally. Again, one day, when much farther from land than such an appearance would justify, a huge white or snow owl came on board, and stayed with us for hours, —in fact, so long, he must have quitted us in the darkness. Again I wished to try my marksmanship, and again the captain objected, not from humanity, but economy. He feared that, in consequence of the motion, I might "miss the pigeon and hit the crow," i. e., miss the owl and blow a hole through his sail, for the bird had perched very low and sat blinking at us like Poe's raven.

The passengers generally were not a set to make much impression. They were not, like those who went out with us in the "Utica," people of mark. Among the latter, I forgot to mention a Mr. Cruger, to whom I shall return again. He was a very intelligent man, gave me a great deal of information, and his parting gift, "Reichard's France," still honors my shelves.

Among the ladies on board the "Virginian" was a Mrs. Brookes—of Troy, I think—who, although a martyr to sea-sickness, was one of the loveliest women, in body and mind, that I ever encountered. She had a pet dog of a peculiar breed, called a "Tea-drinking

Spaniel," much resembling a King Charles, but smaller and more fined down. This animal was so small that I once placed him in the mouth of my Saint Bernard, "Sultan," so that nothing but his curling tail, like an ostrich feather, remained hanging out on one side, while his head, with its enormous protruding eyes and long pendulous ears, like Scotch "sporrans," stuck out in front. If "Sultan" had closed his jaws, the headless and tailless body might have gone down his throat.

"Sultan" stood forty inches high, and his tawny head, with its split nose, peculiar to his own and some sporting breeds, had jaws almost like a lion's; and, like a lion, he would fell any common dog with a single stroke of his paw. He was a tremendous brute, and the contrast between him and Mrs. Brookes's "Tea-drinking Spaniel" realized the idea that "there is but one step from the sublime to the ridiculous."

CHAPTER XVI

I do not think that my trip to Europe did me much good, in any way, except in expanding my intelligence. I went for my health, and as I never have had much to boast of, I think that, in my own, as in thousands of other cases, the doctors in New York sent me to those abroad to experiment on, because they had exhausted their own series of theories. I know I continued to suffer for a long while, in consequence of Dr. Roux's butcher-practice in Paris, and I carry a scar on my left arm, which would pass for the memorial of a minie bullet without the necessity of any lying in connection with it.

This voyage made me very self-sufficient, for at this day the "grand tower," as our people pronounced "tour," was not, as now, an ordinary thing. I used to "swell" upon it considerably, until I was taken down, in my next school, that of Mr. Worth, in Franklin street, by finding that a fellow pupil had made the "grand tower" at an earlier age. This pupil was George Cornell, of St. John's Square, who afterwards became one of the leading Whig politicians of the State.

When Washington Hunt ran for Governor, in 1850, George was on the ticket for Lieutenant-Governor. Hunt won by the "skin of his teeth," and George proved that a "miss was as good as a mile." Poor fellow, this seemed to be the turning point of his fortune. He lost his election; he afterwards lost his fortune; and soon after lost his life, through a professional visit to Brazil, which brought on a fearful disease of the liver. Young as he was, he was an able man among the decent men who were then elected as candidates.

We were a gay set of birds at Worth's school, and he was about as fit to control us as a ram would be to discipline a pack of young wolves. He might buck us over singly, but our teeth were sharp, and his continuations were lank. Imagine the effect upon a school of the late arrival, every morning, of a young buck, mounted on his splendid cream-colored horse, followed by a dashing darkey on its fellow. That darkey, Charles, was a character, in his way, and I must try to do him justice hereafter.

Some of my fellow students at Worth's became very prominent men. John Hamilton, of whom I was very fond, was an exception. John's brother, Schuyler, afterwards was a noted volunteer Major-General. He is a very brave man, a highly agreeable man, and a smart man.

Another fellow student was Bob Benson, the most comical chap I ever knew. If we did not know and wanted to get rid of a lesson, we used to manage it so that, with his consent, he was first called up to recite. With the gravest face he would make such naturally stupid blunders, intentionally, that Worth would get into a frenzy of rage. It is a wonder that he did not often burst a blood-vessel, or have a fit of apoplexy.

He would overwhelm Benson with a torrent of abuse, which shed off the latter's imperturbability like water from a duck's back. Benson would appeal to us as witnesses, and protest against Mr. Worth's language and temper. He would try to explain, and every explanation made the matter worse. We would make believe to prompt him, he would pretend to misunderstand us, and the controversy would go on, increasing in heat, until Worth would own up, whipped, and dismiss the class, apologizing to the others for Benson's interfering with their progress through his stupidity.

Then, when Benson saw Worth exhausted with his passion, he would insist upon an explanation, ape humility, appeal to Worth's better nature, insist upon information on the disputed points, until Worth would snarl out some kind of regrets for his violence, to get rid of Benson's persistent penitence. This scene would

be repeated several times a week. The class would
sometimes be ready to burst with suppressed laughter,
and no stranger, not in the secret, could ever have
believed that any youth could have played his part with
such consummate address, or any master be taken in
thus ten times in a month.

I do not think I profited considerably by my stay at
this school. While I almost reverence my first teachers,
at the Washington Institute, I still bear an intense hate
and loathing to Mr. Huddart, though I acknowledge
his ability. As for Mr. Worth, I neither look back to
him with respect nor dislike; he reminds me, with his
red hair, long white overcoat, and diminutive body, of
Captain Marryatt's description of Captain Vanslyperkin,
in "Snarleyow, or the Dog Fiend."

We had rough play at this school, which was an
isolated building next or near the French Protestant
Chapel of the Saint Esprit, southwest corner of Church
and Leonard streets. There was an alley on the west
side, I am sure. The school would divide into parties,
one body would hold the inner end, and the other
storm the position from the outer. On both sides
the missiles were stones, brickbats, and equally dangerous
articles.

This horse-play went on until, at length, we actually
broke one or more of the cast iron ornaments on the
top of the iron railing on the opposite side of Franklin
street. The next morning the owner appeared in the school
with the fragments, and told Worth that if he didn't
care for the damage done to him, he would have to take
cognizance for the school, for some one would be maimed
or killed. It is a wonder no one was killed.

I had the nickname of "Mad Jack," of which I was
very proud, until Benson, who beneath all his assumed
stupidity possessed an immense fund of dry, sarcastic
humor, added three letters. Had I not nipped the
application in the bud, it would have made it anything
but a complimentary epithet. Nevertheless, my folly
almost justified his addition, for I often volunteered to

lead the storming parties, until, one day, I got a brickbat just behind the ear, which converted me into a "tee-to-tum," so that my followers thought that I was killed. Had it struck two inches above, or below, I should not be here dictating my memoirs.

At this time my dearest friend was not my school-fellow. He was Frederic Anthon, and in some respects he was one of the noblest and most affectionate of men and boys. He was one of the greatest amateur boxers who ever lived, and as a boy, and as a man, no antagonist that I know of could ever stand up before him. Years afterwards, in his prime, he went into the Empire Club in Park Row, and whipped one of the biggest, if not the biggest bully of the gang, on his own "dunghill."

He and I remained bosom friends for many, many years. Dear old fellow, how I loved him! Afterwards, with all his talents, he became, as is the case so often, his own worst enemy, sacrificed his vast capacity, and died the last death any one would have dreamed of, in connection with him. He was six feet tall, powerfully made, and calculated for a leader of men. Why he failed, I cannot imagine, unless it must be attributed to that which occasioned the disgrace of Cassio. I lost sight of him for many years, and finally encountered him, fading gradually away, and so far lost to himself that he scarcely recognized me.

How many happy hours I have passed in his company, and, like every intimate of my early days, he is dead!

His father and mother were the most attached couple I have ever met. They were lovers, down to the day that death separated them. They had a large family, and not one but evinced, in some peculiar way, unusual ability; and yet they cannot be said to have prospered as they deserved. Charles became a professor, and numisma-tician; Henry, the most mischievous boy I ever knew, a prominent lawyer; John, the youngest, acquired an immense influence in the same profession, as a free-mason, and in politics. Phil exhibited large capacity in literature.

All the boys, except Charles, are dead, and I think all the rest of the family. John Anthon, the father, was brother of the celebrated Professor Charles Anthon, who, whatever a few may say against him, was one of the manliest of men, and the most learned of Americans. He was very kind to me when he had a chance. I liked him, living, and I honor him, now that he is dead. I have one or two elegant letters from him, in his peculiarly beautiful handwriting. With all his severity, he was always ready to pardon a delinquency in recitation, if the cause was a manly one, and its acknowledgment truth.

Another intimate friend was Peter Augustus Jay, a perfect specimen of the typical old French nobility—pure blood; handsome, well-made, graceful, easy, agreeable, and as full of elegant wickedness as an egg is of meat. Woman, lovely woman, adored him, and of every class; even those to whom King James would have applied his remark, in the "Fortunes of Nigel," fell in love with him at once. He was a charming fellow; not able, but attractive. He married a woman considered as handsome as I know he was, but she did not live long. He died in Florence, Italy, of what, in those days, was said to be a rare disease.

Gus, in his way, I repeat, was a charming fellow, and almost an invariable favorite.

After my grandfather had lost all his noble sons, things went to sixes and sevens in the stable. Nigger Tom was not the man to maintain order, and, in place of the elegant turnouts which my uncle sported, things got mixed. The saddle horses, somehow or other, always were up to the mark, but the antediluvian collection of vehicles and harness, if they had been kept together until this Centennial year, would have made a lover of antiquities weep for joy.

When the noted Dr. David Hosack died, 23d December, 1835, my grandfather considered it was necessary to go to his funeral with a carriage and pair. So Charlie went to work and overhauled the vehicles,

stored in confusion worse confounded, in our spacious
carriage house, and extricated one which he deemed fit
for the occasion. Its general contour resembled a
modern "Victoria," but as it was mounted in the early
Renaissance style of the opening of the century, it was
somewhat of a curiosity.

My father, my poor uncle Abraham, and myself once
made a trip in it, the length of Long Island. After we
got beyond the reach of civilized ideas, and arrived at
Patchogue, then in the bosom of the pine barrens, our
conveyance became a puzzle and a curiosity. Even our
landlord Roe's sons were dazzled by it, and a circle of
professionals gathered round it, full of deference for a
city equipage.

My uncle Robert was well known down there, likewise
his chums, Jack Lawrence, Jerry Stuyvesant, Cum Suis,
and their preeminent skill in shooting had so impressed
the natives that, if they had adopted the South Sea
Island costume, it would hardly have been questioned as
a fashionable rig. In the Highlands the saying rules,
"If it is not Bran (the Chief), it is at least Bran's
brother," and, consequently, the respect due to the head
of the family must not be wanting to a near kinsman.
On this principle, Bob's brother, my father, like the king,
could do no wrong, and his carriage must be the pink
of fashion.

Doubtless the vision of this strange four-wheeled
"conveniency" lingered for decades in the minds of those
gentle villagers—devoted to raking clams, and using all
kinds of clams in the appropriate manner—something as
the legend of strange ships dwelt upon the minds of our
Indians before the permanent settlement of the country.

The hubs must have been a foot and a half long, and
attenuated, and the fifth wheel was long enough to supply
the loss of one of the fore wheels in case of a smash.
Then, as to the harness, it was made in the day when
leather was cheap, horses were large, and draughts were
heavy. Each trace could have furnished material for
four of the present day, and there was as much stitching

upon it as upon an ordinary light set of harness.

Doubtless the harness belonged to one of my grandfather's state carriages, which he brought out from England two generations previous, such as were hung so high that, from the seat, my Aunt Laight used to say they could look into a second story window. My father-in-law, John Swift Livingston, had some queer equipages still in his stable, when I married, in 1841. One, resplendent with his crest, was styled "Noah's Ark," and I think Noah would have recognized the style.

Charlie unearthed this carriage, and this fossilized harness. Whether the head-stalls were wanting, or whether, having been made for Leviathans—one pair of our traditionary carriage horses, from their size, were named Samson and Goliath—and were too large for any of the degenerate horses of the current era, is not remembered. But the fact is remembered that he selected the most incongruous head-stalls imaginable, and my grandfather proceeded to Dr Hosack's funeral, charioteered by Charlie in such a manner that, when my dear father learned the fact, he lifted up his voice and wept—no, sorrowful to relate, he swore.

The appearance of the Judge at that funeral, with the veneration felt for him, must have been exactly like the resurrection, in this era of light wagons, of a wagon in which our great-grandfathers took the air.

My father, who stood in awe of my grandfather, shook off this feeling, and rose to the occasion. This vehicle and this harness disappeared from the sight of men, and

"Whence it comes, and whither it goes,
Nobody cares, and nobody knows."

On one occasion, Pinckney Stewart, my chum—since dead, like every other chum of my boyhood—and I, were perched on our hen-house, behind the parapet of our rear brick wall, on Greenwich street, pelting passers-by with hard missiles. The heavy gate closed with a latch, and behind it stood Charlie, prepared for action. If an exasperated sufferer descended from his horse, or vehicle, to desecrate the sacred precincts, and avenge his injured

sense of dignity, Charlie was there to administer an
electric shock, such as Sam Weller administered to the
scientist who came to investigate the eccentric lights in
his alley, as described in the Pickwick Papers.

One horseman, to whom and his steed, we had
administered several pebbles, after exhausting the vocab-
ulary of vituperation, without receiving "the gentle
answer that turneth away wrath," dismounted, attached
his reins to one of the rings in the wall, and prepared
to enter our fortress. Charley was all ready for him.
Had he passed the sacred portal he would have got
"one-two-three" that would have astonished him; unfortunately, at this moment, Mr. Stewart, senior, came along
with his wife.

Class distinctions were still potent in New York.
Thus, to show disrespect to the premises of Judge Watts,
excited Mr. Stewart's anger. Mr. Stewart was an irasci-
ble Scotchman. Every· feeling of the dismounted
horseman had been injured. Pink and I disappeared,
for language passed which proved, as Shakespeare said,
"Let Peace ascend to Heaven." We did not witness the
catastrophe. It was reported that the horseman
remounted his steed, a wiser if not a better man, and
Mr. Stewart did not exhibit himself; but he afterwards
did exhibit his temper to Pinckney, and "Pink" was
deprived, for some time after, of the benefits of association with Charlie and myself.

One more little instructive incident; or rather, two.
My room was in the third story front. I was fond of
Carolina potatoes. Mammie brought me up some
which were not cooked to my liking. I opened the
window, looking on Broadway, and dropped the obnox-
ious vegetable on the castor of a respectable negro who
was passing at the time. The aim was good and the
shock was great. It "bonneted" him.

Soon afterwards I heard a violent ring at the door-
bell. The violence aroused my grandfather. I slipped
down stairs and saw a vision of an infuriated negro,
presenting, with one hand, a dilapidated Carolina

potato, and with the other, a much more dilapidated hat.
Kind words were not exchanged, and then the door
slammed with a violence which shook the mansion.
From an adjacent window, I witnessed that negro deliver
a soliloquy, which, from his gestures, was not in the
philosophic vein of Hamlet's.

Another time, in innocent sportiveness, I hit another
respectable colored gentleman on the top of his head with
a hair-brush. It is true that a hair-brush is a proper
thing for the hair, but not when applied perpendicularly
from a third story window. He objected to the manner,
and also rang the bell violently. This disturbed my
grandfather, and I saw another vision of an irate colored
gentleman gesticulating with my hair-brush. My
grandfather told him to keep it, and go about his
business. The idea struck the sufferer as sensible. He
pocketed the insult and the hair-brush, and departed, and
like Charles the Twelfth of Sweden, I combed my hair
with my fingers until my father's wrath was appeased.
One-thousandth part of our capers, attempted to-day,
would put a boy in the House of Refuge.

One horribly rainy night, when the winter mud was
ankle deep in Greenwich street, Fred Anthon and I
attached a cod-line to and inside the bell-knob of Mr.
———, who lived opposite our stable gate. This
strong line we brought into our yard through a gimlet
hole in the gate. When the extinguished lights indicated
that Mr. ———'s respectable family had retired, we
pulled the cod-line, and his bell responded. After a
short delay, a figure in the habiliments of repose, candle
in hand, revealed itself at the open door, responsive to
the summons. After waving the candle to and fro
several times, investigatingly, the door was closed.
Being charitably disposed, we did not desire that the
amiable door-opener should catch a cold through a chill.
Therefore we gave this person ample time to get in bed,
and warm again, before we renewed the bell-pull.

This process was repeated several times. If it was
the same person who opened the door each time, there

11

was evidence that his mood was changed. Irreligious
language was used, and menaces. Unsophisticated
people might ask how the cod-line could escape discovery.
Firstly, it was attached inside the check-plate of the
knob. Secondly, we knew too much not to slacken it
out upon the opening of the door. Thirdly, accurate
investigation, on a winter's night, in a pouring rain,
with an open candle held by a person in the costume of
repose, is next to impossible.

Finally, the master of the house himself appeared,
equipped for service. He was a stout man and he
carried a heavy stick. He did discover the cod-line, and
he started hand over hand, with the determination
adspice finem, adspice funem. We held on like blazes.
When we thought that he was about the middle of the
street, Charles cut the cod-line. Darkness concealed the
development of the denouement, but if the person who
had hold of that cod-line belonged to the church, his
language would have excluded him thenceforward, if the
deacons had heard it.

C——— H———, "the son of the house," had
been a constant companion. His visits ceased; and it
was whispered around that his father had spoiled a suit
of clothes by a sudden fall. It seems to me that I was
reprimanded, and dark hints were thrown out that if
bells were accidentally rung in the middle of wintry
nights again, portions of my frame, connected with the
skull, would ring and be wrung even more violently.
Whatever occurred, this little sportive jest was not
repeated.

I have said that of all the intimate friends of my
boyhood, not one is left, and not very many of my mere
acquaintances. In fact, of these I remember at
present but one, Charles H. de Luze, and it strikes me
that he is a good deal younger than I am. At his
father's house I met a Swiss Count, Portalis, from the
Canton of Neufchatel. His family were royalists, and
I think he had come out to this country in consequence
of some difficulty with the liberals.

This antagonism has since been renewed several times, and finally came to a fight, when those who were inclined to the Royal Government of Prussia were forced into exile, and Neufchatel became an integral part of Switzerland. As may be imagined, a boy did not take much interest in politics, but would be absorbed in Indian curiosities, of which a profusion strewed the Count's chamber. Indian articles from among the tribes of the "far West" were still novelties in New York a half century ago, and he had many very valuable ones. He was among the first of the European travelers who had ventured among the real wild Indians, beyond the farthest settlements, west of the Mississippi and the Rocky Mountains.

He was the only man that I ever saw smoke the real "Kinnikinnick," or "Killakinnick," or "Indian tobacco," which is the dried and prepared bark of a peculiar kind of swamp or prairie water willow, with a small portion of tobacco intermingled. It was positively delicious— far more so than even the famous Latakia, or real Turkish tobacco. I have tried in vain, ever since, to get some at any price. What is sold as "Kinnikinnick," is humbug, and as much the actual article as benzine whiskey is the finest Monongahela.

The interval of nearly two years, between my return from Europe and the next great epoch in my life, is strangely blank to me, and I think it must have been pretty barren of incident. A great part of it was devoted to military studies, of which I had always been very fond. This taste was developed by my cousin, Phil Kearny, afterwards Major-General, U.S.V., killed at Chantilly, coming to live with our common grandfather. I studied and wrote a great deal on the subject, and some of the military maps, plans and drawings, executed by me at this time, and in much earlier years, would do no discredit to a professional engineer.

My campaigns against Kearny were carried out on scientific principles. Strange to say, "Phil" was then, even theoretically, what he always was practically, a dashing soldier. He loved cavalry and he made it his principal Arm. In him the Celt predominated, and in me the Saxon. I preferred Artillery and Infantry, and I wore him out, and honestly I do not think he ever beat me in the end. I was a great fellow for building entrenchments, arming them with artillery, and letting him break his Celtic teeth against the Saxon file.

We fought according to method, reduced to manuscript rules, and if any of our generals, during the Rebellion, could have applied our crude science to actual service, the war would have been more prolific of startling and grand results. Phil would have been a "Grant," in true military application of the same hammering process. He would not have wasted so much life; not because he cared for human life, but because he knew the value of disciplined life.

I would have been a "Thomas," with a good deal more ugliness, always exerted in accordance with the experience which history offers, in return for close study. For those who know me intimately will avouch that, while I am one of the most "orderly disorderly" men that ever lived, there is an astonishing amount of method in my madness. If I failed, it would have been because I never can imagine that antagonists are such fools and rogues as my omniverous reading should teach me that they are.

CHAPTER XVII

In the early summer of 1836, my dear and honored grandfather, John Watts, manifested symptoms of the disease which in three months terminated fatally. Up to this time he had scarcely exhibited any signs of the decay consistent with the attainment of the eighty-seventh year. His real disease was old age, but the technical term was "ossification of the arteries." His limbs became dropsical, and he had to intermit his walks and horseback exercise. At times he was just as active as ever, but I noticed that he used to lie on the sofa a great deal in the daytime, which was not his custom. Still, I do not believe that anyone thought he was going to die.

He had very little faith in doctors, and I wonder that they stood his cavalier treatment of them. He changed them so often that my memory will not keep track of all who appeared and disappeared. A man with $2,000,000 was a rare bird in those days, and the doctors ate an awful amount of "humble pie," in obedience to what I have often heard attributed to eccentricity. There never was a man who had less eccentricity than my grandfather Watts, but if ever a man lived who saw through men more clearly than he did, I have yet to meet him. He was very rough sometimes, but generally to suppleness and hypocrisy. Never, never, never, to the poor!

One of the last, who stayed out till the last, was Dr. Bibby. I was too young to judge of his ability, and as to whether he did any or no good. I suppose that the result was inevitable, and the mitigation of suffering the extent of the power of the ablest.

His name brings up a curious anecdote. "Indian Hemp" was recommended, but where to get it was the question. Finally some one said it was grown in the garden of old Mr. Henry Brevoort, who owned a large plot on the east side of Broadway, extending through to the Bowery, above Tenth street. Grace church stands on part of this ground. Henry Brevoort, his son, was one of the most aristocratic of the aristocrats. His mother was one of the gentlest, kindest, of primitive women, although she was a Langdon, and if that is not good blood, there is none in New England. But the father was a specimen, pure and simple, of a Dutch farmer, or market gardener.

I never saw him—and I saw him often—except in a red flannel shirt, and just such clothes as a well-to-do primitive farmer would be likely to wear. Dr. Bibby gave me some money, told me to jump into his gig, drive up to Brevoort's old low-storied cottage-house on the Bowery, tell the owner that I wanted some Indian hemp for my grandfather, Judge Watts, use diplomacy if necessary, but not return without it. I trotted along briskly, roused Mr. Brevoort from a nap, stated my case, found no demur, and got the Indian hemp, which he dug up with his own hands.

"How much am I to pay?" was then the question.

"I never sells it," Mr. Brevoort replied, "because if I takes money for Indian hemp, it weakens the vartoo." I stated that I was ordered to pay, and we discussed the matter, walking across the garden towards the gig, which I had left on Broadway. I had made up my mind that I had met with a disinterested Christian, had replaced the money in my pocket, and had my foot on the gig step, when I felt a brawny, sunburnt, freckled hand restraining me, and heard these words whispered into my ear, "I never sells Indian hemp, for that weakens the vartoo, but if I gives it, I never refuses a present." I extricated the money confided to me, placed it in the expectant hand, hurried home, related my story, and I have heard it laughed over a hundred times.

At this time old Mr. Brevoort was worth, I suppose, at least a million of dollars, through the increase of value in city lots, and yet no one, to look at him, could have been made to believe that he did not live off the produce of the garden "sarse" grown on his little place.

I have seen a great many persons die—manly men, the manliest of men—without trepidation. I would not mean without trepidation if they displayed physical symptoms of dread, but kept these to themselves, as far as expression in language is concerned.

I doubt, however, in the majority of cases, if those whom I have seen die, actually believed it, even when they were dying. Very often the mind is affected, benumbed; often, again, thought is entirely paralyzed. My two sons, Watts and Frederic, died like perfect heroes, but both, suddenly, when the end came. Frederic for his age, was the most calmly brave human being that I ever witnessed; and what a difference it makes, between dying in the prime of manhood, and extreme old age!

My father-in-law, John Swift Livingston, always said that he wanted to die as soon as it required an effort to live, or as soon as it necessitated a change of his habits. When it was necessary for him to undergo a severe regimen and take stated exercise, to get along at all, he remarked that, rather than go through what he did, he would prefer to die. I believe him. He was the most set in his habits of any human being that I ever saw. He changed his seat with the sun; scarcely took any exercise; was an epicure in everything; and yet he could pass from this inaction to extraordinary exertion, such as would use up the vast majority of ordinary men, without suffering the slightest inconvenience. If ever a man was made of iron he was.

He said to me a few days before he died, "General, these women *will* keep me alive." He alluded to the unremitting attentions of his daughters, for never was a father more faithfully served by his children. Thus he died without fear, for I verily believe that life—through breaking up the rules he laid out for himself—bothered him; or if this word may not seem respectful enough, it became irksome to him.

My grandfather Watts died in a very different way, but equally like a Stoic. He remarked to me, "I want to die, and yet I am not a gladiator." I understood this to mean that suffering, affliction, and his last disease—which, by effecting the breathing, rendered every moment, to say the least, uncomfortable—had gradually weaned him from life; but he did not wish to die like a human brute, which was about the condition of a professional Roman gladiator.

He had lost, in mid-life, a lovely and pious wife, and he had followed to the tomb a family of as noble sons and charming daughters as ever blessed a man. He had only three grandchildren, one, General Kearny's sister, Susan, comparatively a stranger; and he had been partly compelled by legal advice to make a will which was not satisfactory to him.

I shall always believe that Peter Augustus Jay advised him from interested motives. My grandfather desired to leave his property to me for my life, and in trust, something like an entail. I was to take his name. Several trust wills had recently been broken, and Mr. Jay made use of this as an argument to induce grandfather to admit the two Kearny children to equal privileges with myself.

To prove that my grandfather's heart was wholly wrapped up in me, almost his last words were, "Buy John a dog." Some time previous he had made me part with a dog—deservedly, for the dog had flown at him; but, petted as I was, it made me show temper. Remembering this, and full of love to me—the only child of his favorite Justine—in his last moments he strove to please the very lad who had so often rebelled against his wisdom. I trust that I have tried to do honor to his memory, and if it lives, otherwise than through his great benevolence, it will survive through the efforts of one who can never be sufficiently grateful to one of the most sensible, most noble, and most manly of men.

One incident of his illness I cannot refrain from relating. He had relinquished the saddle; he had ceased

to take his daily walk; he had reluctantly come to recline upon a sofa; to desist from waiting upon himself, and, finally, as a last resort, remained most of the time in bed. One day he said to my father, who was as devoted to him as any son, "De Peyster, I must get up and go to my desk." From corroborative circumstances my father was satisfied that he wanted to do something further for me.

My father said, "Mr. Watts, the doctors say that you must not get up; that you cannot." "Cannot?" replied my grandfather, as iron in will as my father-in-law was in body. "Cannot? We will see." He sat up in bed, cast off the cover, threw his limbs out, and, by a supreme effort, essayed to stand erect. My father caught him as he fell. "De Peyster," was his only remark, "all is over." He did not die immediately, but he ceased to struggle against the inevitable, with a calm dignity which never faltered until the last breath.

His daughter, Mrs. Laight, my father, his nephew, Robert Watts, Mammie Trainque, and I were with him when he died. He passed away so easily that I, with my youthful inexperience, did not know when the end came. He expired exactly like a patriarch, with his mind unclouded to the last, breathing affection so vast that it required the full development of my faculties, with years, to know how huge it was.

Without a single iota of the humbug apparent in almost every man styled great, I tell you that John Watts "was the noblest Roman of them all." It is impossible for me to give utterance to the high estimate which I have come to place upon my grandfather, and this opinion is equally shared by my father. They say that no man is a hero to his intimates. He is the only man with whom I have ever been intimate on whose life I cannot lay my finger, or whole hand, or more, and say, in this or that, these or those respects, he was little. There are spots on the sun, but if true manliness makes a man, there was not a spot on my grandfather, John Watts.

I now fell into the hands of my father, and never, since the earth was created, was there a more marked change of policy and administration. That of my grandfather had been the steady course of a vast river, moving with unruffled volume, direct from its source to the sea—the North River, for instance, one of the straightest, if not the very straightest, in the world. I have said, throughout these memoirs, that my father was one of the best of men; but, under my grandfather, he was a vice-president, who had mighty few opportunities for executive exertion. And now the law made him at once supreme, in the double capacity of executor and guardian, and simultaneously there was rebellion.

I had a hard time in some respects, and I do not think that father will ever claim that he conquered me. It was very much like a rebellion which is characterized by great suffering on the part of the rebels, but no crushing defeat, in which time, of itself, brings victory. The expression, "Time and I against any other two," has been attributed to Philip the Second of Spain, and Cardinal Mazarin, Prime Minister of France. In my case it was Time and I against any other dozen, with twenty-one majority in the far vista of humiliation, suffering, and contradiction.

I am afraid I made father very uncomfortable. I know he did me—and very sore, sometimes; but it was the struggle between Antæus and Hercules. My strength was renewed with every fall, and my father had not power to hold me aloft long enough to choke me. I do not blame my father, in the least, for anything, however severe, that he did; for, before Heaven, I believe that his object was to make me something great, and he was only mistaken as to the means.

I said, or ought to have said, that my grandfather was opposed to old Phil Kearny as an executor, but the same Mr. Jay. told him that he must appoint him.

My grandfather's will was one of the noblest that ever was made. The bulk of his fortune was divided between his three grandchildren, in the proportions of about five to me, four to General Kearny, and three to Susie. But old Kearny managed so that, between him, and the Anti-Rent difficulties, and my long minority, which he made to bear the expenses of the estate for years, the shares eventually turned out about equal.

Besides this, my grandfather left a large amount of real estate to his five surviving nephews and four great-nephews—the first, the sons of his gallant brother Stephen, who, a little over twenty-one, as Major, commanded the "Johnson Greens," and led the victorious way to Oriskany. Four of these nephews were in the British service. One, Ross, a Post-Captain; one, John, a Major; one, Gordon, in the civico-military service; one Robert, in the civil service; and one, Charles, poor fellow, too deaf to hold any public position. Of the four great-nephews, one was the noted anatomist, Dr. Robert Watts; one, Ridley, married Miss Sarah Grinnell, and was one of the most unselfish and devoted sons that ever lived; and two, Alexander and Essex, were both afflicted with the incurable "Spanish fever," inertia.

Had their property been wisely administered it would have turned out about double what it did. As it was, I suppose the shares averaged $30,000, which was a fortune in those days for men who had had nothing.

The two gentlemen called in to appraise my grand-father's estate were Robert Reade, my grandfather's cousin, and William Lawrence, who lived in Broadway, just above the corner of Leonard street, west side, next to Contoit's Garden. Both parties passed for men of irre-proachable morals, wore white chokers, moved in the best society, were considered still, at fifty, most eligible matches, and were welcomed, wherever they went, by hoping spinsters, as the most desirable catches.

Robert Reade was still a very handsome man, but devoted to the care of his health. This care grew out of his fear of the gout, which nevertheless caught him at last.

My dear grandfather died on the third of September, 1836, and was buried in his family vault, in Trinity

Churchyard, near the original monument to "Don't give up the ship," Lawrence, there in the very southwest corner. Thither, with the exception of one daughter, Mrs. Henry Laight, his entire family had preceded him. Towards the west, and near the river wall of the yard, my great-uncle, his elder brother, lies buried under a large slab.

This Robert Watts married Mary, eldest daughter of Major-General Alexander, of the Continental Army, and titular Earl of Stirling. I remember his wife very well. She was a little, dignified old lady, who never would allow herself to be addressed otherwise than as Lady Mary.

When I was a boy she lived in the old family house in Pearl street, north side, near the corner of Whitehall, or, more properly speaking, between Whitehall street and Broad. She was the mother of Dr. John Watts, President of the New York College of Physicians and Surgeons. I have his life in the shape of an obituary or eulogy, bound up in a volume of pamphlets in my library.

His brother Robert was with my grandfather when he died. He was as full of wit as it is possible for a man to be, but he was still more remarkable as one of those men who, after having been a fast liver, past middle age, had the will to entirely relinquish every sort of stimulant. It is true that he suffered the torments of hell with the gout. Still, how few are able, even through the lessons of suffering, to restrain the appetite!

His most excellent son, Ridley, although likewise a martyr to the gout, would not yield, but liked a social glass once in a while at his own table, even if he did have to pay for it. In some respects his life has, consequently, been a martyrdom. This Ridley was one of the truest of men. He married Sarah, daughter of Henry Grinnell, of Arctic discovery celebrity. If ever there was a copperhead, it was Henry Grinnell; and Ridley, to his cost, withstood him to his face, as Paul did Peter.

One day, unable to cope with him in argument, Mr. Grinnell shouted out, "You'll go to hell, sir; you'll go to hell!" Ridley instantly replied, with his accustomed calmness and wit, "I have one strong consolation, Mr. Grinnell, which takes the whole sting out of this painful remark. This is, that if you are correct, our separation will not be long." It took five minutes for Mr. Grinnell to get the idea "through his wool," but, when he did, he bounced out of the house in a perfect rage, and did not return for a long while to encounter such another thrust under the short ribs.

His son, Robert Grinnell, was a Rebel Major, and not only severely wounded, but mutilated. He lost a number of bones, not only out of both arms, but both hands, and yet he could roll up a Spanish cigarette as rapidly and neatly as if he had all his fingers, instead of only half the complement. After the war, he drifted down into Arkansas, where he or his father owned some land. Shortly after his settlement there he returned to the North on a visit.

He said to me one evening, at Ridley's, "General, we cannot get a man down in our section who will take the Federal iron-clad oath, and so we are destitute of any postmaster or any postal conveniences in my vicinity. Do you not know some Union soldier who would like to go down there and settle and become postmaster?" I replied that I would see, and on my return to my country place, Rose Hill, near Tivoli, drove out to "Upper Red Hook Landing" to find Lieutenant or Captain John McGill, a veteran soldier, who, having an adventurous disposition, I thought would like to go down to Arkansas. I stated the case, he said he was not afraid, and on my return to New York I announced to my cousin Ridley that I had found a Union soldier who would make a postmaster for Major Grinnell in Arkansas.

"Rid" looked at me in astonishment. "Did you put any faith in Grinnell's idea that a Northerner would get any show in that region? If you have any regard for McGill, don't let him go, for from what the Major says of his neighbors, McGill's term of office would be very short, and with the first excuse they would assuredly cut his throat." I reported progress, and McGill took the hint. He thought he would rather do carpenter's work at the North, with a perfect "swallow," than exchange for a situation which, with better pay and more honor, perhaps, would impair the integrity of his wind-pipe.

I called my place "Rose Hill" after my great grand-father's country seat, between 21st street, Broadway, the old post road to Boston, about 27th street, and the East river. This my great grandfather, John Watts, named after the family seat, "Rose Hill," which, when the family emigrated to America, was on the outskirts of Edin-burgh, Scotland. The quaint old house is still standing, but is now in the centre of a populous district of the Scottish capital. Mr. Hoffman, a Scotch architect, now exercising his profession under the United States Government at Washington, got out from home a plan of this house, and an account of it, which is among my multitudinous papers.

If my residences ever burn up, what a mass of information in regard to the City of New York and its history will follow the treasures of papers, pamphlets, pictures, public documents, heirlooms, and curiosities already swallowed up by the flames! To my knowledge, the Watts family were burned out twice. I witnessed the burning of an immense amount of printed and written matter. Invaluable papers and heirlooms, belonging to the de Peysters, were burnt for kindling by servants, who got access to them, where they were carelessly stowed in the garret. All that different conflagrations spared, of our family silver, was carried off by burglars.

This recalls the magnificent solid mahogany dining tables in Grandfather Watts' old house, and curious old furniture. It was given to poor relatives, and scattered to the four winds of heaven, and I would have bought it back again at any price if I could have done so. These dining tables were a curiosity; at least four, perhaps six, each so heavy that two persons could scarcely lift one. They went together with tenons and mortices, and when joined, with their leaves extended, must have presented (if five) a surface of thirty feet long, by at least five feet broad—sufficient for 32 guests; if six, 40 guests.

My grandfather, John Watts, was born 27th August, 1749, old style. At the age of twenty-five he was the last Royal Recorder of the City of New York. Would that he, some other, or myself for him, had made some notes of his native city in ante-revolutionary times. From his bedroom, in his old Pearl street house, he saw the outbreak of the terrific conflagration which, on 21st September, 1776, laid the better and greater part of New York in ruins and ashes.

A dozen different statements of the origin of this fire have been printed and attested. My grandfather never seemed to have the slightest doubt of the cause, such as he heard it at the time. He said that some of the British soldiers went over on Long Island and brought back a quantity of chestnut fence rails. They were quartered down in Whitehall street, where they kindled a fire, in a low pothouse, with the rails, which they were too lazy or too drunk to cut to a proper length. They just stuck the rails into the fireplace, kindled the end, warmed themselves with the blaze, and, between liquor and heat, soon went to sleep.

Any one who has ever burnt dry chestnut knows how it snaps and throws out small brands. The fire followed the rails out across the hearth into the floor. All the old houses were full of draughts; this was peculiarly exposed, and it took fire like kindling. The wind was from the southwest, which drove the fire towards Pearl street, and the flames spread so rapidly that the Watts family saved scarcely anything at all.

My grandfather was of the opinion that the stories were true of British soldiers throwing persons, suspected of helping on the conflagration, into the flames. He

CHAPTER XVIII

COLLEGIAN AND VOLUNTEER FIREMAN

I was prepared for college by Mr. Vermylia, an assistant to Professor Charles Anthon, in dear old No. 3 Broadway, and entered college in the fall of '36.

Of my class, Freshmen, in Columbia College, few, if any, of my more intimate associates survive. Here again, I came in contact with George J. Cornell.

I think I have mentioned that I got my growth when I was fifteen years old, and I was so large that I used to associate with the Seniors and Juniors as much as I did with my own class. Consequently, I have got them all mixed up in my mind, and while I remember the men, I do not remember their classification.

Ben Kissam was about the handsomest fellow, of his age, that ever took the fancy of a woman. He has since become a lawyer, and I have met him at rare intervals; but all the coarseness of age cannot destroy the marks of his wonderful early manly beauty. The Pythias of this Damon was Ben Romaine, a real nice fellow, but nothing like the same exceptional specimen of humanity as his friend. Worthington Romaine, the latter's brother, is still alive, but Ben was gone at an early date.

As to physical development, by all odds the most remarkable example was Farley or Fairly Clark, in my class; and, strange to say, with his "bull chest," he was the first to go with inflammation of the lungs. Zeb. Ring, one of the handsomest little fellows that eye ever rested on, one of your specimens of elegance, likewise left us, among the first, a victim to chest disease— consumption caught by exposure at a ball. He was as handsome as a picture, and yet he was a good boxer. He was one of those men whose dying words are quoted as examples of Christian endings, and with his last breath he spoke of the "chariots of fire," as in the case of Elijah, to bear him to heaven.

Tom Cooper was another college mate. He was my great antagonist in athletic sports, and set us an example of wearing "love-locks," like the old English cavaliers. This fashion, among those who had perfectly straight hair, proved all that the Puritans said about the "unloveliness of love-locks;" and many of us, who ran with "the machine," docked ours into "soap-locks," fire-boy or fireman's pattern.

I lost sight of Tom for a number of years. When I last saw him he was at the head of the Institution for the Blind, on Eighth avenue, New York City. He lost this, obtained a Captain's commission in the volunteers, and was killed in the Wilderness in 1864. He was a tall and well-made fellow, but there was a streak of queer temper in Tom.

His younger brother, Charlie Cooper, was a regular dare-devil; a fire-eater in the real sense of the word. I forget if he was in college with me, but if not, he was with me every day. He went off to Nicaragua with Walker, "the gray-eyed man of destiny," and I think he was killed there—at all events, I heard so, and we never met again. Charlie had some very attractive traits. Other college mates were Ogden Hoffman, Jr., afterwards United States Judge in California, John Jacob Astor, Jr., Lydig Hoyt, John Knox, John M. Mason (Knox's partner), and Judge Alonzo Munson.

I certainly did not make the most of my advantages in college. The time I ought to have been studying, I was running as a Volunteer Fireman with No. 5 Hose Carriage. Then again, when I was not with the hose carriage, I used to be a great deal among the fancy butchers, and from what I saw, Bergh ought to have made his appearance thirty years before he did.

Terrific cruelty was used before beeves were slaughtered, and many a poor animal was "baited" before he was "butchered." And yet, our butchers, as a class, aside from their business, were not a bad set of men.

They were undoubtedly brutal, but still there was a sort
of chivalry about their very brutality, totally different
from the obtuse cruelty or indifference of the same class
at the present day.

Nothing ever occurred among them like the barbarism
I witnessed in an abattoir at Paris. There I saw a
butcher go into a pen with sheep, throw one deliberately
down, dislocate its hind legs, cross them and jerk them
into a knot; do the same by another, then pick up the
two by the knots thus formed, throw one over each
shoulder, and carry them off, thus, to the slaughtering
tub. It made me sick at heart and stomach. Bergh
would have sent such a savage "up" for three years.

This was the tip-top tide wave of the New York
Volunteer Fire Department, when money was spent
without stint in the decoration of machines and hose
carriages. The Department had won an immense deal
of credit in the Great Fire of 1836, which I witnessed
plainly from the windows of my grandfather's house,
No. 3 Broadway.

I was very sick that night, and the doctors would
not let me go out. Notwithstanding the very severe
cold, I made my escape into the streets next morning,
and saw the militia, and the United States troops from
Governor's Island and the Forts in the Harbor, standing
guard over the ruins and rescued property. Notwithstanding the vast area of flame, I think the burning of
the old Bowery, which I saw twice consumed, and of
the Academy of Music, were grander spectacles.

My father was in the old Park Theatre when it burned
down, and I witnessed the play of "Brutus," with two
Booths in the cast, which was the last night of the
Winter Garden. The performance could scarcely have
ceased when the fire kindled, for the building was a
mass of ruins when the day had well broken.

In the fire of 1836, the rescue of a child occurred,
which has always been attributed to the gallantry of a
volunteer fireman. This claim to the honor of a very
gallant deed is utterly unfounded. My chum, and ship-

mate of after years, Lewis Morris Wilkins, was the real
hero. He had been a midshipman in the Navy, and had
been dismissed for one of his larks, which were as
common as the days. He happened to be passing, heard
the cry that a child was burning in the upper story of
a lofty house, mounted a ladder, plunged into the smoke,
which was already streaked with flame, rescued the child,
and brought it down uninjured. President Jackson
reinstated him for this act of heroism, and the Fire
Department stole the glory for one of themselves.

I may say that I have seen four phases of the New
York Fire Department! With my first remembrance,
say in 1824, I can recall the rows of leathern buckets,
regularly disposed and ready for use, on the wide back
piazza of my grandfather's house, No 3 Broadway. At
this time many of the engines were exceedingly primitive, such as are represented on the copy books of my
boyhood. They formed long lines of engines to the
rivers, and tried to "flow" or "flood" each other, which
was a great feather in the cap of the successful company.
I paid very little attention to the subject at the time,
but we will count this as phase No. 1.

Phase No. 2 was when the Department was gorgeous,
and as yet, as a rule, respectable. This was when I used
to run "wid de ma-sheen." This was from 1836 to
1839, and cost me my health. The fatigue, exposure,
and irregular hours, together with the unavoidable
"drinks all 'round," and "suppers," any time of the
night-morning, wrought some disarrangement of semi-
lunar valves of the heart, and permitted regurgitation
of the blood. The pain I suffered at times was
inexpressible. It seemed as if a claw of iron grasped my
heart and squeezed it.

At this time I weighed more than I ever did in my
life, and then leeched seven inches out of my coat in
one month. I have been, days together, in my wet, half
frozen or wholly frozen clothes; and have run, or double-
quicked—once, a distance estimated at twenty-seven
miles, in less than twenty-four hours.

The scenes I have witnessed, in this service of wanton destruction, unnecessary flooding, frolicking, fighting, and bullying, would fill a good many pages, but tend to no good. The Volunteer Fire Department lasted a great deal longer than it should have been tolerated.

I first ran with "Hose Carriage 5," whose house was in a building where Fireman's Hall now stands, in Mercer street, near Prince. I had some words one night with Carlisle Norwood, the foreman, and went off to No. 9 Hose Carriage, in Elizabeth street, near Broome. No. 5 had a company of tip-top men in every respect—highly respectable. No. 9's company were not such high caste, but they were really nicer men to deal with.

They let me raise a volunteer company, with all the privileges and none of the responsibilities of members. We wore a fire cap a little different from the others; mine hangs up in my library, while I write. It got some hard thumps in its day. I was foreman, Gus Jay assistant, or one of the members.

Curious to say, with all my memory, I never was good at remembering names, and I scarcely recall those of any other members of the company. I meet some of them, once in a while, in the streets, but so seldom that I do not think that half, at most, can be alive. Still, if I do not recall their names, I know that they were very pleasant comrades, and many a happy hour we had together.

In 1852 I came back from Europe and made a report in favor of a paid fire department, militarily organized, with steam engines and fire escapes. I got into quite a controversy in the newspapers, and I think I completely showed up the volunteer system. I went back to Europe to finish my report, and when I came back phase No. 3 was developing—steamers and hand-engines, intermingled, but all drawn by men.

Phase No. 4 is our present system, and I claim that, if it is due to any man more than those who practically administered it, the credit is mine. Doubters, examine my report, and go and ask Orison Blunt, who was a leading alderman at the time, and he will tell you how I worked. I never had the suaviter-in-mode, and so, throughout life, my "thunder" has been stolen, and, wherever it was possible, even my empty honor filched.

CHAPTER XIX

EUROPE AGAIN

The trouble of the heart, of which I have spoken, culminated in November or December, 1838. As soon as I had recovered a little strength from repeated and copious blood-letting, which almost exhausted my young life-blood current, I was ordered to Europe, and suffered to go alone. No, not all alone, for my faithful pointer dog, "Duke," went with me. He was the most intelligent animal that I ever saw, although I did not know how to value him, and was a hard master to him. He deserved what I put up on his monument,

"My truest friend."

He was as handsome as a picture, and he could do everything but talk. They say animals cannot laugh. I have seen him put on a broad grin many a time.

I was to sail on the 25th January, 1839. On that day occurred such a gale as had not occurred on the Atlantic coast since the famous gale of 1816. We have had nothing like it since. We lived, at the time, in a strongly-built two-story house in 12th street, and it trembled like an aspen leaf.

I saw the tin roof torn from a whole row of buildings, on University place, between 13th and 14th streets, and carried through the air like a sheet of paper. I beheld the roof of a building on Fifth avenue lifted many times, —beams, planking, everything entire—just as a person would lift the lid of a chest half open, and then let it fall to again. The roar was terrific, and the damage incalculable.

The same gale occurred about the same day at Liverpool, and swept the ocean, strewing the coast and the Atlantic with wrecks. When we got out to England, on the 12th February, the shore of the Mersey was

still lined with stranded and shattered hulks. In this
estuary, where the spring tide rises about twenty-four
feet, the water did not ebb for twenty-four hours.
Consequently, the vessels that went ashore were carried
far beyond the ordinary high water mark.

Next morning, when the gale had subsided, and I
drove down to go on board of the "Sheridan," packet
ship, Wall street, as high as Pearl, was strewn and
piled with huge blocks of ice, driven on shore by the fury
of the wind, and left there by the tide.

Outside the hook, the waves—although the wind had
shifted to the opposite quarter—were still vaster than
any that I have seen in mid-Atlantic in the fiercest gale.

Our run of sixteen days out to Liverpool was a grand
one for a ship so deeply loaded that her main deck was
almost awash. High above this was the elevated spar
deck, for the "Sheridan" belonged to the "Collins
Dramatic Line," so called because each was named after
a celebrated actor. Their cabins were under the poop,
and this was so lofty that it was a common saying that
one of the Dramatic Line could "lay to" under her poop.
They had top-gallant forecastles, which were airy and
well lighted.

The only trouble was the pitching into a heavy head
sea; an unusually hard dip would sometimes knock out
the stoppers of the hawse-holes, and then everything
would be deluged; for what officer of the deck would be
Christian enough to keep her well off, for an hour or
so, to provide for the comfort of the sailors?

Sailors! bad enough when I first went to sea, in '34,
but still sprinkled with a little respectability. In 1839
the best stuff had been skimmed off into the Navy, and
what was left was little better than "pigswash."

The afternoon that we sailed, while we were beating
down the Narrows, I heard a hoarse whisper in my ear,
"Any man who makes up his mind to be a sailor, and go
to sea, might as well put on his hat and start for hell."
I turned around, and recognized, inside of the tarred
pea-jacket and under the oil-skin southwester, my distant

kinsman, Lewis Morris Wilkins, whose mother was a de Lancey. Lew was a fine specimen of a man—such as the Lion-Hearted Richard said he liked to look upon. He was not tall, but, with that exception, he would have served as a model. Lew was not orthodox in anything, and therefore his language was that of nature. Before I left the sea, I was convinced that he put it mildly, rather than strongly.

A flush spar-deck, commencing a little aft the main-mast, and ending a little beyond the foremast, served as a bridge between the poop and the t'gallant fo'castle— so high out of water that, if the bulwarks in the waist had not been carried around on a level with the rail, forward and aft, the "Sheridan" would have resembled one of the Spanish Caravels, or Galeases, of the Armada. As it was, there being no exterior sign of the depression amidships, the ships of the Dramatic Line resembled enormous sloops of war.

A beautiful picture of the "Sheridan," rounding "the Rock," at the entrance of Liverpool harbor, painted for me by an excellent marine artist, hangs in my library, where I am writing. Her commander, my eldest uncle, Capt. F. Augustus de Peyster, was one of the most noted shipmasters out of the Port of New York.

My grandfather de Peyster having married another wife, while his boys were still young, the little chaps had a mighty rough time of it. At five, my father was already at boarding-school, and, as for "Gus," he was slammed off to sea, as a cabin-boy, when most children are still in the nursery. I was sent to boarding-school at eight, and that is far too early; but I believe Abram, my youngest uncle, was boarded out at three. So much for the tender mercies of a step-mother, and the weakness of a newly married husband!

Here let me refer to my grandfather de Peyster's betrothal. Aaron Burr, Vice-President, who then resided at Richmond Hill, which I afterwards visited, when turned into an Italian Opera House, took him in his carriage, with four blacks, to visit Nicholas William

Stuyvesant, in the Bowery, who, with Burr, were joint-guardians of my grandmother, Helen Hake.

Uncle Gus has written his memoirs, and a portion of them are in the hands of my cousin Maria, but she has written me that the most interesting, relating to his East Indian experiences, have disappeared.

He brought out from Borneo, when I was a little boy, a monkey, about three feet high, which was certainly as intelligent as many negroes. Chief-of-Police Matsell told me he was on board my uncle's ship, in the Canton river, where he saw this monkey, and that he did things that seemed to demonstrate the possession of reason.

"Jocko" had been taught to splice ropes and tie knots. One day a party of Chinese officials had come on board, to visit Capt. de Peyster, and were standing in a semi-circle, talking to him, when one of the cabin boys made signs to the monkey to tie their pigtails together. Now, to touch the pigtail of the lowest Chinaman is an insult, and imagine the row that ensued, when these haughty high-button men started to leave, and fetched up, in consequence of the knots tied in their cues. It required an immense amount of consular diplomacy to unravel the one kind of knot occasioned by the other.

Jocko walked on his legs, by means of a cane, wore "store clothes," and was as amusing as he was gentle and affectionate. Our climate killed him, and he was given to Scudder, who had him stuffed and placed in a prominent position among his curiosities.

Here also was the skin of the hugest anaconda, brought out, or sent from Brazil, by my uncle Abram.

Even after Barnum had the American Museum, corner of Ann street and Broadway, Jocko occupied a post of honor—inside, main story, at the head of the entrance stairs—and he was burnt with the big turtle, the mammoth grizzly, and a host of irreplaceable curiosities, when that establishment was burned.

When scarcely a man in years, Capt. de Peyster was selected to command the "Baltimore Clipper," which was sent out to carry the final dispatches to our represen-

tatives at Ghent, negotiating the Treaty, or Peace, of
1814. To escape the English cruisers, he had to go
north about Scotland, and had a most perilous but
successful voyage.

He was finally selected as Superintendent of the
Sailors' Snug Harbor, and there he continued until very
far advanced in life. His physical strength was tremendous, and he enjoyed excellent health, although I do not
think there was a single patent medicine, advertised in
the papers, with which he did not test his stomach, in
wild attempts to cure imaginary diseases.

In this extraordinary taste for drugs he never had but
one equal, old Mrs. Swarthout, widow of a celebrated
United States Collector in New York. On leaving Mrs.
Toler's house, in Nineteenth street, where she had been
staying, she requested to be excused for a few moments,
and, when she got into the carriage, she said she went
back and swallowed all the residue remaining in a row
of vials, because it was wicked to waste so much stuff
that had cost money. This lady lived to a very advanced
age, and why, is a marvel, because she was always sick,
always drenching herself, and always ready with a dose
for anybody who would listen to her. I believe she took
as much medicine, while I knew her, as would have
filled the room in which she lived.

For a ship loaded so deep, the "Sheridan" made a very
quick passage, but we had extraordinary weather. In
the daytime it was often calm, or there was a very
light breeze, and at night strong favoring gales. A
great deal of snow fell, accompanied with lightning and
thunder, as vivid and heavy as is customary in the
summer season.

One night the snow came down in such quantities, in
huge flakes, and consequently moist, that it was absolutely dangerous to be on deck. It would collect up
aloft until its own weight broke it loose, and then it
would sometimes come down in masses, equal to the size
of a barrel, and strike the deck with a "thud" that made
things shake. I often wondered how any human being

could get aloft or lay out on the yards in such a state of
things. And yet we were making sail, and taking in
sail, and making it again, all night.

The atmosphere was full of electricity, and we had
corposants, or whatever they call the lurid fires which
show themselves aloft at sea, all over the ship—at the
mast-heads, at the yard-arms, in fact, the extremity of
every spar—and the ship went careening along, rolling
so that if her top-mast, stun or studding-sail booms had
been out, she would have dipped them continually, on
either side, and all the time she was illuminated as
if she had been lit up with Bengal lights for a marine
festival.

The "Akbar," a large ship, sailed a few hours before
us, and a few days out, when day broke, we sighted her
about three miles to windward, and ran along on a
parallel course with her pretty much all day. She looked
exactly like a perfect toy ship, and just as big as one.
From morn till afternoon the wind was light, but
favorable, and we tumbled about on a smooth sea. All
at once Capt. de Peyster called all hands, and the way
we shortened sail was a caution.

Things had scarcely been made snug when the gale
struck us from the nor'-west, the "Akbar" disappeared,
our own ship was enveloped in the mist or sleet, which
the wind brought with it, and in an instant almost, from
wallowing in a sluggish swell, the "Sheridan" was bowling
along like a race-horse. There were few other incidents
of importance on the voyage, and the "Sheridan" made
her two hundred and forty or sometimes two hundred
and sixty-eight knots (or sea miles) a day. Once in a
while she got up to twelve knots an hour, but she was
too heavily laden, or, more properly speaking, too deep
by the stern, and dragged too much water after her,
to keep this up long.

We had very few passengers; two, that I was most
with, were Messrs. Pierce and Fontaine, from Mobile,
going out to Liverpool to establish a house in connection
with the cotton trade. Pierce was a tall, black-haired,

genial man, and Fontaine a rather small, red-haired
man. Both were rough diamonds—Pierce a regular
Southerner—and both very agreeable to me.

Another passenger was an Englishman, whom I shall
never forget, who realized the idea of Paddy's mother,
in Lever's novel, whose religion consisted in taking
whiskey in her tea. This Briton held the same faith,
but belonged to another sect, whose tenets substituted
brandy. In those days passage money covered liquors,
and he was not a man to throw away any advantage.

He fortified his coffee at breakfast, he "toted his tod
neat" at lunch and at dinner, he qualified his tea, and
he wound up his day's work with cocktails, mixed on
Father Tom's principle—plenty of sugar, plenty of
liquor, and then every drop of water you put in spoils
the drink. The result was that, when he turned in at
night, it would have taken more than the strongest blast
of Boreas to wake his innocent slumbers. By the time
he got to Liverpool, I think the owners had lost money
by him, in stimulants alone.

George Cornish, the first officer, who succeeded
Captain de Peyster in the command of the "Sheridan,"
was a genius and a bully comrade. He said he was an
American, but if he was born under the "Stars and
Stripes," it was astraddle of the northeast boundary
line. Both he and Uncle Gus are dead—Cornish, in his
prime. George was a fancy man, and, although a prime
sailor, he dropped the ship as soon as he got ashore.

He traded in everything, from apples up to summer
ducks, and from dogs down to potatoes. He was very
kind to me all his life. He was a pugilist, dog-fighter,
fox-hunter, in fact "a sport," in the better sense of the
word, and in mundane things he knew, as St. Paul said
of spiritual, "when to and when not to abound." He
was built like a "John Bull," and there was a good
deal of the "bull" about him.

He finally gave up the sea, went out to England,
married a rich widow, and she was too much for him.
He had only one child, a daughter by a first wife, left

an orphan at an early age, whom he cared for tenderly. With the exception of unredeemed red hair, she was quite an interesting girl, and made a good wife to a sort of kinsman or connection of Captain de Peyster, named Robinson, a fine fellow.

I once drove Cornish out to see the place where his first wife was buried. She died while he was away, and was laid in the grounds of the old Eastchester Church. It was a bitter winter day, and we struck the venerable isolated edifice about nightfall. I don't think I ever saw a more dismal spot. It was solitary and gloomy enough to make a man shudder. This must have been thirty-five years ago, and yet so strongly did that drive and that church impress themselves upon me, that the other night (10th July, 1876), my kinsman, de Lancey Neal, told me that my description of it was perfectly correct, after such a lapse of time.

The life of Capt. Cornish would have furnished the materials for a dozen novels. When a youngster he was kidnapped, and placed aboard a slaver as a cabin boy. His vessel was finally driven ashore by a British cruiser, and he had to foot it, along the coast of Africa, for a long distance, before he reached a white settlement—I think, Sierra Leone. He came near being hung, and, it strikes me, only escaped on account of his youth.

A curious thing happened to him and me in 1842. I had a house that year at Yonkers, and was driving him into town, one day, in a one-horse wagon, when suddenly we smelled smoke. We both had cigars, but were so interested in conversation that we had forgotten everything else but the subject. So oblivious were we, that, before we discovered the fire, a whole lot of articles in the wagon were burned, likewise the bottom, and even the captain's pantaloons. This may sound like a "fish story."

I do not remember the second mate, any more than if he had never existed. The third mate was Lewis Morris Wilkins. I have said enough about him, and will only add that he was never happy unless he was in a

row, and that, whatever were the color of his eyes, one
or more were generally black. He might have married
a rich heiress, who was very much in love with him, if
he had only let wine and women alone. When "half
shot," he was as dangerous as a loose tiger.

One night, after a supper party at my rooms, he got
hold of a poor "leather-head," as the old-fashioned New
York night watchmen were called, from their head
coverings. He took away his cap and club, made him
walk home with him, and when the poor devil thought
his last hour had come, he dismissed him with something
equivalent to a gentle kick, such as Sam "Veller" gave
the "Fat Boy," in the "Pickwick Papers." I was told
that he frightened the poor man out of his seventeen
senses.

I was in England, from the middle of February to the
end of March, 1839, and I never remember such weather.
On St. Patrick's Day (17th March), it did everything
that it could do. There was sunshine, rain, sleet, sunshine, hail, sunshine, snow, sleet, sunshine, rain, sunshine,
and a gale of wind. Nevertheless, St. Patrick was
honored with a very lengthy procession, and the usual
amount of drink.

Meanwhile, there were lovely days, sandwiched between
this rough weather, that were perfectly balmy, and the
hedges were as green as they are in New York State in
the latter part of May. The day I drove out to visit
the Earl of Derby's estate was exactly what is described
as "Heaven above, and Hell or death below"—just the
kind of weather to kill a person with weak lungs. The
sky was cloudless, the air warm to tempt, and the earth
saturated with moisture to kill. In the sun, it was our
June, and in the shade, November. I had to go up to
London to see Sir Benjamin Brodie about my heart.

I never suffered more with cold in my life; a damp
snow fell; there was no heating apparatus in the cars.
Uncle Gus and I had the coupé. When I woke up,
towards morning, I found myself alone in the darkness.
He had the money, and I felt exactly like a sick traveler,

stranded in a strange land, without means and without
friends. Finally I set to "stamping" to warm my half
frozen feet; and pretty soon I heard a growl. It was
"Uncle Gus." He had coiled himself up, in his enormous shaggy sea-coat, and had gone to sleep on the floor.
He might have cursed my hair off, for all I cared—I,
poor sick youth, was so glad to find that I was not, as
I supposed, deserted and alone.

All I remember of London, this time, is that I saw
Liston, whom I did not think deserved his comic reputation; Keeley, who certainly deserved his; and the
Matthews—people say, father and son, uncle and nephew,
say I,—the latter, the man who ran away with Dolly
Davenport's wife, and got his "eyes blacked" and himself
"bum kicked" by the husband. Mme. Vestris was his
wife, then, a remarkable actress, and an astonishing
favorite.

I never could see enough in Mrs. Davenport to justify
Matthews in running away with her. She was a mimini
pimini, mincing, prinking, exponent of maudlin, senti-
mental, seduced country girls. These Matthews made
me laugh so that I danced with the pain of the
merriment, and nearly got a head put on me, for I
stamped on an Englishman's toe, and nothing restrained
his fury but the fact that I was a foreigner.

I also went to see the "Three Temptations," or
"Paradise and the Peri." It was got up at enormous
expense, and some of the groupings were magnificent.
The angels had enormous swan wings, and in a fight
with the devils, who opposed red-hot clubs (candles
inside of gauze work), they suddenly elevated their
wings, just as you see angels' wings sometimes represented as upraised in pictures. This was done to scare
the devils, but the audience burst into roars of derisive
laughter, shouting "goose feathers."

In the last scene the whole stage was supposed to sink
into hell. All went down into flame except the hero
and his faithful Azola, the Peri. The machinery was
very ably managed. Yates, the manager, was called out

when the curtain fell, and appeared, to return thanks, in perfect dishabille. I particularly remember his terminations—yellow slippers, down at the heel.

While in London I consulted Sir Benjamin Brodie, and I think, from his manner, that he dissented, *in toto*, from the opinion of the New York doctors. Still, as Dr. Smith had sent him out a barrel of American apples, he felt it would be a breach of courtesy to condemn, in so many words, the treatment of his professional trans-Atlantic brother.

On my return to Liverpool I had a very pleasant time, at the Waterloo hotel, with a number of packet captains, who stood at the head of their profession, which was one of mark at that day.

Among them, I recollect several distinctly; the first, Captain Cropper, of the "Columbus," which had once been commanded by my uncle. He was a noble specimen of an American sailor. The second, Capt. Rathbone, was jaunty in his ways, and, when he was got up for a high-caste dinner party, looked as little like a sailor as a veteran mariner could appear. He was a dapper little man, and, on these occasions, he sported black tights, and silk stockings and pumps, and then no one would have dreamed that he had ever smelt or felt the salt water.

The third, Capt. Delano, was considered a tip-top swell, and yet a more driving sailor never walked a quarter deck. They said it was delightful to hear Delano swear. As Dick Bottom, in "Midsummer Night's Dream," phrased it, he could "roar you gently as a sucking dove."

He would commence, sotto voce, with the mildest maledictions on Jack Tar's optics and hide. Then, as his voice mounted into a distinct whisper, his anathemas took in other portions of the microcosm than, in ordinary conversational tone, he comprehended—the inner John Brown—until, finally, the old salt spoke out, and then everything material and spiritual was consigned, in unmistakable language, to the hottest place known. He was not an economical captain for his co-partners, for his bill for spars and sails, expended in order to make a speedy trip, was something startling.

Capt. Kean, of the "Elizabeth," was another quiet little fellow, who spoke of the perils he had encountered, on his last voyage from the States, in as quiet a manner as if he had been taking a summer jaunt. He had been caught and battered in the ice, which had been making south much earlier and farther than usual. As will be seen, we encountered some giant monsters of icebergs on our return passage.

Our hotel was kept, nominally, by a man, but, in reality, by a very smart woman; her husband was a perfect specimen of a brandy-soaking John Bull, who sat, the whole day and evening, in the office, or whatever they called it, by the side of the fire. He gave me a disgust toward his countrymen, and I thought nothing could be more ignorantly arrogant, until I fell in with two said-to-be intelligent Irishmen.

One was the captain of the "Wild Irishman," that towed us to sea, who asserted, in such a stupid manner, that New York, already up to Fourteenth street, could be placed in one quarter of Liverpool, that I gave him up. The other was a very handsome specimen of a man, and, as the world goes, was not a fool; and yet his ideas of geography were about as much developed as those of a remarkably handsome whaler, who had been out for three years, and only knew that he had been somewhere, but whereabouts it was he did not know.

I have told a little story about the Devil and the wind in Rome, in connection with Fire Island, to show why there is always air stirring in front of the Jesuits' Church. To me Liverpool seemed to be always buffeted by a gale, but the reason why I never read. This "Pool of the Liver," a mythical bird in the city "arms," never rejoiced in an unruffled bosom, when I was around. It was a perfectly horrid hole, but the police appeared to be excellent.

One little adventure, and I am done with the town. Mr. Prue, the ship's butcher, offered to get me a first-rate fighting bull terrier, and I went up to his slaughter-house to see some dogs tried. He had a Peccary, or Brazilian hog, and he said that the best test of a dog would be to let him tackle this pig.

The latter was a little bit of a brute; could not have weighed over twenty-five pounds, but his tusks were almost as long and thick as his legs. He seemed to know what was coming, and went in a corner and crouched, muzzle out. No dog ever went in at him twice. He would shear off their hair as if it was done with a pair of shears, taking hide and flesh with it. Then two dogs were loosed at him; he slit one's shoulder open, and punished the other so severely that he skulked away completely whipped.

It was scarcely possible to conceive the mingled caution and agility, calculation, courage, and ferocity displayed by the pig. It is very likely that, if three or four dogs had been loosed upon him at once, they might have killed him, but he certainly would have ripped open two.

This baiting took place in an arched alley, and by this time the men and dogs were so excited that they made it a perfect reverberating hell of sound. All at once we heard an ominous rapping at the heavy, double-doors which shut us in from the street. Someone reconnoitered and said it was the police. The butchers cried, "Scamper!"

Fortunately, there was another way out into another street, and the way the mingled crowd of men and dogs skedaddled was remarkable. No such time was made at Castle Bar, where some of the English ran eighty-seven miles in forty-eight hours, nor by either side at Montchery, nor at Bull Run. This was my last attempt at selecting a bull-terrier, and, if Peccaries ever say their prayers at night, Prue's must have invoked blessings, that evening, on the police.

The "docks" at Liverpool were stupendous then, and yet they tell me that they were pigmies to the giant basins which now exist. It was a beautiful sight, at slack high water, to see the vessels haul through the gates, making sail as they hauled; then brace yards, and schoon away. While I write, I can see the "Heart of Oak," an English barque. She was handled like magic, and she shot away like an arrow, between wind and tide, which runs in the Mersey from seven to ten miles an hour, according to the season, direction, and force of the wind.

To give you an idea of how it blows in this estuary, and what a sea runs in it, a sloop loaded with guano, coming in in a gale, although she had some feet to spare under her keel, thumped to pieces on the bottom, in consequence of the height and force of the sea, and consequent shallowness of the troughs.

One of our few cabin passengers, on our return voyage, was a Mr. Crowther, and I cannot sum him up more emphatically, in concise, appropriate, descriptive language, than by qualifying him as a huge human hog.

On this passage we had very few cabin passengers, not many second cabin and near five hundred as wild, uncouth "Paddies" as ever were caught in a trap, baited with a bottle of whiskey. When they would swarm up in fine weather, forward, they would bring the "Sheridan" so down by her head that she would not steer, and the captain had to let them up by relays.

I never did, nor do believe in Darwinism, but, if he had been on board that ship, he would have sworn that any animals, walking on two legs, who could live in such filth and vermin, were below even the "missing link." Choirs of them would get on the "t'gallant fo'castle," and scream what they considered songs, whose burthens were the joys of going to "Columbee," and the prospects they had before them in "Ameriky."

Not one said he was a king, or a son of a king, for there were too many there to contradict them; but from the airs they gave themselves, before I got sick, and after we passed the "Banks," I have no doubt that, in twenty-four hours after they had landed, every mother's son of them swore he was a direct descendant of Brian Boru.

As I kept an accurate log of my return passage, I will skip that, and simply say that it terminated, abruptly, off Sable Island, or Cape Shore. I had never been seasick, but got very bilious on the ocean. Dr. Brodie had ordered me, in such a case, to take three pills, for which he gave me the prescription. I took one, and was lying in my berth, as weak as a cat from its effects, when a sea struck me under the counter, and chucked me clean out of my bunk, and through the cabin door, against the stationary seats alongside the table.

I picked myself up, made my way on deck, and stood for a few minutes, on a wet mat, talking to the man at the wheel about this shock, its cause, our course, etc., when I recollected that I was then in my bare feet, and that I had been taking medicine. I went below and turned in. In a little while it was agony to gather up my legs, and greater agony to stretch them out again. In the morning I had aggravated dysentery.

What I suffered, no human being can tell. I had had charge of the medicine chest, and my dog, "Duke," was my "surgeon's mate." When they wanted to look up the treatment of dysentery, they found that Mr. Duke had torn out the page relating to this disease. There was no doctor on board, and they had to treat me by guess. A second cabin passenger, who had seen some cases of the malady, prescribed flour, boiled into a concrete ball, then scraped, and administered in boiled milk. This, for sustenance, and laudanum for remedy, was all that passed my lips for ten days, until we reached port.

I soon became delirious, and the visions which I saw were so exquisite and so vivid that I can recall them to my mind, with perfect distinctness, after thirty-seven years. I saw armies and fleets manœuvre, as if my darkened stateroom was a vast field of exercise, or a vaster basin. Everything was as distinct as if my eyes had become invested with microscopic and telescopic power, and when, at intervals, the agony of the disease awakened me to consciousness, I longed for another dose of the narcotic to restore me to the bliss of dreamland.

In one of my lucid intervals I found the captain sitting beside me. "Am I going to die?" I asked. He intimated very coolly that he thought it was most likely such would be the case. "Uncle Gus," I rejoined, "don't throw me overboard." "No danger of that; I have made all the preparations necessary," was his comforting answer. "I shall start the water out of a butt, get up some sacks of salt (coarse salt, in sacks, was a portion of our cargo), and carry you in pickle."

He says I bore this gentle intelligence like a man, without a whimper or a word; that I turned my face over to the ship's side, and was soon lost in my fairyland, induced by opium.

Another time I had struggled into my senses, when I heard a cry of "Fire!" No one who has not heard that cry, on shipboard, can imagine its startling horror. It wilts the bravest, in the full possession of their strength and senses. Add to this the tossing of an angry sea, and the howling of the wilder wintry wind, and imagine its effects on an invalid, chained to his berth, and hourly drained of his life-blood! If I never was frightened, before or since, I acknowledged the corn then.

There was a lady on board, and I would be disgraced, if my memory was not defective on names, if I did not note hers here. I never saw her after we landed, but she watched over me like a ministering angel. The vast joy of getting ashore obliterated everything but the fact that I was home again. It was long before I got about, and when I did get out I lost all trace of her.

How I got ashore is the strangest part of the story. I was almost in a comatose state, and, in some respects, very much neglected. A lady is not exactly the nurse for a man afflicted with this infernal malady, and a large portion of the time I was left to the tender mercies of a rough and not over-attentive cabin boy. I had become a pretty good sailor, while about, so much so that I was permitted to act as a volunteer fourth mate. Consequently, I could understand pretty much all that was going on, simply by listening to the sounds on deck, coupled with the motions of the ship.

One morning, about four bells, I knew that the ship had been thrown aback, and I heard a strange voice. I sent the cabin boy on deck to learn what had occurred. He came back and told me that the pilot was on board, and that we were entering Sandy Hook.

Now comes a most astonishing proof of the power of mind over matter. I sent for a cup of black tea, and some toast. I drank a cup, and ate a slice. Strengthened and refreshed, I got up, and, by instalments, I dressed. My teeth had begun to crumble; I cleaned them; I washed myself; I crawled on deck.

By this time we were abreast of Quarantine. The Health Officer gave immediate permission for me to go ashore. How I got there, I don't remember. Something tells me it was in the visiting doctor's boat. From it I walked on board the ferry-boat.

Uncle Gus was with me, and when we got to the foot of Whitehall street, he put me alone into a hack, and ordered the driver to take me to my father's home in Twelfth street. I got out; rang the bell. The door was opened by an old servant. I made my way into the hall, and there my will and strength gave out, and I fell like a log on the floor. They carried me up to bed, sent for Dr. Gilbert Smith, and for a long time I continued to battle with the malady, gaining ground, however, each day. Oh, the horror, the agony, the despair, of my last ten days on board the "Sheridan." If I had given up for one minute, not I, but my corpse, would have come home.

I left home in a sad condition of body and feelings, and I returned so near a corpse, and so nearly resembling one, that, when I recovered strength enough to crawl out into the sun, and sat down on a pile of beams in front of a building erected on the same block with my father's house, the Irish laborers took up brick-bats, and bid me be off, or they would pelt me for a walking skeleton, that would bring the "pestilence" among them.

They were so much in earnest, and I so utterly helpless, that I crawled home again. I do not believe I had an ounce of flesh on my bones, and my skin hung on them like loose clothes.

I have never entirely recovered from the effects of this attack of dysentery.

Sam Weller somewhere speaks of a fat man, who was butted in the stomach by a boy with a big head, and remarks that his insides were never right afterwards. To this I say, ditto.

I believe the joy of getting home saved my life, but the treatment I had experienced was pretty rough— pretty rough, pretty rough—for a rich man's son!

Uncle Gus was not an unfeeling man, but I have always found that men made of leather, catgut, oak and iron, cannot sympathize with the sick, or, perhaps—not to be uncharitable—cannot comprehend sickness.

Not many minutes after he left me, the Captain encountered my father, in Wall street. After a few words, and salutation, father asked, "Well, Gus, how is John?" "John! I have brought him home, but he is about as good as dead." "Gus," said my father, "if you were not my brother, I'd knock you down on the spot." Then he posted home, and he certainly was stirred up, when he saw me.

CHAPTER XX

In 1841, soon after his marriage, General de Peyster purchased the property at Tivoli, New York, which remained his country home, and which he called "Rose Hill," after the ancestral home of his mother's family in the suburbs of Edinburgh. From this time until his death, in the spring of 1907, his summers were spent in Duchess County, which was also his legal residence, while his winters were spent in his town house in New York, number Fifty-nine East Twenty-first Street.

In a letter to J. B. Lippincott & Company of Philadelphia, dated 19 June, 1877, the General gives the following account of the village of Tivoli:

"Tivoli is a recently incorporated village, combining two post office villages about a mile apart; one, Tivoli, a steamboat landing on the Hudson River, and a station on the Hudson River Railroad, and the other, Madalin, formerly Myersville, so called after one of the original settlers on the plateau back.

"Tivoli is in the Township of Red Hook, the northwestern Township of Duchess County, New York. Madalin is famous for its strawberries, the finest variety sent to market, and produced in enormous quantities on account of some fitting quality of the clay soil. Tivoli was laid out as a city about the beginning of the century by an old Frenchman named Delabygarre, but his plans turned out to be dreams. The population of the incorporated district, a little over a mile square, must be about 1,500. It is bi-sected by White Clay Creek, upon which, in Madalin, there is now a grist, saw and plaster mill. About the year 1800 there was a large grist mill and a saw mill at its mouth, and thence a rude canal to the main channel of the Hudson, about a mile distant, through a 'fly' which is now filled up.

"There are five churches; one, a beautiful stone Gothic Episcopal Church, St. Paul's original Parish Church, with a beautiful series of vaults of several of the oldest families in the country; second, Trinity Episcopal Church, built of brick, which is, I think, a sort of dependency of Trinity Church in New York, and an invasion of the old Parish; third, fourth, and fifth are Baptist, Methodist, and Dutch Reformed Churches, respectively, all built of wood. The latter, known as the 'Red Church,' was built on the site of the oldest place of worship in this region, and has attached to it a cemetery finely situated and quite extensive.

"There are no banks and no manufactures of any account. On White Clay Creek there is an old woolen factory, and near it a sulphur spring. Shortly after 1800 there was a porcelain factory at Tivoli. There is a boys' school in the village, and St. Stephen's Episcopal College is at Annandale, about four miles away. There are no newspapers.

"General Montgomery's mansion is about four miles south; Chancellor Livingston's, and also his father's, two miles north of the village. All three, as well as others, were burned by the British in 1777. The only house spared by them was the mansion of my ancestor, Robert Gilbert Livingston, still standing.

"The first regular passage steamboat—second steamer —was built within the limits of the corporation. I can tell you all about this, and I don't believe another man can.

"In 1777 the British anchored their fleet opposite Tivoli (then Upper Red Hook Landing), and their vessels extended four miles up and down the river.

"A number of travelers, native and foreign, have pronounced the scenery surrounding Tivoli more beautiful than any they have seen elsewhere. Opposite Tivoli is the re-entering angle of the Katskill Mountains, and the highest peaks. The old Mountain House is just to the northwest; Saugerties, at the mouth of Esopus Creek, opposite. Two miles back of Tivoli is 'Turkey

Hill,' a trigonometrical station of the United States Survey. Thence the Highlands of four States, New York, Connecticut, Massachusetts, and Vermont are visible on a very clear day, and, on extraordinary occasions, it is claimed that the White Mountains of New Hampshire can be discerned. The view to the west, north, and east is wonderfully fine. There is a desecrated cemetery in old Tivoli, in which people, among whom is one of whom I know, were buried, many of them being born over two hundred years ago; but one interment has occurred there within the memory of an old settler who died two or three years since at the age of ninety-nine.

"One of the first groves of mulberries for the nourishment of silkworms planted in the State of New York is on my property.

"I could tell you a great deal more, but I guess I have told you more than you want already. If I have not, advise me, for I am full of folk and historic lore on subjects connected with my race and name."

In a letter written to a Mr. Ridley, 9 June, 1877, the General speaks of his country home as follows:

"My place never looked more beautiful than it does now. It is an extraordinary place in one respect, it requires so little expenditure to keep it in beautiful order. I have been cutting down a great many trees and letting the light in, for after a heavy rain, under the dense roof of foliage, it is very chilly. As Cousin Phil* said, it looks out upon the most beautiful scenery that he ever saw. Every day, however, adds to the damage of the river. Right under the bank where Henry Barclay used to live, they have run out a causeway which extends half across the river to the outer edge of the westside flat. This causeway stops up the Little or Glasgow Channel, so that between this new dock and Saugerties Creek, in a few years, it will be all dry ground. At the end of the causeway there is a large square steamboat dock and

---

*Major-General Philip Kearny.

ferry slip, and on the dock a hotel or tavern and sheds. It is a perfect 'eye-sore.' A week ago they had a grand 'pow-wow' to celebrate its completion, with a band of music and a cannon. This was to welcome the first day boat that landed. The object of this dock, which is said to have cost $22,000, is to divert through Saugerties from Catskill the travel to the mountain houses."

The best years of the General's life are associated with "Rose Hill." It was the centre of his activities in connection with the New York State Militia. Here he accumulated one of the most interesting private libraries in the possession of an American, adding to the books inherited from his grandfather and his father thousands of volumes acquired in the prosecution of his military and other studies. On the rear of his house he built an annex in the shape of a tower, mainly devoted to his library, and here were dictated and written the greater portion of the hundreds of books and pamphlets which he issued. From "Rose Hill" also he conducted a correspondence with many of the most distinguished scholars and military writers of Europe, as well as with nearly all the eminent Union officers of our Civil War.

The following interesting account of "Rose Hill" appeared anonymously in the Poughkeepsie Weekly Eagle, of 30 December, 1871. Anyone who has visited the place will appreciate the picture.

"A few days ago I happened to be detained at a station on the Hudson River Railroad named Tivoli, opposite the Saugerties Iron Works, and, having a few minutes on my hands, I wandered up into the woods, north of the depot. I found a good graveled road climbing a steep hill, carried along the edge of a slope, supported in places by a wall embodying cyclopian stones, and, continuing on underneath an evergreen foliage, came upon a dwelling which well repaid my walk. It was as queer a conglomeration of styles as can well be imagined; some forty paces long, cross-shaped, recalling European mansions commenced in one age, continued in another, and completed a century or centuries afterward.

"ROSE HILL," TIVOLI, NEW YORK
Country Seat of General de Peyster

The main building is in the Italian style, the north wing simple or rude as well may be, the southern somewhat more tastily finished; while in the rear, over the roadway, soars a tower, reminding the visitor of the keep of an early modern manor house.

"There was no one about; and so I wandered around and marvelled at the taste of the owner and builder. This tower, by guess, sixty or seventy feet high, is a square, with one corner cut off, with heavy iron balconies, richly carved keystones, with deeply cut armorial bearings, marble and stone sculptures let in without regard to artistic design as if dictated by caprice; and, queerest of all, in a niche, aloft, sat a huge Aztec idol, such as is only seen in museums. Shut up and alone, no questions could be asked; but peeping in through a grated window, imagine the surprise at seeing brass guns grinning out between the bars. No other building like it, I will be bound, is to be found along the Hudson. A short distance north of the house are extensive—it might be said enormous—stables and farm buildings overlooking the river, with gate posts crowned with huge eagles or vultures.

"These constructions would be in exact keeping with the house were they in stone instead of wood.

"From the house, across a deep ravine, by a bridge some forty paces long, a path climbs a hill to a neglected flower-garden, beginning to be overgrown with a new growth of forest, and beyond this again another garden and orchard. The former must have once been beautiful, with beds marked out with luxuriant box; but everything seems neglected except the necessaries, such as roads, buildings, which were in good order. The roads were wonderful for such broken ground, and seemed to twist off in every direction, up steep hills and through woods of grand trees. Within the same area it would be almost impossible to find more natural beauties, almost altogether undeveloped by art. Doubtless, the place was once in better condition, for under this gloomy vault of lofty pine and hemlock stood a

14

marble monument; in another place, a pretty little summer house; and in a fresh grassed opening I stumbled over a cistern. Again, out a way, in a level field, in fine order, there was quite a pretty pond, which must have been excavated—not natural, although quite a growth of swamp willow was growing on the sides. Toward the southwest, adjoining the grass land, niched in this country seat, a very attractive Gothic church stood amid fine trees, with a row of massive funeral vaults, as unlike the usual appendages of American country churches as the mansion which first attracted my attention.

"While wondering, and admiring the strangeness of my surroundings, my watch told me that time was up, and so I hurried back to the station, pausing once or twice to note and admire some of the finest views of inland scenery, mountain and river, remembered in the course of long journeyings. In my haste I nearly pitched over a precipice, and, trying to recover my road, stumbled into a cemetery devoted to dogs and parrots. Mercy, thought I, is the owner an Egyptian! From his house, he might have been an eclectic admirer of all the orders and creeds of the Old and New Worlds.

"But, enough; I made my way through the noble woods, almost as shady in the bright autumn sun as many forests in summer, so numerous were the lofty evergreens, and, on asking at the depot, learned that the owner of this curious place was a General de Peyster. Curiosity demanded more particulars, but the train was at hand and I was off, with my greed for information unsatisfied. And so, at my first leisure, I send you this memorandum of a visit to one of the most beautiful natural situations, and survey of one of the most eccentric or unusual of mansions. With money and art the place might be made one of the finest in our land. As it is, it is queer, but doubtless most comfortable, and everywhere scrupulously clean and orderly. This, however, must be said: From the front of the house, on a point by the way, there is a river view, backed by the

Kaatakills, unexceeded in extent and beauty; to the southward the river resembles nothing less than one of the seven lakes which have called forth so much good and bad poetry.

"Whoever the owner of this glorious spot may be, I thank him for as pleasant an hour as ever compensated for missing a train."

General de Peyster's connection with the Militia began with his appointment as Judge-Advocate of the Twentieth Brigade, New York State Infantry, with the rank of Major, dating from the sixteenth day of September, 1845. A copy of his commission follows.

"THE PEOPLE OF THE STATE OF NEW YORK,
"TO ALL TO WHOM THESE PRESENTS SHALL COME:

"KNOW YE, That pursuant to the Constitution and Laws of our said State, We have appointed and constituted, and by these Presents do appoint and constitute John Watts de Peyster, Judge Advocate of the 20th Brigade of Infantry of our said State, (with rank from 16th September, 1845) to hold the said office in the manner specified in and by our said Constitution and Laws.

"IN TESTIMONY WHEREOF, We have caused our Seal for Military Commissions to be hereunto affixed. Witness SILAS WRIGHT, Esquire, Governor of our said State, General and Commander-in-Chief of all the Militia, and Admiral of the Navy of the same, at our City of Albany, the 18th day of September, in the year of our Lord one thousand eight hundred and forty-five.
                                "SILAS WRIGHT.
"PASSED THE ADJUTANT-GENERAL'S OFFICE.
    "THOMAS FARRINGTON,
            "Adjutant-General."

From the beginning Major de Peyster evinced a remarkable interest in the Militia, as might have been anticipated from the youthful enthusiasm with which he had engaged in military recreations, such as the

carrying on of mock battles with his cousin, afterwards
General Philip Kearny.   His devotion to the service, and
his manifest abilities, fitting him for command, were soon
recognized by the men.   Within less than a year's time,
he was elected Colonel of the Regiment.   The letter
notifying him of his election, dated at Tivoli, 15 August,
1846, and signed by P. H. Lasher, "Brigadier-General
and Presiding Officer," was as follows:

"At an election this day held, in pursuance of the Act
to organize the Militia, at the house of William A.
Moore, in the Town of Red Hook, Duchess Co., S. N. Y.,
you were duly chosen to fill the office of Colonel in the
111th Regiment, 20th Brigade and 7th Division of the
Militia of this State.   As presiding officer at said Election, it becomes my duty to notify you of your election
and to request that you will signify your acceptance
within ten days after the receipt hereof, otherwise you
will be considered as declining."

We also here give the commission issued by Governor
Silas Wright:

"THE PEOPLE OF THE STATE OF NEW YORK,
"TO ALL TO WHOM THESE PRESENTS SHALL
    COME:

"KNOW YE, That pursuant to the Constitution and
Laws of our said State, We have appointed and constituted, and by these Presents do appoint and constitute,
John Watts de Peyster, Colonel in the 111th Regiment
of Infantry of our said State, with rank from August 15,
1846, to hold the said office in the manner specified in
and by our said Constitution and Laws.

"IN TESTIMONY WHEREOF, We have caused
    our Seal of Military Commissions to be hereunto
    affixed.   Witness, SILAS WRIGHT, Esquire,
    Governor of our said State, General and Com-
    mander-in-Chief of all the Militia, and Admiral
    of the Navy of the same, at our City of Albany,
    the 25th day of August, in the year of our Lord
    one thousand eight hundred and forty-six.
                            "SILAS WRIGHT.

"PASSED THE ADJUTANT-GENERAL'S OFFICE.
    "R. E. TEMPLE,
        "ADJUTANT-GENERAL."

Colonel de Peyster's regiment was recruited in the towns of Red Hook, Milan, and Rhinebeck, Duchess County. Among his personal reminiscences he has left an amusing account of his experience as a colonel of militia.

"In 1846," he says, "I found myself in command of the 111th N. Y. S. Infantry. I had lain awake the whole night before 'officers' training,' studying out the manœuvers which were to be practised next day. I had some respect for myself, more for my commission, and I believed I could make something of this regiment. At 'officers' training' all the commissioned and non-commissioned officers of the regiment met for instruction. If the regiment was full, these constituted a body of about one hundred and twenty-five men, of whom the Colonel took command as instructor. Many of the officers had served six or seven years; some had attained middle-age; all were men of good understanding. I think I was the youngest man on the parade ground at Lower Red Hook.

"From early morning until sundown, I had done my best to drill that body according to book. I thought I had made some impression. Just as I was about to dismiss them, my Adjutant, Van Fredenburg, quite a tall, good-looking fellow, approached me and asked me to allow him to put the regiment through some of the manœuvres to which they had been accustomed; that the officers were disappointed. He did not say in me, but his looks, echoed by the looks of others, implied it.

"Anxious to see in what I had failed, and knowing that the Adjutant was, compared to me, an old hand at the business, I consented. His face lit up. He communicated the permission to the expectant line, and their faces lit up. The music struck up with an alacrity and liveliness I had not heard in it all day, and them, imagine my astonishment, when, after all my pains to instil some common sense into that hundred and upwards, my Adjutant led off, and those dignified, respectable, one hundred and twenty-five men-in-arms, many, fathers of families, solemnly, in the presence of a thousand people, performed the very evolution that I had seen in Cooperstown—'hunting the fox.' I thought I should have dropped.

"I made a spiteful dash for the Adjutant, but he was already in the centre of the coil, and around him were twined those one hundred and twenty-five men, with faces glowing with delight, making themselves supremely ridiculous, as solemnly as if they were executing some evolution before the eyes of Frederick the Great. I left the field. I ordered my horses and drove away; but, long after I left the village, I heard those drums and fifes filling my abandoned warriors with enthusiasm, in the prosecution of a series of manœuvres, my ignorance of which, doubtless, filled my command with as much contempt for me as I felt for them.

"When company training came, I drove through my whole regimental district with my annihilated Adjutant, and I guess there was no 'hunting the fox' while I was by that day. When regimental training came, I had a mutiny. I may tell the story at length in its appropriate place, but it was put down in a way that somewhat astonished the command. This occurred in the morning, and after it, and throughout the afternoon, there never was a better behaved regiment in the United States service.

"I honestly and truly believe that those infatuated men really and conscientiously thought that this boy's play was something supremely—what it was the custom then to style—'military.'

"Next year the 'uninformed' militia was disbanded forever, and it was time.

"A new law and a new system came in, under which something practical might have been accomplished. It was tried with amendments, for three or four years, but was deemed too severe on the people. In 1851 there was another new law, and with it passed away everything like the general disciplining of the people, contemplated by the 'Fathers,' in our first organizing Congresses."

Colonel de Peyster proved himself to be a successful disciplinarian. He began at once to bring his regiment into a state of great efficiency, and it became apparent that he was a practical and rapid organizer of effective troops.

The military laws of 13 May, 1846, and 13 May, 1847, effected a complete reorganization of the New York Militia. The entire State was re-districted; numerous regiments were disbanded. The One Hundred and Eleventh Regiment, the command of Colonel de Peyster, passed out of existence. The radical nature of this change may be realized from the fact that the new Twenty-second Regiment, New York State Infantry, under the command of Colonel George Decker, covered not merely the territory formerly under Colonel de Peyster's command, but embraced all the northern towns of Duchess County, and the southern half of Columbia County, including the city of Hudson, a territory which, under the old system, had contained fifteen or sixteen regiments.

The law of 13 May, 1847, provided that the commanders of disbanded regiments might retain their supernumerary rank by reporting themselves before 1 May, 1848. Colonel de Peyster so reported himself to the Adjutant-General, on the sixteenth October, 1847, and to Colonel Decker, of the Twenty-second Regiment, on the seventeenth. To the latter he wrote:

"I hereby report myself as Col. of the late 111th Reg't, N. Y. S. I., and as having duly reported myself to the Adjutant-Gen'l of this State, under Section 21 of the Militia Law passed May 13, 1847, prior to May 1st, 1848."

Assistant Adjutant-General Van Vechten's acknowledgment of the receipt of the letter in which Colonel de Peyster reported himself, is dated at Albany, 18 October, 1847, and reads:

"I have to acknowledge the receipt of a communication from you, by this Department, on the 16th inst., reporting yourself as Colonel of the 111th Reg't, under the old organization, and as wishing to retain your Supernumerary rank, under Section 21st of the Act passed May 13th, 1847."

The official certification that Colonel de Peyster had been rendered supernumerary, dated 9 September, 1848, is signed by Adjutant-General Samuel Stevens.

"I HEREBY CERTIFY," it runs, "that J. Watts de Peyster, of the County of Duchess, did on the first day of December, 1847, report himself to this Department as holding a commission of Colonel in the Militia of the State of New York, and having been rendered supernumerary by the provisions of the act passed May 13th, 1847, entitled 'An act to provide for the enrollment of the Militia, and to encourage the formation of Uniform Companies, excepting the First Military Division of this State,' is entitled to all the privileges conferred by any preceding law."

The military laws of 1846 and 1847 were designed to effect a radical reform of many prevalent abuses, and to lay the foundation for a genuine State soldiery. Their enactment created widespread opposition. Many officers who had been deprived of their commands were dissatisfied, and so changed were the old organizations that the rank and file, as well, became rebellious, and even mutinous.

The situation was still further complicated by the anti-rent agitation, then at its height. The new Twenty-second regimental district embraced one of the disaffected regions, where excitement ran highest. A considerable part of the territory was wild and mountainous. Many of its inhabitants, identifying themselves actively with the anti-renters, assumed a lawless and desperate character, setting all authority at defiance. Colonel Decker, commander of the district, was unable to control these turbulent elements—could not, in fact, maintain proper discipline even amongst his own troops.

Under these circumstances, as a military necessity,

Colonel de Peyster, the youngest Colonel in the district, was assigned to its command over the heads of a number of officers of his rank holding commissions antedating his. The order of the Adjutant-General to this effect was as follows:

"STATE OF NEW YORK, HEADQUARTERS,
"ADJUTANT-GENERAL'S OFFICE.

"Albany, Sept. 3d, 1849.

"GENERAL ORDERS:
"No. 119.

"Pursuant to the provisions of Section 1st of the Act passed April 10th, 1849, the Commander-in-Chief hereby assigns the command of the 22d Regiment, N. Y. S. M., to Col. J. Watts de Peyster.

"Col. George Decker will forthwith deliver to Col. de Peyster all the books and papers belonging to said Regiment.

"By order of the Commander-in-Chief.
"SAM'L STEVENS,
"Adj't-Gen'l."

A little later, the power of prescribing the uniforms of his officers and troops was conferred upon Colonel de Peyster by an order of Adjutant-General Samuel Stevens, dated 8 November, 1849:

"The Commander-in-Chief hereby orders and directs that until further Orders the uniform of the Officers, non-commissioned Officers, musicians and privates of the 22d Regiment shall be such as shall be prescribed by Col. J. Watts de Peyster, the Commandant thereof."

Authority for a further reform of the same nature was granted by General Orders No. 328, dated at Albany, 31 January, 1851, and signed by Adjutant-General L. Ward Smith:

"The Commander-in-Chief hereby orders and directs that Col. J. Watts de Peyster, Colonel commanding 22d Reg't, shall have the power to prescribe the undress uniform, and to make such alterations, &c., in the full dress uniform, arms and equipments of said Regiment as he shall deem advisable, and also that at all parades and Courts Martial or of Appeals, full or undress uniform may be worn, as may by him be determined in Orders."

So successful as a disciplinarian was Colonel de Peyster that, within a year from his assignment to the command of the Twenty-second Regiment, he received the special commendation of the Adjutant-General. The latter stated that, with the exception of Colonel Willard of Troy, who had been an officer of the United States Army, Colonel de Peyster alone, of the regimental commanders of the State, had succeeded in reducing his troops to proper discipline and in completely enforcing the law in his district. In recognition of this achievement Colonel de Peyster was authorized to wear a medal.

An incident which occurred illustrates the difficulties which confronted him, and his method of meeting them. At a general parade all but one company of the regiment broke out into open mutiny, refusing to obey orders. Colonel de Peyster was prepared. Knowing that one company could be relied upon, to this he had issued ball cartridges. He announced this fact to the mutineers, and drawing up his faithful company, threatened to open fire. The men instantly submitted, and from this time forward their commander heard no more of rebellion in the ranks.

In the summer of 1850 Governor Washington Hunt wrote to Honorable George Cornell, the unsuccessful candidate for lieutenant-governor upon Hunt's ticket, that "if he had an army of thirty thousand regulars, he knew no officer to whom he would entrust their command with such perfect confidence as he would to his friend, Colonel de Peyster." The following summary of Colonel de Peyster's military services to the State is an official document issued by the Adjutant-General of the State, 31 December, 1850.

"I, SAMUEL STEVENS, Adjutant-General of the State of New York, do hereby certify, That Col. J. Watts de Peyster, then Commandant of the 111th Reg't

JOHN WATTS DE PEYSTER, 1849
Colonel of the Twenty-Second Regiment, New York State Militia

of Infantry, was placed in command of the 22d Regimental District for previous efficient services which had been rendered by him: That the former Colonel was superseded in consequence of his mal-administration and neglect, which had completely disorganized the District, but which Col. de Peyster, by his energy and determination, very soon reduced to a perfect state of discipline: That while in command of the 22d Reg't, Col. de Peyster had cast, at his own expense, a MOUNTAIN HOWITZER of elaborate workmanship and improved pattern, at the foundry of the Ames Manufacturing Company, Chicopee, Massachusetts: That with this Howitzer he made many experiments, and his Report, based upon those experiments, induced the State Authorities to introduce MOUNTAIN HOWITZER BATTERIES into their service: That during the same period, Col. de Peyster's attention was directed to testing the mooted question, as to what firearms were best adapted to Foot and Flying Artillery.

"That during the winter of 1849 and 1850, Col. de Peyster was sent by me to inspect the U. S. Armory for the manufacture of Small Arms, at Springfield, Massachusetts, and examine and report upon the serviceableness of altered Percussion Muskets and decide whether it was expedient for the State of New York to receive the altered Arms, as part of the quota of Arms due from the General Government, instead of new Flint Lock Muskets, and that upon his Report muskets with flint locks altered to percussion were introduced into the State service.

"That during the time Col. de Peyster has held a Commission, his efforts have been constantly directed to the improvement of the Municpal Military Organization of the State of New York: That he has introduced tasteful, salutary and economical reforms in the uniform, arms and equipments of the troops under his command, and that many of the changes in uniform, &c., which by order of President Taylor were adopted in the United States Army, were advocated and published by him some time previous to their approval by the United States War Department.

"That Col. de Peyster had constructed at his own expense a new Garrison Carriage, somewhat similar in its arrangement to the Romme Naval Carriage; and that, in 1849, he projected a Field Carriage for a light Howitzer, which was subsequently adopted by the United States Ordnance Department, and known as the Mountain Howitzer Prairie Carriage."

The Adjutant-General mentions the fact that Colonel de Peyster had been appointed to report upon the advisability of a change in the arms used by the troops of New York. The results of this investigation were embodied in the following official report:

"Headquarters, 22d Reg't N. Y. S. T.,

"Tivoli P. O., Duchess Co., 7th Feb., 1850.

"To the Brig'r Gen'l Hon. Samuel Stevens, Adj't Gen'l of the State of New York, Albany:

"My dear Sir:

"I returned yesterday from having visited and inspected the machinery and muskets in the U. S. Armory at Springfield, Mass. Pursuant to your instructions, I hereby make my Report respecting the U. S. muskets, whose locks have been altered from flint to percussion, which the General Government are willing or anxious to issue to the State of New York, instead of the flint lock muskets hitherto furnished by them. After leaving the U. S. Arsenal at Watervliet, I was averse to this State's receiving the muskets with altered locks at the same price as the muskets with new flint locks, but careful and farther examination has proved to me that the altered arms are superior to flint lock muskets at the same price, and in two respects superior even to the new percussion muskets.

"1st. The main spring of the altered lock having power sufficient to strike fire with the flint, is more effective, and renders the explosion of the cap certain.

"2d. The nipple or cone being inserted in the top of the barrel, the fire from the cap is communicated to the charge in the most direct and consequently most certain manner, whereas in the new muskets it is not direct but circular—thus:

"The only advantage, besides appearance, possessed by the new percussion lock musket, is the bayonet stop and the safety notch, which restrains the hammer sufficiently from off the cap to prevent an accidental explosion in case of the hammer being struck by anything, thus causing a soldier to make three movements in cocking, viz:

"1st, Safety notch;

"2d, Half cock;

"3d, Cock.

"This is a very advantageous addition in Cavalry arms, and has been adopted in the U. S. Carbines, and Sappers and Miners' musketoons.

"I would advise the receipt of bright instead of bronzed barrels, in consequence of the difficulty of keeping up a perfect color, even on parade, much more in the field— for which reason bronzed barrels have been discarded in the French and the United States service, as I was informed at the Springfield Armory, where I saw a new Regulation French musket, with bright barrel.

"Having reported my reasons as above for advising the receipt of the altered lock muskets,

"I have the honor to be, respectfully,

"Your obed't Serv't,

"J. Watts de Peyster,

"Colonel commanding 22d Reg't N. Y. S. M."

CHAPTER XXI

Colonel de Peyster's connection with the Militia meant much more to him than merely an opportunity to wear an officer's uniform. From the beginning of his career, he earnestly studied the conditions in the State with a view to the introduction of needed reforms. This continued for a number of years until at length, believing that he could accomplish no more for the State troops, he addressed his efforts to a wider audience—the military spirit of the Nation.

While in command of the troops of Duchess and Columbia Counties, first as Colonel and afterwards as Brigadier-General, he experimented with firearms and field pieces, at his own expense, and reported the results to the military authorities of the State. He was indefatigable in exercising his troops, established a reputation as a bold and skillful horseman, and became a conspicuous figure throughout his regimental district. In his reminiscences, dictated in 1876, he refers to his rides and drives over the country.

"I can bring plenty of witnesses," he writes, "who will swear that no man living ever could tool more handsomely, one horse, pair, spike team, tandem, trandem, or four-in-hand. I never got to six, but many a time have I cut figures of 8, backwards and forwards, in the circumscribed barnyard of Artillery General Wainwright, U. S. V., run four-in-hands through the fields, and jump them over stone walls and ditches, before a sleigh. And then in the pigskin on Posy, across country! I never knew but one man, my Galway hunting groom, Matthew, who could follow me. I came off safe, while he got a fall which broke one or more ribs and crippled him for life. Posy could take five feet six, standing, clean and clear.

"Once, in 1849, I was practising with artillery, at Round Pond, three or four miles east of Upper Red Hook. The battery was on the west side of the pond, the target on the east. There was a crowd of people watching our firing, among them an ex-Captain of the United States Dragoons. I had occasion to ride over to look at the target. When I got round near to it I encountered a rail fence, which extended out into the water. I rode out into the pond, supposing I could soon get to the end of the fence and turn it. When I got into water so deep that it was about up to my mare's neck, I discovered that the fence continued on under the water, so that I had either to jump the fence or turn back. The latter course my pride forbade, so I charged the fence and Posy carried me over safely. I visited the target and returning jumped the fence again. This was a wonderful feat of horsemanship, jumping a fence of ordinary height in deep water; but Posy could jump five feet six, standing, and was perfectly fearless. Few are alive who were eye witnesses, but Philip H. Teator, U. R. H., spoke within two or three years of having seen this jump.

"I had afterwards a black mare named Dolly, who was Posy's equal in courage. Posy would stand in the midst of a Battery, firing with ball, without flinching, and Dolly would stand in the middle of a band of music and seemed to enjoy it, and I could ride her up to a Locomotive and rest her nose on the cylinder, when her head was enveloped in steam. Dolly was as cunning as a trick horse in the circus, would walk a plank, and, at the signal of the reins, without a word, break into full run before a wagon, and stop without a word at a certain touch of the reins. She died of goitre. I thought I ought to have Posy shot when she got decrepit, but I will never again kill a pet. Life, even in misery, may be as sweet to animals as to human beings.

"I had two steeple-chase grounds on my own place, and yet I was fifty years old before I got a 'sockdolager.' A brute of a horse jumped into the air, kicked at the same time, and came down with so much force, on a gravel road, that his fore legs gave way and he landed square on his head. I landed plump on my face, and smashed it up generally. This was six years before I write, and I am not entirely over the consequences yet.

"I got up, washed the gravel out of my mouth, and the blood off my face, rode that infernal chestnut into good behavior, then drove him twelve miles, came home, went to bed, and had a fever. I couldn't eat for weeks, and eventually I lost four or five back teeth. My head was bent square back by the fall, and the doctors said that if I had weighed twenty-five pounds heavier, my neck must have been inevitably broken. I have lain three times like dead by the side of my fallen horse, but I never got such a jar as this. I have never been the same rider since, for the agony that I suffered at intervals for years is something beyond the power of the pen to express.

"Sleighing was my delight. I built two sleighs, different sizes, with runners shod with pot-metal, having long curves, somewhat on the Esquimaux pattern, and in them, with a pair of jumping mares, I could cross the country as in steeple-chasing. Stone walls, board fences, logs of the largest size, saplings that would bend under the weight of the sleigh, everything but a new post and rail barrier, were no obstacles. I could jump a ditch eight or ten feet wide, four-in-hand, and on horseback scarcely anything could stop me. I have done things that astonished experts.

"Now I cannot ride with comfort, especially since I broke four ribs, running into a barbed wire fence in the woods, and I have to go jogging along the roads, which to me is tame work. My second son, Colonel Fred, who distinguished himself so greatly during the Civil War, especially for his ride of seventy or eighty miles, if not more, at the time of the Battle of Bull Run, first, to be present in that conflict, was, I must concede, an even more extraordinary rider than I was, great as was my reputation for cross-country work. My eldest son,

Colonel Watts of the Artillery, was another remarkable rider.

"The following is an instance of my reputation as to hazardous riding and driving. One day, within two years, I started with Dean R. W. Oliver, of Nebraska, to drive my pair of black mares, Molly and Folly, to go from Rose Hill, my home, and drive to the Hermitage, on the north shore of Roeliff Jansen's creek, one of the most curious of the old Livingston homesteads, so embowered with Balm of Gilead trees, perhaps one hundred years old, that it is in deep shadow even at the brightest noontide. On the way I stopped at the Lutheran church to ask an old acquaintance the shortest road to Dale's Bridge, which I had to cross. 'How far is it?' 'Two or three miles,' was the answer. 'Two or three miles!' I replied, 'Why it must be six or eight! You are fooling me! Two or three miles! Yes, as the crow flies.' 'Exactly so,' he answered. 'That is the way you go when you want to get to a place. Do I not know how you cross country? Have I not often seen you jumping and clearing everything in the way?' He was right. But those days are 'done gone.'"

On 9 May, 1851, Colonel de Peyster was commissioned Brigadier-General with rank from 7 May, 1851, by Governor Washington Hunt. This was the first appointment of the kind in the State, elevation to the rank having theretofore been by election. We give a copy of the Governor's letter to General de Peyster, dated 12 May, 1851.

"It gives me pleasure to transmit to you the enclosed commission, creating you the Brigadier-General of the 9th Brigade, which has been forwarded to me here by the Adjutant-General for my signature.

"The subject of uniform, &c., which you suggested to the Adjutant-General, will be considered and acted upon after my return to Albany, with every disposition to give effect to your views."

A copy of the commission follows:

"THE PEOPLE OF THE STATE OF NEW YORK,
15

"TO ALL TO WHOM THESE PRESENTS SHALL
      COME:

"KNOW YE, That pursuant to the Constitution and
Laws of our said State, We have appointed and consti-
tuted, and by these presents do appoint and constitute
J. Watts de Peyster, of Tivoli, in the County of Duchess,
Brigadier-General of the Ninth Brigade of the Militia
of our said State, with rank from May 7, 1851, to hold
the said office in the manner specified in and by our said
Constitution and Laws.

      "IN TESTIMONY WHEREOF, We have caused
      our Seal for Military Commissions to be hereunto
      affixed. Witness, WASHINGTON HUNT, Gov-
      ernor of our said State and Commander-in-Chief
      of the Military and Naval Forces of the same, at
      our city of Albany, the ninth day of May, in the
      year of our Lord one thousand eight hundred and
      fifty-one.

"(L. S.)   "WASHINGTON HUNT.

"PASSED THE ADJUTANT-GENERAL'S OFFICE.
      "L. WARD SMITH,
         "Adjutant-General."

We also give General Orders, Number 354, dated at
Albany, 19 May, 1851, and signed by Adjutant-General
L. Ward Smith, which assigned General de Peyster to
the command of the Ninth Brigade:

"The Commander-in-Chief hereby orders and directs
that so much of General Orders issued June 12, 1847,
as assigns the command of the Ninth Brigade to
Brigadier-General Jacob S. Scofield be and the same
hereby is countermanded.

"Brig. General J. Watts de Peyster having been duly
appointed and commissioned will assume command of
the said Brigade, and the officers attached to the several
Regiments comprising said Brigade will report to him
for duty.

"Brig. Gen'l de Peyster is charged with the duty of
promulgating this order.

"By order of the Commander-in-Chief."

As brigade commander, General de Peyster was given full authority to prescribe the uniform and equipments of himself and Staff, as had been the case while he was colonel. General Orders, Number 362, dated 2 June, 1851, and signed by Adjutant-General Smith, delegated this power to him:

"The Commander-in-Chief hereby orders and directs that J. Watts de Peyster, Brigadier General of the Ninth Brigade, Third Division, N. Y. M., shall have the power to prescribe the undress uniform of himself and staff, and to make such alterations, &c., in the full dress uniform, equipments and horse furniture thereof, as he shall deem proper and advisable, and also that at all parades, and courts martial, full or undress uniform, in whole or part, may be worn or may be determined in orders."

This commission as brigadier-general, together with a subsequent appointment as military agent of the State, came as a disappointment, although they led to consequences of the greatest importance to the entire country. Colonel de Peyster had been instrumental in securing the passage of a militia bill creating the office of Inspector-General, and, with the election of Governor Hunt, it was understood that he should be appointed to this office. For political reasons another was appointed, who, it was understood, would make his military duties subservient to the more important task of furthering the interests of his political party. General de Peyster has given us an account of the matter in his reminiscences.

"In 1850-1851 I had been very instrumental in passing a Militia bill. I had received the only medal for faithful service ever issued in the State of New York, and I was well known to Thurlow Weed through my friend, Senator Beekman. I had accomplished the creation of the office of Inspector-General. I was to have it. Thurlow Weed asked me if I was an adroit politician, good stump-speaker, and aware of the political opportunities afforded by the office, if given to a cunning politician, who, through the performance of the duties of the office, had

an excuse for visiting every township in the State. I
answered, 'I am neither a wire-puller nor a stump-
speaker, but a soldier, by instinct and experience.'
Thereupon he compelled Washington Hunt to appoint
Benjamin F. Bruce Inspector-General, a slab-sided wash-
basket. You will understand the simile if you have ever
seen a loose-knit wash-basket (as I have) in a seaway.
It gives out and takes in water, and twists and squirms
as if it had no normal shape.

"As a sop to Cerberus, Hunt selected me as the first
brigadier-general, by appointment, in the State, and
made me Military Agent to Europe. I was endorsed
by the general government, with the amplest powers,
such as were never before given to a State officer, and
have not been since. My Report foreshadowed very
many improvements since carried into effect, and I was
ahead of the United States Commission in recommending the Napoleon gun, which was the gun of the Civil
War, a paid Fire Department, with steam fire engines,
the present system of fighting infantry, &c. Jefferson
Davis, then Secretary of War, wrote me a most complimentary letter, and Governor Hunt gave me a
magnificent gold medal."

Soon after receiving his commission, Brigadier-General
de Peyster was designated, 29 July, 1851, to visit Europe
and report upon such features of the various militia
systems there as might be adopted, with advantage, in
America—virtually an appointment as Military Agent of
the State of New York. In the fall of 1851 he went
abroad. Previously, however, during the spring and
summer of 1851, as brigade commander in the field, he
maintained the high reputation which he had already
established for efficiency. The following tribute to his
attention to details was issued from the office of the
Commissary-General of the State of New York, dated
12 August, 1851, and signed by Brigadier-General D.
A. Lee, Commissary General:

"GENERAL J. WATTS DE PEYSTER, both while
in command of the 22d Regiment, N. Y. S. Troops, and

since promoted to the Command of the 9th Brigade, has been distinguished for his constant attention to the details connected (with) Ordnance and Ordnance Stores. His returns have been the most correct of any received at this office."

On 29 July, 1851, the date of General de Peyster's commission to visit Europe, a certificate enumerating his services to the militia of the State, up to that time, was issued by Adjutant-General Smith.

"I HEREBY CERTIFY," wrote General Smith, "That J. Watts de Peyster was on the 18th day of September, 1845, commissioned Judge Advocate with the rank of Major, from the 16th day of Sept'r, in the same year, in the Staff of Philip H. Lasher, Brigadier General of the 20th Brigade, 7th Division, New York State Infantry,

"And on the 25th day of August, 1846, commissioned Colonel of the 111th Regiment, 20th Brigade, 7th Division, New York State Infantry, with rank from the 15th day of Aug't in the same year under the Organization of 1835,

"And on the 3d day of September, 1849, for meritorious conduct, assigned to the Command of the 22d Regiment, 9th Brigade, 3d Division, New York State Troops, under the Organization of 1847-49.

"And on the 9th day of May, 1851, for important service, commissioned by His Excellency, Washington Hunt, Governor of the State of New York, and Commander-in-Chief of the Military Forces thereof, Brigadier General of the 9th Brigade, 3d Division, New York State Troops, with rank from the 7th day of May, in the same year, under the Act of April 16th, 1851, amending the Organization of 1847-49,

"And that in order to Indicate Service he is entitled to wear the Medal designated therefor, inscribed with the figure (6) six."

Special Orders, dated 8 September, 1851, and signed by Adjutant-General Smith, describe the medal, or "Badge of Distinction," referred to in the above certificate. We learn from it that this decoration was conferred "for zeal, devotedness and meritorious military conduct displayed in organizing a difficult District." We give the text of these Orders.

"For zeal, devotedness and meritorious military conduct, displayed in organizing a difficult District, and in pusuance of certificates of service granted on the 29th day of July, 1851, and sanctioned by Washington Hunt, Commander-in-Chief of the Military Forces of the State of New York, J. Watts de Peyster, of Tivoli, Duchess County, Brigadier General N. Y. S. Troops, is hereby authorized to wear on his left breast the following Badge of distinction, viz: A medal of gold one (1) inch in diameter, the obverse chased and inscribed in the center, four-tenths (4-10) of an inch long, with the figure six (6), denoting length of service, and below with the number of current year, 1851—and on the reverse,

" 'For Zeal, Devotion and Meritorious Service.

J. Watts de Peyster,
            Major, 16th Sept'r, 1845;
            Colonel, 15th Aug., 1846;
            Brig. Gen'l, 7th May, 1851.' "

In addition to his field work as a brigade commander, General de Peyster began to wield his pen, in the furtherance of reforms and the dissemination of correct military ideas. In 1850, the winter of 1850-51, and the spring of 1851, a number of articles by him appeared in the United Service Journal. These were the first of a long series of military writings which he was to continue to put forth for more than half a century.

CHAPTER XXII

As we have seen, General de Peyster records the fact that his appointment as Military Agent was "a sop to Cerberus," the office of Inspector-General, created for him, having been given to another on the ground of political expediency. No one, however, who carefully studies the reports made by General de Peyster as Military Agent, and their important bearing upon the Civil War, which soon afterward overwhelmed the country, can fail to recognize a guiding Providence in this readjustment of plans. Valuable as his services would have been as Inspector-General, this office, necessarily, must have centered the General's efforts upon minor details, and, in view of the prevalent antagonism to reforms, insuperable obstacles and final disappointment must inevitably have confronted him. The influence of his military reports, on the other hand, was far-reaching, national in scope, and peculiarly opportune, in view of the rapidly approaching struggle between the North and South.

A copy of the General Orders granting leave of absence to General de Peyster to visit Europe is here given.

"By order of the Commander-in-Chief leave of absence for two years (or as much longer as may be necessary to carry out the instructions received from this office, provided same shall not exceed three years) is granted to J. Watts de Peyster, Brigadier General of the 9th Brigade, 3d Division of the Military Forces of the State of New York, to enable him to visit Europe and Inspect and Report upon the Ordnance, Artillery and Municipal Military Systems of the countries he may deem advisable to visit.

"As Brigader General de Peyster has been engaged for some time in experimenting with Artillery as adapted to the State Service, he will pay particular attention to everything connected with that branch of the service.

"Wm. P. Wainwrght, Colonel of the 22d Reg't, N. Y. S. Troops, will assume the command of the 9th Brigade during the absence of Gen'l de Peyster and promulgate this order throughout the 9th Brigade District."*

Governor Washington Hunt granted leave of absence and issued special orders, as follows:

"STATE OF NEW YORK,
    "EXECUTIVE DEPARTMENT,
        "Albany, 29th July, 1851.
"TO ALL TO WHOM THESE PRESENTS SHALL
    COME:

"KNOW YE, That whereas J. Watts de Peyster, Brigadier General of the Military Forces of our State of New York and Commandant of the Ninth Brigade District therein, has applied to us for leave of absence, to enable him to visit Europe for the restoration of his health; and Whereas we have the fullest confidence in the ability and experience of General de Peyster, whom we have promoted for important service:

"NOW THEREFORE, leave of absence for two years, or as long as he may deem expedient from the date hereof, is hereby granted; and Brigadier General de Peyster is hereby ordered and directed, with a view to promote the efficiency of the Municipal Military Systems of our said State, to inspect and report upon the systems of Ordnance and Artillery of the countries he may visit and also to examine into the organization of the French National Guard, Prussian Landwehr, Swedish Indelta, and all other similar Municipal Systems of Police and Defence, for the purpose of submitting the information thus acquired to the authorities of our said State.

"And we do hereby commend General de Peyster to the favorable consideration of the Powers he may visit, and desire that he may receive from the Representatives

---

*The above,—General Orders, No. 411—are dated at Albany, 29 July, 1851, and signed by Adjutant-General L. Ward Smith.

of the United States therein, all proper aid in discharging the duties herein specified.

"IN TESTIMONY whereof we have caused our privy* seal to be hereunto applied. Witness, WASHINGTON HUNT, Governor of our said State and Commander-in-Chief of the Military and Naval Forces of the same, at our city of Albany, the twenty-ninth day of July, in the year of our Lord one thousand eight hundred and fifty-one.

(The Great Seal
   N. Y. S.)   "WASHINGTON HUNT."
"STATE OF NEW YORK, HEADQUARTERS,
     "ADJUTANT GENERAL'S OFFICE,
              "Albany, July 29, 1851.

(The Great Seal
   N. Y. S.)   "Passed the Adjutant General's Office.
               "L. WARD SMITH,
    "Adjutant General of the State of New York."

These credentials from the State officials were supplemented by others from the National Government. A letter dated from the Department of State, Washington, 9 September, 1851, and addressed "To the Diplomatic Agents and Consuls of the United States in Europe," was signed by Acting Secretary of State W. S. Derrick.

"This letter," he wrote, "will be handed to you by J. Watts de Peyster, Brigadier General of the Military Forces of the State of New York, and Commandant of the Ninth Brigade District therein, who has been recommended to this Department by Washington Hunt, Governor of the State of New York, as one of the most useful and accomplished officers in the Military Organization of that State.

"Gen'l de Peyster goes abroad under orders from Gov'r Hunt, to inspect and report upon the Systems of Ordnance and Artillery of the countries he may visit,

---

*This was a clerical error. The great seal, only used when the Governor exerts his highest prerogatives, was actually affixed to these credentials.

with a view of promoting the efficiency of the Municipal Military Systems of his State.

"I take great pleasure in commending him to you, and in bespeaking for him during his sojourn in your neighborhood such facilities for promoting the object of his mission, and such good offices as it may be in your power to afford him."

General de Peyster also carried seven letters of introduction, dated at Washington, 10 September, 1851, and signed by C. M. Conrad, Secretary of War. Each letter was a duplicate of the following:

"Allow me to introduce to your acquaintance, General J. Watts de Peyster.

"General de Peyster holds a high military rank in the Militia of his State (New York), and is about to visit Europe on a mission from the Governor of that State, with a view to the acquisition of such information relative to the militia systems and establishments of different foreign countries as may aid in improving and perfecting that of his own State.

"You will oblige me, and render a service to the State of New York, by affording him all the aid and facilities which your official station will enable you to afford in the attainment of his object."*

Thus equipped, General de Peyster sailed for Europe in the fall of 1851, and spent the winter of 1851-52 in the study of foreign military systems. He returned in the spring or early summer of 1852, and at his country home, "Rose Hill," prepared two reports, addressed to Governor Washington Hunt. They were privately printed for General de Peyster, and, in this form, were submitted to the Governor, who expressed his appreciation of the valuable service rendered to the State by

---

*The seven letters were addressed, respectively, to Hon. William C. Rivers, Envoy Extraordinary, Paris, France; Hon. Daniel B. Barnard, Envoy Extraordinary, Berlin, Prussia; Hon. N. D. Brown, Envoy Extraordinary, St. Petersburgh, Russia; Hon. William B. Kinney, Charge d'Affaires, Turin; Hon. Charles N. McCurdy, Charge d'Affaires, Vienna, Austria; Hon. Francis Schroeder, Charge d'Affaires, Stockholm, Sweden, and Hon. E. Joy Morris, Charge d'Affaires, Naples, Italy.

JOHN WATTS DE PEYSTER
In 1852

presenting to General de Peyster a special gold medal. This graceful tribute he announced in a letter dated 10 November, 1852.

"I esteem it at once a pleasure and a duty," he wrote, "to express to you my high appreciation of the value and importance of your recent Report on the Military Systems of the countries which you have visited in Europe. The ability and fidelity with which you discharged the duty confided to you, and the enlightened zeal which you have manifested in promoting a better military organization, entitle you to the most distinguished approbation.

"As an additional testimonial of the just estimate which I have placed upon your official services, and as a tribute of my regard for you personally, I have ordered an appropriate gold medal* to be prepared and presented to you; and in consideration of the friendly sentiments which this token is intended to express and perpetuate, I trust you will deem it worthy of your acceptance."

The first of these reports, on the Military Systems of Europe, was dated from Tivoli, New York, 1 July, 1852. The second, on the French and Florentine Fire Departments and their application to the City and Rural Fire Services of the State of New York, was dated from Tivoli, 16 August, 1852. These reports were brought to the attention of Governor Horatio Seymour, Governor Hunt's successor in office, on 1 January, 1853, by L. W. Smith, Adjutant-General of the State, in the latter's Report for the year 1852.

"In pursuance of the orders and instructions of the Commander-in-Chief," writes the Adjutant-General, "Brigadier General J. Watts de Peyster, of Tivoli, in the county of Duchess, Commandant of the Ninth Brigade,

---

*Description of medal: Gold, massive, one and seven-eighths inches in diameter. Obverse: Shield and motto of the State of New York, and trophies, with inscription, "Washington Hunt to Brigadier-General J. Watts de Peyster, as a testimonial in honor of his efforts to improve the Military System of New York." Reverse: In the center, the crest of the State of New York encircling, as if embroidered on a belt, the inscription, "A Tribute to Official Service and Personal Worth."

N. Y. S. M., has submitted to your Excellency's predecessor two full and interesting military reports: one upon the subject of the organization of the National Guards and municipal military systems of Europe, and the artillery and arms best adapted to the State service, and the other respecting the organization of the French and Florentine fire departments, intended to show the practicability and utility of a thorough military organization of fire companies. At home and abroad, the time, talents and energy of this accomplished officer have been devoted to the promotion of the interests of the militia. These reports contain a large amount of valuable information. They are the results of General de Peyster's recent personal investigation in Europe, published at his own expense, and transmitted herewith for the use and examination of the Legislature.

"Many of his suggestions for changes in militia laws are entitled to the consideration of those who may undertake the revision of the militia laws of the State."

The two reports were published by the State of New York, 26 March, 1853, as Senate Document Number Seventy-four. In this form they are paged continuously, and together form a bulky treatise of two hundred and forty-seven printed pages, with several additional pages, I-IV, of errata. The list of errata the author introduces with the remark: "There is no excuse for these, or any, errata, as the State edition of this Report was printed from the private edition, which latter was carefully revised, corrected, and published at the expense of the author."

The digest of these reports, given in the several chapters following, has been made from the above-mentioned State edition—Senate Document Seventy-four, of the year 1853.

CHAPTER XXIII

THE MILITIA OF EUROPE IN 1851

The present chapter contains a summary of General de Peyster's report upon the militia of the States of Europe. While the account still retains historical interest and military value, the reader must bear in mind that it is not necessarily an accurate description of the systems now in operation, but of those which were in existence prior to 1851.

SWEDEN

The Swedish Army is divided into three bodies: the Vaerfvade, or Standing Army, stationed in and about the capital, Stockholm; the Indeldta, or Militia; and the Landstrum, which is the conscription of uniformed militia.

The Indeldta, organized by Gustavus Adolphus, is famous for its morality, perfect discipline, and fine appearance. "Morning and evening they celebrate religous service. Generally the Commanding Officer calls one of the soldiers out of the ranks and the whole corps, taking off their caps at once, this man repeats the Lord's Prayer, after which they all sing a hymn, very beautifully, and the parade is dismissed."

The militia, drawn from the peasantry, receives pay only when called out, which is during a few weeks in summer, after the fields are sown. It consists of cavalry, infantry, and seamen, these latter recruited from farms along the coast. The commanding officers, who give their whole time to the service, receive lands from the Crown. The cavalry is furnished with arms by the Government, but provides its own horses. The men are drilled, for short periods, in company with the troops of the standing army, an advantage which General de

Peyster considers of inestimable value, and the regulations of the army are adapted for their use. The
Landsturm consists of men from twenty to twenty-five
years of age, and its officers are those of the Indeldta.

NORWAY.

Although the greatest military successes of Norway
have been achieved with the rifle, the nation is enthusiastic in regard to cavalry, and the militia is equipped with
horses, each man using his horse for work and pleasure.
The horses are under Government inspection, four times
a year, and the soldiers receive pay for their maintenance
only during the time of service.

PRUSSIAN LANDWEHR.

The Landwehr, or Militia of Prussia, is a part of the
regular army, which enrolls some 500,000 men who are
ready for service, in case of war, although ordinarily
most of them are not withdrawn from their life as
civilians.   Every Prussian enters the army for five
years; in times of peace this is shortened to three. After
the first period of service, which is between the ages of
twenty and twenty-five, the soldier belongs to the First
Levy (Erstes Aufgebot, i.e., "first called out") till the age
of thirty-two.   He is then of the Second Levy (Zweites
Aufgebot), where he remains until the age of thirty-nine;
and lastly is enrolled in the Landstrum.   This latter is
the great body which is called out in case of war, and in
which the men are eligible for service from the age of
seventeen to twenty and until fifty.

The officers of the Landwehr are retired officers of the
regular army—non-commissioned officers, and the Jagers,
or sharpshooters, men above the ordinary intelligence.
They must have certificates from their late commanding
officers attesting that they are fitted to act as officers,
and in most cases they must have a certain income.
There is still another class of militia officers, young men
of education, called Freiwillige (volunteers), who are
required to pass an examination.   From time to time

they are sent back to the regular army for the purpose of receiving training. They are eligible, in war time, until the age of thirty-nine. During peace they are considered to be on furlough, and their commands are taken by specially detailed non-commissioned officers of the regular army, who constitute the Stamm, and are only temporarily connected with the Landwehr, receiving pay as army officers.

The Landwehr cavalry is composed of squadrons of ninety-six men each, all lancers, who are specially drilled during their last year of service in the army. Their officers are the same as those of the infantry. The artillery is drilled at the stations of the regular army.

There are three militia drills. First: The one-day drills, of which there are about twenty during the year, from the middle of April to the middle of July, and from the 1st of September to the middle of October. These take place on Sunday—with economy of time, at the expense of morals—provided that they are not allowed to interfere with the morning service, and that the men may go and return by daylight. Second: The Musters, also held on Sunday. They take place twice a year, and the lists are corrected, residences ascertained, orders and articles of war read and explained. On dispersing, the men are required to return directly to their homes. Third: The Grand Drill, which occurs at least every other year and lasts from two to four weeks. It is sometimes held with that of the regular army. For the convenience of the farmers, the time set is the latter part of May or the first of June. The men are in uniform, which only differs from that of the army in its facings, collars, etc.

The "Warnings to Drill" are served by the civil magistrate, in cases where the person to be served is not at his home. The magistrate also receives all excuses for non-appearance at drill, and the person wishing to be excused must attend the drill unless he receives notice of his exemption. During these drills the men are paid fifteen silver groschens a day (about thirty-six cents).

The uniforms of the privates are furnished by the State and are expected to last ten years. They are kept at the armories, and, unless condemned as worn out, are never taken away by the men.

Absence from drill, without excuse, is punished with three days' imprisonment on bread and water, or a judicial proceeding is instituted. In either case the magistrate of the district is informed. Omission of notice of change of address is punished with three days' arrest, or a fine of about one dollar. On drill, the discipline of the army is enforced. When vacancies occur among the officers of the Landwehr (not the Stamm), the civil authorities choose three candidates, one of which is selected by the corps of officers. The candidate must have served in the regular army and must be of good character. The choice is then ratified by the Crown. Promotions are made in the order of seniority.

Quakers are exempted from all service by payment of a tax of three per cent. of their yearly income, and many Jews also pay for the same privilege.

General de Peyster does not consider the system of Prussia suitable for the United States. "Only by introducing her whole military system," he writes, "the basis of which is a standing army of more than a hundred thousand men, could we copy it. Its object is not making soldiers, but preserving from rust those already trained. From the army, as from a great school, is, in every year of peace, sent out some fifty thousand men (more or less), with an experience of two or three years' service, and from the same source come officers eminently qualified to command them. We have no such school for either, but, if we can only provide officers, we have a vast advantage in the material for soldiers."

An addenda to the report briefly characterizes the Landwehr as a body trained by the preliminary service of its members in the regular army, as privates of the line, and as consisting of every male of the whole population, between the ages of seventeen and fifty, unless debarred by bodily infirmity, with the exception of the clergy, schoolmasters, and the only sons of widows. Rank or occupation does not exempt from the service, and no substitutions can be made. By a system of levies, the Prussian citizen is made available, during his whole life, as a soldier in the service of the State.

MINOR GERMAN STATES AND FREE CITIES

The Landwehr of Wurtemberg resembles that of Prussia in many respects. In the Grand Duchy of Baden it has not been regularly instituted, but the cities maintain voluntary guards. There is no regular military organization in Hesse-Darmstadt. In Saxony there are two Reserves, much like the Landwehr of Prussia, with burgher guards in all the cities. In Hesse-Cassel there are civic guards, much like the National Guard of France. In the Kingdom of Hanover, and in many Duchies, there is no militia system proper, but the army seems to be organized like that of the Sardinian States.

The military authority of the free cities, Hamburg and Lubeck, is vested in their war departments, of which, in the former city, the chief burgomaster is President. In the latter, the war department is administered by a staff of officers. In Bremen military affairs are directed by a commission composed of Senators.

In 1832 these free cities, together with the Duchy of Oldenberg, entered into a compact to form a brigade. They maintain a militia of over thirty-eight thousand men.

AUSTRIA

In Austria the militia is utilized as a frontier guard, originated by Prince Eugene, of Savoy, for defence against the Turks, and carried into effect by Marshal Lascy. During times of peace it is used for maintaining the quarantine and customs regulations. It is so well organized that only about four thousand men are needed to protect eight hundred miles of frontier. These support themselves and pay taxes.

The land is divided into fiefs and given to families, sometimes consisting of several married persons, who live under the same roof, in community. The eldest man and woman, called the house-father and the house-mother, have control of all the other members. These families perform service for the State in repairing roads, and bridges, draining swamps, etc., during one day in the year for each English acre they own, and eight days for the village. They are not allowed to sell these fiefs. The land tax amounts to fifteen or thirty shillings a year, and furnishes the uniforms; the arms, boots, etc., are supplied by the State.

In times of peace the borderer is required to go to the military stations, for seven days at a time, for drill, his family supplying him with food. During war with the Turks, or during the plague, the number of men is increased to six thousand, and sometimes to ten thousand. In war the militia forms part of the regular army, and may be sent out of the country. The regular force amounts to forty thousand, but, with the addition of the Reserve and the Landwehr, it is nearly one hundred thousand. In the short time of four hours the entire force on the frontier can be mustered out by signal fires and alarm bells.

RUSSIA.

Russia's militia system differs but slightly from the military communities of Austria, with the addition of light cavalry, recruited from the Tartar tribes. It was established by the Emperor Alexander in 1818, under the direction of General Araktschejef, the Minister of War. Afterward, in 1821, General De Witt organized a better system, which depended on the distribution of large tracts of land by the Government. General de Peyster suggests that this system could be adapted for our western and Mexican frontiers, which, at the time he wrote, were the scene of Indian fighting.

The land was given to the Russian heads of families at the rate of about forty-five acres each. One village was built for each squadron, and furnished with a church, school, hospital, stables, magazine for forage and crops, residences for officers, and one hundred and eighty farm houses, with out-buildings. In the centre of the land awarded to the regiment is the barracks, riding school, etc.

The major-general, who corresponds to our brigadier-general, and his staff, live near the two regiments which compose his brigade, and the headquarters of the general commanding are in the centre of the district occupied by the troops. The stock, implements, etc., required for the cultivation of the land, are furnished by the Crown, and the farmer must contribute to the general magazine of the village, and to the repairing of roads, etc. After these demands are met, the remainder belongs to him.

To each farmer is assigned a soldier, to be maintained by him, but when not on duty, his services are to be given to the farm. The colonists, as well as the soldiers, must wear a uniform, and are clean-shaven, under the military law, although the former are in no other way under military authority. A staff, or cadre, administers the laws, and is the civil authority. The brigadier-general decides any difficulty which occurs between the colonel of the troops and the colonel of the district. In each village is a tribunal, composed of the chief of the squadron, president, the priest, three military judges, and three colonists, who hear the civil cases. All criminal cases are tried by a council of war.

The male children are well educated, taught a trade, and also brought up to be soldiers, each village furnishing eight for every thousand of population. In case of the sickness or death of a soldier, the son of the colonist, or some other member of his family, must take his place. There are colonies composed of veterans, connected with the forts, and also among the Cossacks, on the Siberian frontier.

FRANCE.

The law of 22 March, 1831, entirely reorganized the National Guard of France, and but few changes have

been made since that time. By a decree of the President,
11 January, 1852, the Guard was disbanded, and immediately reorganized under a system almost identical with
that in use before its disbandment, except in regard to
the uniform, which was almost entirely changed.
General de Peyster gives translations of the articles of
the law which accomplished the last organization.

The National Guard is divided into two parts: first,
for service in the interior of the commune; second, for
service by detached corps, in aiding troops of the line.
The intention of the Government is to make this body
a local force. It can be dissolved by the President, but
may be reorganized in two years. The Minister of the
Interior is at the head of the National Guard, as the
Minister of War is of the army, and it is therefore under
the authority of the mayor's prefects and sub-prefects.
In some cases, however, it is under the command of the
military authorities. It cannot take arms, or assemble,
without orders from the commandants, who cannot order
it out without a requisition from the civil authority.

Every man from twenty to sixty years of age must
serve, with the exception of magistrates, ministers of the
gospel, students of divinity, officers, active or retired, of
the army and navy, officers in the employ of the Government, those over fifty years old who have served for
twenty years, and all who have bodily infirmities. All
persons convicted of crime, and vagrants, are ineligible.

The National Guard is divided into two parts, the
ordinary and extraordinary, the latter only being called
out in extremity, and consisting of persons who cannot
serve habitually, such as domestic and body servants, etc.
Substitution is allowed between members of a family,
provided they are of the same company. Foreigners who
enjoy civil rights must serve. It is considered an honor
to be enrolled in its ranks, and the register of each
commune in the Mayor's office is open for inspection by
the public for the correction of omissions, etc.

The enrollment is made by the council of examination,
composed of officers differing in the cases of companies,

battalions, etc. Each year, in January, the names of
men in their twentieth year are enrolled, although they
do not serve until they attain the age of twenty, and
also those persons who have come to the commune during
that period. The names of those over sixty, and of those
who have died or left the district, are removed from the
rolls. Appeal from the decisions of the councils of
examination may be made to the jury of revision, of
which there is one in each canton, and of which the
President is the Judge. At Paris this jury is presided
over by the Chief of the General Staff.

The National Guard is organized by platoons, companies, battalions, and legions of infantry. Special
corps of cavalry, artillery, engineers, and firemen
(Sapeurs Pompiers) can only be created by the Minister
of the Interior. Along the seacoast the population is
drilled, and corresponds somewhat to our marines.

There is no honorary ranking in the National Guard.
Arms are supplied and inspected by the Government.
When serving with the regular paid corps, it takes
precedence over it, although the general command is
under officers of the highest ranks in the regular army.
In each legion and battalion, a council of administration
gives an annual report of the disbursement of funds.
All regulations are determined, for the Department of
the Seine, by the Minister of the Interior, and for those
of the other departments, by the mayors. On recommendation of the commander, special laws are made in
time of war.

Perfect discipline is maintained, but the soldier has
the right to prefer complaints to the chief of his corps.
Punishments consist of extra duty, for light offences,
and imprisonment for those which are more grave, or
the offender may be arraigned before a council of discipline, which may punish in the following manners: first,
reprimand; second, reprimand *avec mise a l'ordre* (i.e.,
stating the grounds for the order or sentence); third,
imprisonment for from six hours to three days; fourth,
degrading; fifth, removal from the Muster Roll. When

there is no prison or place of detention, a fine may be paid in lieu of imprisonment.

Officers may be punished for non-performance of duty, infractions of the laws, absence from post, inaccuracy in returns of offences committed by subordinates, disobedience, want of respect for superiors, and abuse of authority. The families of those wounded in service are pensioned by the Government.

SARDINIAN STATES.

General de Peyster declares that the militia system of Sardinia possesses all the weakness of that of Prussia, and none of its strength. It is composed of volunteers, with bounty, and a conscription draft. The term of service is sixteen years. A conscript must serve two years, without interruption, after which he is at the disposal of the Government for eight years, in his home district. He is then enrolled in the Reserve for six years longer.

TUSCANY.

The Tuscan Active Civic Guard is almost identical with that of the National Guard of France, which was the model after which were patterned the militia of Revolutionary Europe in 1848. The uniform, laws, and, in some cases, the language, were adopted, and even now the traveler in Naples, Rome, and Tuscany, sees the loose red trousers and fez of the Zouave, introduced into France by Napoleon.

HOLLAND.

The militia system of the Netherlands General de Peyster considers the simplest and most effectual of Europe. Every regiment of the line has, attached to it, dormant militia companies, which, at times, join the ranks of the regular army, and in a remarkably short space of time acquire the skill and military spirit of veterans.

TURKEY.

The militia system of Turkey is very similar to that of Prussia. There are six armies, each consisting of two services, the Active, and the Reserve, the latter, much like the Landwehr, composed of men who have served for five years in the Active force. After leaving the Active service, they do not receive pay for seven years, for reasons of economy. The regiments are raised from the same localities, so that the men are personally known to each other, and a spirit of comradeship is kept up. Many improvements are due to French officers, exiled for political reasons.

REGENCY OF TUNIS.

The Bey of Tunis is practically independent, and the Regency exists only in name. A large proportion of the army is under military discipline, copied from the systems of Europe. It consists of about twenty thousand men, exclusive of the Arab tribes, which are only utilized in case of necessity. These would add forty or fifty thousand more to the fighting force. Cannon and clothing for the troops are manufactured. There are powder mills and a fine barracks in and near the capital, one of which would contain five thousand men.

The regular army consists of eight thousand men, chiefly under the instruction of French officers. There are three regiments of infantry, of from one thousand five hundred to two thousand men each. The arms and equipments are modeled after those of Europe, but are heavy and old-fashioned. The soldiers, drawn from the lowest classes of the population, present an unsoldierlike appearance, but manœuvre very fairly, considering how opposed the drill is to their habits of warfare.

At Tunis, under the eye of the Bey, a show of discipline is kept up, but in the country districts the lawlessness of the soldiers is a terror to the population. This is almost entirely caused by the treatment the troops receive at the hands of the officers, who give them

miserable rations and cheat the Government of the funds
provided for that purpose. Notwithstanding this treatment, they are not without courage, and at the time when
war was expected with Sardinia, their camps and
defences were very creditable.

General de Peyster made an inspection of the barracks
of the cavalry, which arm consisted of about nine
hundred men. He found the barracks clean, furnished
with iron bedsteads, and the arms kept in good condition.
In the regimental workshops the soldiers made their own
clothing. In the armorer's shop the carbines examined
were equal to those of the French. The hospital was well
conducted. An assistant, educated in Italy, was engaged
in compounding medicine. The stable consisted of a
shed, built around an enclosure; the horses were hardy
and serviceable. General de Peyster's visit was
unexpected, and he found the barracks in its everyday
dress.

The artillery consists of a single regiment of about
one thousand men. The militia (Turcos) are called
Zouaves. Rank is denoted by crescents, suspended from
the neck, formerly the custom in the Turkish army also.
The latter now makes use of epaulettes, on account
of the enormous expense of crescents, ornamented with
diamonds, for the highest ranks.

CHAPTER XXIV

General de Peyster's comments upon the militia of the countries visited by him, his suggestions of features which could be adopted with advantage by the State of New York and other States of the Union, and his proposed reform, based upon his studies, are of the greatest value. A considerable part of these deductions and recommendations, with which his report begins, we give in their author's own language.

"STATE OF NEW YORK.

"No. 74.

"IN SENATE, MARCH 26, 1853.

"Report

"As to the organization of the Militia, &c., by

"Brigadier General J. Watts de Peyster.

"Headquarters, 9th Brigade,

"3d Division, N. Y. S. T.,

"Tivoli P. O., 1st July, 1852.

"To His Excellency Washington Hunt,

. "Governor of the State of New York, and Comman-

"der-in-Chief of the Military Forces, thereof:

"Your Excellency:—In pursuance of the instructions contained in the General Orders No. 411, and powers conferred upon me 29th of July, 1851, &c., &c., to investigate the Organizations of the National Guards and Municipal Military systems of Europe, and the Systems of Ordnance and Artillery best adapted to the Military Service of this State, I have the honor to submit the following Report on the subjects to which my attention was specially directed.

"After examination abroad of laws and publications relating thereto, reported results, and consultation with officers of rank and experience who have given their attention to similar matters, the best conclusion at which I can arrive, is that there are no systems which in themselves are applicable to our institutions and population.   The most efficient differ but little from the laws which govern the regular forces of the same nation, while those which resemble our own system, like it, cannot be relied on in pressing emergencies.

"I will hereinafter endeavor as succinctly as possible, to explain the present different European organizations, referring for minute particulars to documents collected throughout my military tour and submitted herewith.   I will then respectfully submit my own views of the wants and weakness of the military force of our State, and the means by which its efficiency can be promoted, in the statement of which I do not presume to rely on my own judgment, but append a list of those military authorities which justify the positions I have assumed; still I doubt if the present Militia Law of the State is constitutional, or if any organization can become so whose provisions differ from those of the Acts of Congress, relating to the Militia of the United States, approved May 8, 1792, and March 2, 1803.

"In Military States no dependence whatever is placed on that popular force which we term Militia.   The National or Civic Guards are equivalent to our uniformed volunteer companies.   Even they are barely tolerated, and have been disbanded as soon as the government possessed the requisite authority, as powerless for good and fruitful of evil, or else placed under the same severe laws which govern the regular forces.   And except in the Sardinian States, they can be disbanded at any moment, in whole or in part, by the order of their sovereign.

"In Sweden, Prussia and the minor German States, that organization (whose characteristics resemble Militia) is an integral part of the regular army. In all these there are elements worthy consideration and application at home.   In Austria and Russia the Military Colonies are governed by such absolute laws, and subjected to

such severe discipline, that they can only be considered
as an armament subsidiary to the regular forces. From
these systems we can glean almost nothing whatever, for
laws, oppressive even in appearance, could never be
enforced in this State.

"In France the ranks of the National Guard are filled
by the middle classes, and thus it has possessed a moral
power it never could have exerted as a military force.
At the present moment it exists, from hour to hour, as
a concession to the Bourgeoisie, but it will be dissolved
the moment its members evince the slightest disposition
to reason on the acts of the President. Many of the
provisions of this system are beneficial, and should be
incorporated in the present or any future organization
of our Militia.

"In the Sardinian States the National Guards of
Genoa, 5,000 strong, are a very fine body of well disciplined men, but I can say but very little in favor of their
appearance in other cities of the kingdom. Even those
of Genoa are considered of little value in a really
Military point of view, except for the defence of fortified
places, in which, even, they have shown but little
reliability, for in 1849 they suffered the impregnable
lines of their native city to be taken by escalade by a
detachment of riflemen, altho' it was reported at the time
they were animated with the best spirit against the royal
army; still, I must confess, in appearance and real
discipline they are superior, as a body, to our uniformed
volunteer corps.

"In case of war, or internal difficulty, the French and
Sardinian National Guard are immediately placed
under Generals or Colonels of superior rank of the
regular army. In Tuscany, the States of the Church
(Roman), and Naples, the National and Civic Guards
have been entirely disbanded, as too insurrectionary in
their tendencies, and all the Laws relating to their
organization in the two latter suppressed, and their
possession or sale declared illegal under the severest
penalties.

"The Tuscan National Guard did not appear to have accomplished any of the objects of its mission, but the Roman National Guard were said to have been very good, and maintained tranquility in the city, even during the turmoil of the Carnival.

"The organization of the Neapolitan National Guard in 1848 was the affair of a day, no sooner conceded to the people, than it was destroyed in the bloody conflict which overthrew the constitution by which it was granted. But in 1820-21 (my authority is Gen. Guillaume Pepe) they not only enforced tranquility in the interior, but even sent eighty battalions to the frontier, of which thirty fought the battle of Rieti, from morning until sundown. This statement is all very well, but if they were such good troops, where are the results?

"Now there is not a more degraded population than that of the two Sicilies. The fact is, our citizens do not appreciate the want of intelligence, self-government, and morality of the masses abroad; and a comparison between them and our own population would be unjust and derogatory to the latter. In Europe, unfortunately, liberty is ever translated as license, and the people are so destitute of that moral sensibility and submission to the laws which form the safeguard of our institutions, that the freedom which we enjoy, if granted to them, would inevitably terminate in what is best known as Red Republicanism. Therefore, I deem it most advisable to suggest a basis of an organization, which, at the same time, would comply with the requisitions of our constitution, and establish such a Militia as would serve for the protection of property, the defence of the State, and afford an auxiliary police force for the repression of riot, or the enforcement of Law.

"The principal defects of the existing Militia Laws of the State of New York, are as follows:

"First: The almost total absence of discipline, which does not mean instruction in manual exercise and evolutions alone, but also subordination, and submission to orders, regulation, and laws.

"Second: The weakness of our military penal code, in consequence of which the superior cannot enforce obedience, or maintain that respect due to his rank.

"Third: The election of officers. Officers, both of the army and of the National Guard itself in France, declare that whatever discipline and reliability existed in that institution, were, in a great measure, destroyed by conceding the election of officers. The café and the wine shop now exert their pernicious influence, where formerly ability and character were considered sufficient recommendations.

"Fourth: The want of an institution to supply and practically educate a nucleus of officers, i.e., a State Military School or College.

"Fifth: The want of means to pay and sustain a sufficient Military force, which fund can only be supplied by a direct capitation tax, or assessment on property, collected in such a manner as to prevent the odious features of a military tax, and equally distributed in proportion to the districts in which it is raised.

"Sixth: The fact that, depending upon the volunteer system, portions of the State are left without any military force whatever, for the protection of person and property, in districts destitute of military spirit.

"This could be easily remedied by resorting to draft, or ballot, to fill up the ranks of the few companies necessary as police, etc. The recruits could be supplied from the class of young men, for youth possesses the qualities best calculated to form an active and enthusiastic soldier, where health is not hazarded by the exposure and fatigues of an active campaign. Enlistment might, therefore, be permitted as early as the age of sixteen. The most effective citizen soldiery which ever shouldered a musket were the Parisian Gardes, Nationales Mobiles, the generality of whom were what we should term boys.

"Fathers of families, and men whose business is dependent on themselves alone, are certainly unfitted for the hazards of a soldier's life, and it is unjust to expose

them against their will, to dangers which can be avoided.
The first draft should therefore fall upon the male
population between sixteen and twenty-five or thirty.
But in the case of invasion, every citizen then owes a
sacred debt to his native land.

"Next, for what service are our Militia best suited by
their habits and constitutional tendencies? As Riflemen
they may be made very effective; as Guides, Estafettes,
Scouts, &c.; a few platoons or even corps of Cavalry may
be organized to advantage; but as Cavalry and Infantry,
to act in masses in the open field, from the very nature
of their organization, they can never be reliable. As Foot
Artillery, the intelligence, activity and adaptability of our
people can be fully developed, and all their powers
exerted in the highest degree for the protection of our
coasts and the defence of our most important positions.
It is needless to dwell upon the weakness of Militia in
the Field, or their strength behind fortifications. In
the notes hereto appended will be found the views of
military writers who have so ably explained these ideas
that it would be presumption to do otherwise than quote
their arguments and expositions of facts.

"The wars of 1848-49 in Italy, and, I may say,
throughout Europe of that period, are like the handwriting on the wall, as a warning of the slender
dependence that can be placed upon the bravest Militia
when exposed to Regulars in the open field, while the
exploits of the National Artillery and Volunteer Corps,
in defence of cities and lines, are written with glorious
characters in the blood of their assailants. The siege of
Venice, the defence of Rome, of the Sicilian cities of
heroic Brescia, and the lines of Curtatone, are incon-
testable proofs of the value of National Guards when
serving with Artillery, whereas every attempt at field
operations, or the opposition of popular armaments in
the formation of Cavalry and Infantry, to Regulars,
terminated in such disastrous defeats that, were it not
for the awful sacrifices which they cost, the only term
which could be applied to their efforts would be
'ridiculous.'"

General de Peyster suggests the establishment of a fund for the support of the militia by a State tax; arbitrary enrollment of citizens, who may be called on in the case of disturbance; and methods of drafting. He advocates the organization of fire companies under military discipline, and the instruction of corps of sappers and miners. All drills should be regulated, and the rosters, accounts, etc., should be verified under oath. Officers should pass an examination before being commissioned, and ordnance and pay departments should be organized.

He maintains that the State uniform should be made distinct from that of the regular army, advocates gray as the color to be used in the State of New York, and a system of stars to indicate rank.

He urges a stricter code in the militia, with punishment by fines, imprisonment, etc., and the awarding of medals and badges for good service.

"Some other term should be applied to uniformed corps than that of Militia," he writes. "It has an injurious effect abroad, as the word Militia is only applied to the last resort of nations, which implies the final levy or uprising of the population, with scarcely any organization. 'National' or 'Civic Guards' is not advisable, but 'State Troops,' 'State Volunteers,' 'State Guards,' 'State Service,' or some other equivalent title that would indicate an honorable profession."

He makes an earnest plea for the enforcement of discipline, and speaks of the great weakness of the Italian army, in its wars with Austria, from its lack. Only through subordination to superiors can a military force be made perfect. Even courage itself is secondary. He quotes the words of Napoleon, who declared that no army could be successful or glorious which is composed of "Baionettes raisonnantes" (Reasoning bayonets). He advocates the organization of the militia under the regulations of the army, and says, "In no country is the proper organization of a well-instructed popular military force so necessary as in the

United States, and in no part of the United States, as
in the State of New York, which will always be the
theatre of the first hostilities, particularly in the event
of a war with England, which God forbid!"

He declares the election of officers by subordinates to
be ruinous in its effects on discipline, and that the State
officers too often look upon the militia as a political
hobby. He discountenances the formation of independent target companies in cities, which, he says, in times
of disturbance, will be found in the ranks of the mob.
He refers to the Seventh Regiment of New York as an
example of the good effects of discipline.

The establishment of State military schools, in connection with the public schools, he strongly advocates, and
he speaks of the graduates of West Point, who, as officers
in the Mexican War, changed the raw recruits into a
trained soldiery.

He considers that the best weapon for an intelligent,
brave people is the rifle. It was with this that our
nation fought in the Revolution, the Indian Wars, and
the War of 1812. With this the Vendean peasantry
overcame the Republican armies in 1793, and, in
Germany, it repelled the French troops. He believes
that the rifle should be provided with a bayonet, and
that it is specially adapted for our country militia.

He says that cavalry is almost entirely unfitted for use
in the militia of our country districts, and that unless
a people is thoroughly accustomed to horses, and, like
the Arabs and Tartars, have almost spent their lives
in the saddle, when suddenly called into the field it will
be unreliable. Not only is special training necessary for
the men, but for the horses. The most efficient weapon
for cavalry is the lance, and a simple company of lancers
could easily disperse the most violent mob in case of
riot. He quotes the narrative, by Captain Carleton, of
the Battle of Buena Vista in the Mexican War, as follows:
"Had the Arkansas * * * and Kentucky (mounted)
volunteers never been allowed horses, they would have
been able to make a stand."

"The other purpose of my mission," he writes, "was the examination of what Artillery is best adapted to the Militia. The object of the Militia in war is, or always should be, entirely defensive. I am far from wishing to imply the solecism that Light Artillery is not necessary for defensive war, and most eminently serviceable in supporting raw troops; but there is so little probability of its ever being brought to any useful perfection in the Militia, that their time and attention had better be devoted to the other great support of imperfectly disciplined levies, the throwing up of supporting Field works, whenever practicable, and the management of batteries of position (heavy field pieces) connected therewith. Where the very considerable expense of horsing and thoroughly drilling a section of Light Artillery can and will be borne, let it be done by all means; but I apprehend there are not many such localities."

He discusses the French field batteries. He proposes the howitzer as the most suitable for use in street fighting, citing their utility in Paris in 1848.

Citizen artillery, he adds, has always won the admiration of soldiers by its success. In the European wars of 1848-49, at Rome, and at Venice, its efficiency was demonstrated. In our country it defended Forts Moultrie and McHenry, and secured the victory of Stonington. He considers the Massachusetts system of foot artillery the best adapted for the militia, and that field batteries should be discouraged, on account of the great expense of equipment and horses. The men should be taught the making of ammunition, and the raw supplies should be sent by the Government. In cases of riot, artillery is indispensable, on account of the effect it produces upon the imagination of a mob. He advises the formation of artillery corps by the workmen at State arsenals.

The hospital department should be carefully regulated, with well-instructed surgeons, ambulance corps, and every care for the welfare of the troops. He earnestly urges the necessity of having only physicians of education appointed to the medical staff.

17

He suggests the system of military telegraphy in use in France and England, which consists of squads of soldiers raising their coats on their bayonets, and, by this means, representing certain words or sentences which may be seen by squads near by.

He gives a careful outline of the essential points which should be adopted in training the militia of this country, based upon his study of the Prussian system. We should have a First Levy, like that of the Landwehr, to form a cadre or frame for the whole force. This could be recruited with volunteers, under trained officers, and provided with armories. Uniforms should be furnished the men, and kept at these armories, except when in use. Squad drills, once a week, should be held; company drills, every two or three months; and a regimental drill, lasting several days, once a year.

Officers could be trained at camps of instruction; and a polytechnic institute, with drill and discipline like that of West Point, combined with other studies, would send out pupils well equipped for service as officers, engineers, and instructors in the public schools. They might serve the State for a term of years, in compensation for their education.

The militia officers might join in the yearly encampment of these institutes, and military instruction in the public schools would be a valuable factor, in preparation for the militia service. The company district should be divided, as in the Prussian system, in order that every man may conveniently attend the drill.

"In one respect, however," says General de Peyster, "we would be far from recommending the Prussian system, which allots sacred time to this purpose. * * * Much might be said (as we know) on their reasons for so doing, but it may be questioned whether, among similar influences, this does not keep down the character of the soldiers. * * * At any rate, we have no Silesian weavers, working for six cents per day, and find themselves, nor have we that other proof of lack of time—that men taught to read in the public schools remain, from want of practise, always at the measure of a child six years old in the facility with which they do so."

He decries the idea of a system which would attempt the military training of our whole nation, saying, "It would cost millions and can never be necessary nor possible, until that woeful day of which curious patriots talk calmly, when, by a division of the Union, two or three rival nations put armies on their frontiers and accustom their people to taxes. At the same time, if we do not wish to pay foreign enemies for teaching us the art of war, we must learn it ourselves, and practise before they come. In short, although we do not need a nation of soldiers, we need such a number of those who really are so that we cannot be taken by surprise and must wait until the end of the war until we are fit to oppose our enemies."

He urges the enlistment of young men, over sixteen years of age, in the militia, where the interests of military exercises would supplant those of a more harmful character. With the appropriation of a fixed sum from the State for the support of the militia, it might be made "a body of privates not known since the days of Greece and Rome, to whom their art is neither a pastime nor a trade, and, though a serious occupation, enthusiastically enjoyed and most devotedly cultivated."

In closing the report, he quotes the words of the Statistique Militaire, "Let us follow the example bequeathed to us by the ancient Romans—abandon without regret our own customs, if better can be substituted."

CHAPTER XXV

ON FIRE DEPARTMENTS

General de Peyster's report on the Parisian and Florentine fire departments was made at a time when a paid fire department, with steam fire engines, was unknown in the State of New York. His recommendations led to a complete reform of this branch of municipal service. His report begins as follows:

"Head Quarters, 9th Brigade,
"3d Division, N. Y. S. T.
"Tivoli P. O., Dutchess Co., 16th August, 1852.
"To His Excellency, WASHINGTON HUNT,
"Governor of the State of New York, and Commander-in-Chief of the Military Forces thereof:

"Your Excellency:—Having been several years connected with the New York Fire Department, and acquainted with all its details of duty and material, from that time I became interested in the improvement of that neglected branch of the public service in the rural districts, the more especially as the continued command of military districts, under the Laws of 47, 49, 51, 52, and the previous organization of 1835, afforded constant opportunities of appreciating the necessity of aid against fire and the absolute inefficiency of the present system to cope with serious circumstances, requiring *coup-d'oeil*, tactics, and discipline, although well enough perhaps on ordinary occasions.

"Quicksightedness (coup-d'oeil), a most precious gift of nature, which can be attained, however, to a great degree by practice and observation, is seldom available in this State for the arrangement of an attack on fire, through the recklessness and insubordination of inferiors. Tactics, written or traditional, there are scarcely any; and discipline—I maintain, and every casual and accurate

observer will corroborate my assertion—discipline in its
real signification and application is not understood (I
might even add, dreamed of, in the rural fire-corps) in
our military and fire organizations. Against slight
obstacles small means may compass success, but triumph,
or even safety, can never be derived, under trying
circumstances, from systems or institutions which lack
the key-stone, obedience, and the corner-stones, responsibility and law. It is in order to insure these elements,
that I urge so strongly a thorough military organization
for our rural fire companies."

He alludes to the unnecessary numbers of firemen in
small communities, declaring that in the small village of
Rhinebeck, New York, the number of men in the fire
department almost equals that of the city of Florence,
while with better discipline a smaller number would
suffice. The history of the fire department of Paris is
traced from its beginning, as a volunteer force, to its
incorporation as a part of the regular army.

In the Middle Ages the terror inspired by fire was
almost as great as that by war or the plague. In Paris
the alarm of fire was tolled from the belfry of the Hotel
de Ville, and echoed by all the parish churches, while
the wardens of the night, the ringers for the dead, as
they were called, joined the cry of fire to their chant,

> "Sleepers awake, devoutly pray,
> For those whom God has called away."

The Capuchin monks gave their services in attending
those injured in fires, and some of the trade guilds
organized corps; but there was no regular provision
made against its fury until the year 1699, in the reign
of Louis XIV, when M. Dumaurrier Duperrier, a provincial gentleman of noble family, on his return from
Holland, described the fire engines he had seen, and was
rewarded by the King with the right of their construc-
tion and sale for thirty years.

The first engines were mounted on four wheels (at
present they have but two), and manned by workmen
in the employ of M. Duperrier, a tax for their

compensation being levied upon the sufferers from the flames who had received aid from them. In 1705 a fire broke out in the house of a mechanic contiguous to the Church of Saint Anthony the Less, which caught that edifice, spread rapidly, and was only arrested after having occasioned great damage. This fire is remarkable as having been the first in Paris at which fire engines were used. In 1786 a physician and a surgeon were attached to the corps. In 1790-91 the theatres were obliged to employ the firemen. In 1792 the firemen were armed with sabres. In 1793 the candidates for service were obliged to pass an examination.

Soon after this the corps was re-organized by a decree, and, later, was given a standard and a uniform. After the Revolution, 6 July, 1801, Napoleon, as First Consul, entirely re-organized the Corps, raised the pay, and increased the number, by two hundred and ninety-three men, through the addition of a supernumerary force. It was then composed of three companies of one hundred and fifty men. The regular firemen were divided into two classes, to each of which sixty supernumeraries were attached, thirty of which received uniforms and rations, but were not paid, while the others maintained themselves, and were exempt from conscription after two years, becoming entitled to fill vacancies in the active force as soon as they occurred. The fire department was under the direction of the chief of police.

In 1811 the force was augmented by a battalion of four companies, on account of the destruction by fire of the palace of the Prince of Schwartzenberg. In 1813 the ancient house of the Capuchins, in the Rue de la Paix, who had given their services in the first attempts to fight fire, was assigned to the Second Company. It was visited by General de Peyster, in company with the United States Secretary of Legation, in April, 1852. Here he witnessed the drills and gymnastic exercises of the firemen.

In 1821 a royal ordinance decreed that the fire corps should be included in the army. The Restoration brought many improvements, among them the attachment of canvas water buckets to each engine. Previously water was brought in wicker buckets by hackney coaches from the public stands. Scaling ladders and the *sac-de-sauvetage* (sack of safety) were introduced at this time. In 1841 a royal ordinance increased the force to twenty-one officers and eight hundred and eight men. In 1848 the firemen were deprived of muskets, which had superseded the sabres of earlier date, as inappropriate to the service. In 1850 the battalion was disbanded by a decree of the President, and re-organized under the administration of the Minister of War.

General de Peyster compares the system of Paris with that of New York City, the latter being the largest and best regulated of our country. He considers that of Paris superior in every way, and says, "The superiority of a military to a volunteer organization is verified by continued experience and innumerable examples." The Parisian fireman quells the fire with as little damage to the property by water as possible.

In our department there is a reckless use of it, which not only causes as much damage as the fire itself, but wastes the water supply. The fireman of Paris is trained to regard his calling like that of a soldier, while the volunteer fireman, necessarily, does not give his best energies to the service.

"When a conflagration breaks out in Paris the measures of the firemen are truly strategetical. They take possession of the threatened locality, without control or interference, and * * * against an enemy which pardons neither the most trifling error nor momentary hesitation, in danger of sacrificing their lives * * * they exercise the absolute right of troops under arms and command on their field of battle. And such is the legitimate confidence which they inspire that the population, reassured by their presence alone, obey their injunctions * * * and keep themselves aloof, so as to cause neither let nor hindrance. Whilst, on the other hand, every one deems he has a right to advise volunteer firemen, who are often his neighbors, and of whose experience and capacity he has legitimate cause for suspicion."

Again he says, "The same cross of honor which rewards the gallant and successful soldier, sparkles on the breast of the devoted and generous fireman—the same infamy which awaits the deserter and coward, impends over the faithless and insubordinate Sapeur Pompier."

The personnel of the fire department of Paris is described as consisting of, first, the Sapeurs Pompiers (firemen), incorporated with the army; second, the Sapeurs Pompiers Municipaux (independent corps of firemen), civil in character; and, third, the Sapeurs Pompiers Gardes Nationaux (militia firemen), connected with the National Guard. This corps has also the care of the aqueducts.

A description of the independent fire corps follows. General de Peyster uses a translation of its Regulations, submitted to the Prefect of the Department and the Minister of the Interior, which embraces organization, duties, discipline, and administration. He gives a translation of the rules and regulations for towns and villages, as likewise of the Sunday regulations. He also gives, from the code of the National Guard, extracts which apply to the fire corps. A description of the Parisian fire engines and other apparatus concludes the account.

FIRE DEPARTMENT OF FLORENCE

The firemen of Florence form a municipal guard maintained by the city and composed of artificers and mechanics. They have a military organization, and not only protect the city from fires, but maintain the health ordinances, superintend the lighting of the streets, and attend to the operation of the floodgates of the river Arno during freshets. They also attend fires in the country districts near the city. The fire department is under the city government and also that of the Tuscan troops, and partakes of the character of a volunteer

municipal and military force.   A translation is given of
the regulations governing it.

"After much study of the principles of the herein-
before mentioned systems," says General de Peyster, in
conclusion, "and examination of the acts regulating fire
companies in this State, I am satisfied that the incorporation of the fire department in the rural districts with
the State military organizations would bring order out
of chaos.   To accomplish this, I herewith submit
suggestions for an act calculated to attain so deserving
an end, to which are appended my reasons for believing
its passage would be generally popular, and its advantages eagerly embraced throughout the State."

He gives an outline of an act to reorganize the fire
corps in the State of New York.   It contains suggestions
for organizations, uniforms, etc., and gives the laws of
the State, of that time, respecting fire companies, and
a report from Captain Horton, of Company B, 22nd
Regiment, made to General de Peyster, and dated 12
September, 1852, upon the condition of "the fire
organizations and apparatus within the bounds of the
9th Brigade district."   This report shows the district
to be very poorly equipped, while in many cases the
corps were only nominal, to give their members the
privilege of exemption from taxes and militia service.

In the fall of 1852, soon after General de Peyster's
reports had been transmitted to Governor Hunt, the
field and staff officers of his brigade expressed their
appreciation of their commander's labors in behalf of
the militia by tendering to him a medal.   Their letter
to him is dated 22 November, 1852.

"It is with a lively sentiment," they write, "of your
devotion to their interests, and a high appreciation of
your efforts toward establishing in the State of New
York that only harmless and secure provision for the
defence of a Constitution and Liberty, such as an
American enjoys—a peace-loving but in time of need
fighting militia—that the Field and Staff Officers of the
9th Brigade beg your acceptance of the medal voted by

them at their last Officers' Drill, Oct., 1852, with an
expression of their deep interest in the success of your
present journey, both for establishing your health and
advancing the service."

CHAPTER XXVI

MILITARY AGENT OF THE STATE OF NEW YORK

In the early fall of 1852, soon after receiving General de Peyster's reports, Governor Washington Hunt extended the General's leave of absence to enable him to prosecute further his military researches abroad, at the same time conferring upon him the official title of Military Agent of the State of New York. The commission from the Governor, revising and renewing the powers, which previously, on 29 July, 1851, he had conferred upon General de Peyster, is as follows:

"STATE OF NEW YORK,
"EXECUTIVE DEPARTMENT.
"Albany, 1st September, 1852.
"TO THE PEOPLE OF THE STATE
OF NEW YORK:
"TO ALL TO WHOM THESE PRESENTS SHALL
COME:

"KNOW YE, That whereas J. Watts de Peyster, Brigadier-General in the Military Forces of our State of New York, and Commandant of the 9th Brigade District therein, hath applied to us for a renewal of his leave of absence, to enable him to return to Europe, and make a tour of such countries as he may be advised or deem advisable to visit for the entire restoration of his health: And whereas we have the fullest confidence in the ability and experience of General de Peyster, whom we have promoted for valuable improvements in Organization, Armament, and Uniform, while Colonel Commanding the 22d Regimental District of our State, and subsequent important service:

"Now, Therefore, leave of absence for two years from the date hereof, or as long as may be required for his recovery, is hereby granted, and Brigadier-General de

Peyster is hereby constituted MILITARY AGENT of our said State of New York, and ordered and directed, with a view to promote the efficiency of the Military System of our said State, to INSPECT, EXAMINE and REPORT upon the Military and Naval Systems of Defence, the Ordnance Departments, Artillery and Armaments in general, the Organizations of the National Guards and Municipal Military Police and Fire Systems of the countries he may visit, and purchase such publications, maps, charts, arms, equipments and apparatus as may to him appear advantageous, for the purpose of submitting the information thus acquired, and specimens selected, to the authorities of our said State.

"And we do hereby commend General de Peyster to the favorable consideration of the CIVIL and MILITARY AUTHORITIES of the countries he may visit, and desire that he may receive from the Diplomatic Agents and Consuls of the United States, abroad, all proper aid and such facilities for promoting the object of his mission as well as such good offices as they can with propriety afford him.

"IN TESTIMONY whereof, we have caused The Great Seal of the State of New York to be hereunto affixed.

"Witness Washington Hunt, Governor of our said State and Commander-in-Chief of the Military and Naval Forces of "(The Great Seal the same at our city of Albany, the N. Y. S.) first day of September, in the year of our Lord one thousand eight hundred and fifty-two.

"WASHINGTON HUNT.

"State of New York, Head-Quarters, Ad'j Gen'l's Office,
"Albany, Oct'r 18, 1852.

"(L.S.) Passed the Ad'j Gen'l's Office.

"Abm. Van Vechten,
"Ass't Adj.-Gen'l of the State of New York."

The co-operation of the departments of the national government of War and State was again invoked in

order that European sources of information might be
made as completely accessible as possible. The following
letter, dated 4 November, 1852, Governor Hunt addressed
to Hon. Edward Everett, Secretary of State.

"Having confidence in the ability, judgment, and
discretion of Brig. Gen'l J. Watts de Peyster, I have
granted him certain powers, and leave of absence, to
enable him to travel abroad. On a previous visit, made
under similar authority, Gen'l de Peyster obtained a large
amount of valuable information, which he has embodied
in two elaborate Reports, made to me on the subjects
entrusted to his charge.

"I should feel gratified if you would grant him a passport, in accordance with the facts, setting forth that he
is a Brigadier-General of the Militia of the State (of
New York) and a Military Agent of the same, and give
him a Circular to our U. S. officers, as will advance the
objects of his mission and afford him facilities for
travelling.

"If you should not deem it improper, and inconsistent
with the custom of your Department, by gratifying the
wishes of Gen'l De Peyster in this respect, I should feel
greatly obliged."

On the same date the Governor addressed a similar
letter to Hon. Charles M. Conrad, Secretary of War, in
the course of which he said:

"He has devoted much time and money to promote
the efficiency and the organization of the Militia of the
State, and is one of the most accomplished officers we
have.

"I should feel obliged if you would give to Gen'l de
Peyster a Circular to the U. S. Diplomatic Agents and
Consuls abroad, such as will advance the objects of his
mission, and afford him facilities for seeing all that may
be interesting, and render agreeable his sojourn in the
countries he may visit."

On 11 November, 1852, Secretary Conrad referred the
matter to Secretary Everett.

"Allow me to introduce to your acquaintance Lieuten-

ant-Colonel James Mulford, of the New York Militia,"
he wrote. "Mr. Mulford has business with your Department
connected with his official station, and brought me
the enclosed letter from Governor Hunt, of New York,
the request contained in which should properly have been
addressed to yourself.

"The gentleman mentioned in Governor Hunt's letter
—General de Peyster—visited Europe last year, in order
to collect such information in military matters as might
aid in the re-organization of the Military System of his
State, and, at my request, a passport was furnished him,
in which he was designated by his military title of Major-
General,* New York Militia. He again solicits a similar
favor, which I hope it may be in your power to grant."

As a result the following letter, dated at the Depart-
ment of State, Washington, 11 November, 1852, addressed
"To the Diplomatic and Consular Agents of the United
States in Europe," and signed by Secretary of State
Everett, was delivered to General de Peyster.

"This letter will be handed to you by J. Watts de
Peyster, Brig. Gen'l of the Military Forces of the State
of New York, and Commandant of the Ninth Brigade
District therein, who has been recommended to this
Department by Washington Hunt, Governor of the State
of New York, as one of the most useful and accomplished
officers in the Military Organization of that State.

"General de Peyster goes abroad under orders from
Governor Hunt, as Military Agent of the State of New
York, with a view to promote the efficiency of the Military
System of said State, and to inspect, examine and report
upon the Military and Naval Systems of Defence,
Ordnance Departments, Artillery, Armaments, etc., etc.

"I take great pleasure in commending him to you, and
in bespeaking for him during his sojourn in your vicinity,
such facilities for promoting the objects of his mission,
and such good offices, as may be in your power to afford
him."

---

*A clerical error for Brigadier-General.

Sailing for Europe in the fall of 1852, General de Peyster prosecuted his researches during that season and the winter of 1852-'53, returning to the United States in the spring. The results of his investigation are embodied in a third report, addressed to Governor Seymour.

CHAPTER XXVII

Printed at his own expense, General de Peyster's third report is dated from Tivoli, 1 June, 1853. While it is described by its author as a "supplement" to his preceding reports, it occupies no less than one hundred and eighty-three printed pages. Subsequently, he drew up and printed a section on the Prussian and Berlin fire departments. This is dated 23 March, 1854. It is designated as Chapter X, paged from 184 to 215, and intended as a continuation of the Report to Governor Seymour. Still later, under date 27 April, 1854, General de Peyster made another addition, printed under the title, "John Edward Purser's Fire Escape."

His work as Military Agent, on the occasion of both visits to Europe, was carried on by the General in spite of ill-health, and while under the strain of much physical suffering. His report was drawn up under the same handicap, and he speaks in it of "continued ill-health, and at times entire inability to use my pen." The document begins as follows:

"Head Quarters, 9th Brigade, 3d Division, N. Y. State Troops,

"Tivoli Post Office, Dutchess Co., 1st June, 1853.
"To His Excellency, Horatio Seymour,

"Governor of the State of New York and Commander-in-Chief of the Military and Naval Forces thereof:
"Yr. Excellency:

"In pursuance of General Orders, No. 411, and powers conferred upon me, 29th July, 1851, revised and renewed 1st September, 1852, etc., etc., by His Excellency,

JOHN WATTS DE PEYSTER IN AUSTRIAN UNIFORM, 1853

WASHINGTON HUNT, Governor and Commander-in-Chief, etc.,*of the State of New York, to inspect, examine and report upon the Military Systems of Defence, and Organizations of the National Guards and Municipal, Military, Police and Fire Systems, etc., etc., best adapted to the Military Institutions of this State, I have the honor to submit the following Report and Corollary Information, collected in the course of my Tour, which may be considered a supplement and material part of my preceding Reports, dated 1st July and 16th August, 1853.

"The present Report will endeavor to furnish analyses of the English and Swiss Militia Laws; the Prussian (Berlin), Swiss (Genevese), Russian (St. Petersburg), and supplementary information with regard to the French (Parisian) Fire Departments; the Laws of 1851, relating to the Military Reorganization of the Kingdom of Sardinia; as well as such other subjects as may appear valuable as suggestions for improvements in the Militia Establishments of this State."

The introduction briefly discusses the needs of the different divisions of the Militia of the State of New York, recalling some of the recommendations of the earlier reports, and reënforcing them by facts and arguments derived from later researches.

"Every day's experience and observation in Europe," General de Peyster declares, "confirmed my original opinion of the value of Mountain Howitzers." His attention was specially directed to the improvement of the carriage, and this led, later, to the introduction, by him, of the prairie carriage.

He again emphatically commends the rifle as an offensive weapon, and urges the formation of corps of sharpshooters.

---

*"I am indebted to His Excellency Washington Hunt, late Governor, not only for my promotion to the rank I now hold and selection to represent our State (militarily) abroad, but for extraordinary facilities for seeing and studying foreign systems and organisations, obtained through his recommendations from the General Goverment. To the Hon. Charles M. Conrad, late Secretary of War, also, I owe my warmest thanks for his letters to American representatives abroad, and continued assistance in enabling me to fulfill the object of my mission."

18

The uniform of riflemen in the United States he considers utterly unsuitable. "Examine them in detail: Metallic ornaments, bright buttons, glistening lace, unsuitable on any military dress, mortal to their wearers when opposed to adversaries skilled in picking off their opponents! Then scrutinize foreign uniforms, sombre green, like the dense foliage, dark blue, appropriate 'to the forest gloom,' or grey, swallowed up in the first wreaths of 'war's sulphurous canopy.'" He advocates grey as the most appropriate color for the uniform of the State of New York,* giving the following reasons for this choice:

"Over and above the many cogent reasons urged in * * * my Report of 1st July, 1852, for the adoption of grey as the appropriate color for our State uniform, the following additional recommendations may not be without weight. At morning and evening twilight, in foggy, muggy, and rainy weather, a body of men thus clothed would be undistinguishable at a very short distance, and amid the smoke of battle they would be swallowed up at once in the clouds of kindred hue. Grey and yellow, or gold, form the richest dress in the world: without bullion, it is the cheapest, taking into consideration its serviceability; it is national to a great degree, and last—not least certainly—it is the least fatal to its wearer. Grey, it is stated, was the uniform of the English troops in the reign of William III. It is now worn by the Austrian Riflemen, and good reasons must have dictated the choice, for it was not appropriate to any province of the Empire.

"It would appear from numerous observations, that soldiers are hit during battle, according to the color of their dress, in the following order: red, the most fatal; the least fatal, Austrian grey. The proportions are, red, 12; rifle green, 7; brown, 6; Austrian-bluish-grey, 5."

On the subject of chaplains, he says, "Where Colonels

---

*This suggestion was not lost upon Jefferson Davis, who became Secretary of War in 1853, and grey uniforms were adopted in the Confederate armies.

have Chaplains attached to their Staff, they should be called upon on all suitable occasions to discharge their duties and celebrate divine service at the head of their regiments. * * * No Christian people does, or should, neglect their duty to the Lord of Hosts, or forget their entire dependence on Him. It ill becomes us, who have partaken so largely of his bounties, and found Him a 'Banner' and 'Defense,' on many a hard fought field, to forget the respect due to Him who gives or withholds the victory."

The introduction contains suggestions for the organization of the medical department of the militia, discusses the subject of orders and badges of merit, urges a military plan of fire organizations, and renews the suggestions for changes in the militia laws, made after consultation with many militia officers, as "the best and perhaps the only basis for the organization of a reliable force."

A description is given of the musketoon of the French Cavalry, introduced into France after General de Peyster's visit in 1852. In his careful analysis of its points of advantage, his remarkable technical knowledge of the principles of firearms is apparent to the most ignorant. It is this broad, yet detailed, grasp of his subject which makes the military writings of General de Peyster so valuable. In this connection, he urges the need of a change of arms as follows:

"As a matter of primary importance, I beg leave to call your Excellency's attention to the Armament, etc., of the New York State Militia, and cannot too strongly urge upon the State authorities the necessity of perfecting everything connected not only with the arms themselves, which are in many respects inferior to those issued to the United States Regular Troops, but other material, which should be complete in every respect, and so kept up as to enable the Militia to take the field at once in case of riot, insurrection, or war.

"If the Regular Troops, thoroughly acquainted with the use of their arms, and their details, require perfect weapons, how much more the Militia, composed of citizens, so superior in every respect to the Army Personal, worthy, both as a body and as individuals, of every attention and every endeavor to place them on the most efficient footing and best enable them to preserve their lives, so valuable to their families and friends and the State, and at the same time discharge their duty with fidelity and success.

"As the Infantry—or rather the Corps serving as such —are most numerous, the first remarks are somewhat due to them. Almost, if not all, the Regiments use flint-lock muskets, which have become almost antiquated in Europe, where the Neapolitan is the only army which retains these obsolete locks; and even there the Swiss troops, on whose valor the Royal House rely for the preservation of their throne, are armed with the most approved percussion-lock fire-arms. This State could well afford to have all the efficient flint-lock muskets in its arsenals and armories immediately altered to percussion."

The report proper is divided into ten chapters. The first two treat of the militia system of New York. Chapter I contains amended suggestions for changes in the laws relating to that body. General de Peyster advocates a poll tax for the purpose of raising a fund for its support, and also a property tax. The recruitment is to be made from the list of voters. The compulsory service, in the militia, of non-commissioned officers of the line would insure rapid improvement in the training of the men. He favors the mountain howitzer, as best adapted for rural artillery, and the transportation of ammunition on carts.

He proposes that the fire departments be placed under the direction of militia officers. The rosters, returns, accounts, etc., are to be verified under oath, and officers commissioned only after passing an examination. He also suggests the organization of a pay department, an ordnance department, and the awarding of medals. He proposes an order of merit, to be called the "Excelsior," with appropriate decorations. His suggested amendments likewise provide for the establishment of a State military school.

In Chapter II he makes suggestions based on his studies of European systems. He strongly condemns the election of officers by the men, which completely destroys discipline, and deplores the absence of schools where they can be trained, saying, in this connection, "Every foreign State, it matters not how circumscribed in territory or restricted in resources, maintains schools for the instruction of those destined for the career of arms."

Chapter III contains an analysis of the militia laws of England. General de Peyster dclares that "at no time during the existence of the English monarchy * * * since the days of Alfred the Great, has England been destitute of an Armed Force, answering, in many respects, to the present Militia." From his examination of the acts under which the English militia has been organized, he believes them to be the basis of our original militia laws. An examination of the system in England from the earliest times follows.

Under the Saxon law, one soldier was furnished from every five hides of land. A hide is believed by some authors to have been the area of land necessary to sustain a single family for one year. The Venerable Bede is an authority for this belief. It was supposed to consist of from fifty to one hundred acres. The fighting force, in Saxon times, was composed of the Ceorls, the lowest class of freemen, and commanded by the Eolderman, the governors of shires, who were elected at the Folk-Motes (Assemblies of the People).

After the Conquest, under the feudal system, the militia was provided by the nobles, who sent their vassals to the field at the order of the Crown. General de Peyster points out that this system was equivalent to a tax upon property. It continued until the time of Cromwell, when the same right was exercised by the Parliament. At the Restoration, the authority over and command of the militia returned to the Crown, and every person who had £200 or more a year was obliged to furnish one foot soldier; those who possessed £500 and over, furnished a cavalryman; those who had less than these sums gave contributions.

In 1756 the militia was re-organized. The acts of George the Third followed, consolidated by the act of 26 June, 1802. In 1809, during the wars of the time of the French Revolution, a force of four hundred thousand men was at the disposal of the State. "Under the Act of 30 June, 1852, the militia was augmented to eighty thousand; not only the officers, as with us, but also the non-commissioned officers and privates taking the Oath of Allegiance, whose rank and file sworn in and enrolled for five years, in contradistinction to the old method of draft or ballot, are filled up, as far as possible, by voluntary enlistment, and the deficiency supplied by draft or ballot among men under thirty-five years of age, with certain exemptions, and in cases of invasion, imminent dangers, &c., can be raised to one hundred and twenty thousand."

The report treats of the provisions respecting officers, armories, desertion, formation of corps, yeomanry, etc. Fines and other penalties, exceeding £20, can be collected by actions brought in any court of record. In less amounts, any Justice of the Peace can, in default of payment, confiscate the goods and chattels of the offender, or commit him to jail.

Chapter IV is devoted to a description of the militia of Switzerland. "There is no country in the world," writes General de Peyster, "from whose * * * militia system the State of New York can learn so much as that of the Swiss Confederation, the only Government of Europe * * * truly analogous to our own." Switzerland is composed of independent cantons, whose populations present characteristics widely differing as to language, occupation, modes of worship, etc., and yet which are united in a Confederation which has held its own amid the turmoil of European wars. It is the only nation in the world without a standing army, and maintains its independence with its citizen soldiery alone.

General de Peyster regards a regular army as a necessity in our country, but urges that the Swiss militia system might well be imitated by us in its most admirable points, namely, perfect discipline and military instruction for officers and men in military schools. The Swiss militia is divided into the Elite, corresponding to our regular army, and the Reserve, somewhat resembling the Landwehr of Prussia.

The remainder of the chapter consists of the provisions of the Swiss federal law in regard to military organizations, staffs, and officers, medical department, time of service, armament, equipment and uniforms, instruction and inspection of troops, and the Department of War.

Chapter V, treats of the military organization of the Sardinian States, and gives a description of the tactics and methods of instruction. This chapter is based upon the original manuscript of Lieutenant-General Alexandre de la Marmora, Commander-in-Chief, at Genoa, of the Military Division, who instituted the Corps of Piedmontese Bersaglieri, or Riflemen, from which the famous French Chasseurs (originally d'Orleans, now de Vincennes) were copied. These instructions, translated by an officer, formerly of the Piedmontese army, for this report, are by General de Peyster modified slightly to harmonize with the tactics of the United States Army. The instruction is divided into three schools: the School of Quadriglia (a division of four men), the School of the Platoon (one-fourth of a company), and the School of the Company (one hundred and thirty to two hundred men). A description of the instruction of these schools is given in a series of lessons.

In a note under "Errata," General de Peyster pronounces this exposition of the Sardinian system "valuable, as showing the operation of an Organization analogous to that of Prussia, but better suited to a Constitutional or Republican form of Government."

Chapter V also contains an account of public instruction in Russia. "Public Instruction appears to have first assumed a station among the governmental institutions during the reign of Boritz Feodorowitsch Godunow (Bovis Godounove) about the year 1598. The accession of the present dynasty of Romanow gave a powerful impulse to the Russian System of Public Instruction, which was warmly patronized by the Czar Michael Feodorowitch, 1616, and his son and successor, Alexis Michaelowitsch, 1645. During the reign of the latter, Nicon, Patriarch of the Russo-Greek Church, distinguished himself by his zeal for the propagation of learning.

"In 1634, the Metropolitan of Kiew, Peter Magila, founded in his province (Exarchie) the first Theological Academy. The Hyeronomite (Greek title for a Magistrate of distinguished position), Simeon Polotski, Preceptor of the Czar Feodor Alexiowitsch, a celebrated Professor of his age, instituted at Moscow the Slav-Greek-Latin School of Theology. The immortal reformer of Russia, the Emperor Peter I (1682-1725) called The Great, has, on this and on many other grounds, laid the foundation of an edifice, to which his successors have constantly added, until the Russian System of Instruction merits an important position among the similar establishments of other European nations."

Peter the Great founded many public schools and schools of art and science, among which was the Naval School, afterwards called the School for Pilots. In 1724, he instituted the Academy of Sciences at St. Petersburgh. In 1732 the First Corps of Cadets was organized; in 1752 Empress Elizabeth Petrowna founded the Corps of Naval Cadets, and, in 1755, the University of Moscow, the first established in Russia. Empress Catherine II, in 1762 founded the Corps of Artillery and the Engineer Cadets, the College of Moscow, the House of Instruction, the Academy for Young Ladies of Noble Extraction, the Commercial School and College of St. Petersburgh, and the Russian Academy. Emperor Paul I in 1798 established the Institute of the Order of St. Catherine for the Education of Young Ladies of Noble Extraction, and, in 1799, the Academy of Surgery and Medicine.

In 1802 the Ministry of Public Instruction was established by the Emperor Alexander, who also laid the foundations of many other institutions of learning. In 1808 the Corps of Military Orphans was organized, and, in the next year, the School of Bridges and Roads. In 1820 the Michael Artillery School was founded; in 1822, the School of Chevalier (noble) Guards. Soon afterward the Patriotic Institute, the Corps of Forest Rangers, a School for the Deaf and Dumb, an Orphan Asylum, etc., were established.

"Beneath the sceptor of the reigning Czar, Nicholas I," says General de Peyster, "the Empire of Russia has begun a new era, not only in regard to Public Instruction, but in every point of view." Nicholas I. founded, among other things, the Military Academy and many Corps of Cadets at various cities. Statistics follow, which General de Peyster declares "will enable our State Officers and Legislature to appreciate the present vast development of Public Instruction in Russia."

"Like our own," he says, in closing the chapter, "Russia is a nation of yesterday. Each is advancing to power. * * * Each must one day come in collision with antagonistic principles and races. * * * But how is each preparing for the struggle? * * * Russia, with limited means, when compared with ours, but with marvellous foresight and unflinching perseverance, trusts to the sword—that arbiter which has ruled, and ever will rule, the mind, until the latter, purified and true to itself, understands its mighty mission to free and ennoble, not crush and prey upon, mankind; and, with her 72,000,000 of inhabitants, maintains thirty-seven Governmental Military Establishments (1,292 Instructors, and 12,010 Pupils), besides hundreds of Institutions tending more or less to the same ends, to prepare her youth for the career of arms; by which, alone, she is aware that her sway and progress can be maintained and can triumph.

"On the other hand the United States, possessing, or soon to possess, 25,000,000 souls, has two (one, Military, glorious unit! and one, Naval), unequal to the wants of such a population, and far unequal to the mission we have arrogated to ourselves, of protecting every political refugee, worthy or unworthy, who casts himself into our arms, thrown open to receive him; and the State of New York, the 'Empire State,' with her lofty motto, 'Excelsior,' with 3,000,000 of inhabitants, *NONE!*"

Chapter IX describes the military conditions of Spain, which General de Peyster characterizes as deplorable, the army being filled with corruption, and the people deceived by those who should be their guides. From a letter written in 1843, he quotes as follows:

"In general, the Spaniard possesses all the qualities requisite to form a good soldier; gay amid privations, content with his simple rations; and, provided he has a paper cigarette, he will never complain, but execute forced marches of seven or eight Spanish leagues without a murmur * * * In as great proportion as the soldiers possess the necessary qualities for their calling, the officers are deficient in them. The grades are, even to-day, the exclusive patrimony of the privileged classes. One often sees Commandants who are not twenty years old, and Second Lieutenants who play with a top in public! * * * It would seem as if in Spain the epaulette had the faculty of stifling all zeal. From the moment that an individual changes the lace (*les galons*—the chevrons of the sergeant and corporal) into the epaulette, a metamorphosis is accomplished, contrary to that which takes place everywhere else; he is at once good for nothing except to tyrannize over his former equals, or to censure the conduct of his superiors * * * The highest rewards have too often been the rewards of the basest intrigues or the most cowardly treasons."

The conditions found in Spain General de Peyster makes the text of the following suggestive homily:

"From Spain can be derived little, if any, information in regard to the organization of a military force, great as were the effects and marvellous the results of the uprising of her people against that Scourge of God, Napoleon; nor are the following pages presented with a view to that end; but in other respects her history, her former elevation, her present decay, teem with lessons the most important and impressive.

"She is a living example of the depth to which a nation can fall, whose councils are swayed by bigotry, intolerance, and ingratitude in every branch of the public service; whose upper classes have slept away their patriotism and manhood; whose navy, which once sovereignized the ocean, linking her establishments and colonies, which girdled the earth with their grandeur and riches, has been precipitated from the heights of glory to the depths of insignificance by the folly, venality, and ignorance of her rulers; whose army, whose discipline, valor, and determination challenged the admiration of the civilized world, has almost become a by-word for inefficiency and mutiny, through the want of proper institutions for military education, the effects of favoritism and politics; in a word, the continual interference of ambitious demagogues and unprincipled agitators with that organization which, of all others should be free from such treasonable and destructive influences.

"Like the column of iron, when defective, no army can be trusted in a crisis, whose discipline has been flawed by any such causes. To us, in this respect, she presents a terrible example; for, in no country have the people been more deceived with regard to their military organizations, by political leaders and the press, than our own.

"To attain great or insignificant, but temporary offices, how often has falsehood, or, what is equally culpable, concealment of the truth, been resorted to, with regard to the value of our regular army! Again and again, in our National Congress and State Legislatures, have fluent orators, experienced in its weakness and viciousness, dared to place a volunteer system on the same level with a regular permanent organization. We have seen Generals and subordinate officers, created by the stroke of a pen, replace chiefs and leaders grey with mental and physical labor, sacrificed for political reasons alone, with a full knowledge of the injustice of the substitution or promotion. On a paltry question of momentary expediency, perhaps the election or appointment of an inefficient, but available candidate, how often have the Militia of this State been sacrificed, or the efficiency of the New York Firemen tampered with!

"As in Spain, men to whom our country should look for the truth have so blinded the eyes of our people, too often averse to the most wholesome restraint, to the real strength of military organizations, that those experiences which seem to have been sent by Providence to awaken us from our errors, through the insidious, interested explanations of false teachers, have served but to lull us into a more dangerous apathy.

"The day will come, however, when, thrust into a contest with a great military power, we will awaken from our dream of security to expiate the criminality of our rulers with such sacrifice of life and treasures as the history of nations has not yet chronicled—peradventure with the sword at each other's throats. Of this truth, the annals of Spain and of her armies furnish continual examples, throughout the last two centuries, and teach us that when a military organization is ever exposed to, and entirely dependent on, the selfishness, influence, and corruption of mere politicians, farewell to discipline, farewell to reliability, and, in the end, farewell to every sentiment of justice and honor!"

Equally notable is General de Peyster's eloquent plea for discipline:

"In England, when the Militia is embodied, Her Majesty can put the forces under the command of such general officers as she may be pleased to appoint. In France, Holland, Prussia, the German States, in fact all whose laws I have ever quoted, except Switzerland, the sovereign assigns generals, colonels, or other field officers of the Regular Army, to the chief command and leading of divisions and brigades. In the Swiss service there is no higher grade than that of Colonel—even the Commander-in-Chief, in reality, ranks as such.

"We are the only people who are sufficiently unwise to entrust our military forces to the guidance of ignorance, conceit, recklessness, and political intrigue. As to the staff corps, the Army is, or should be, the example for the Militia under present circumstances; although the principle, militarily considered, is wrong. In the former, the staff officers are, with very few exceptions, provided for by law, supplied by subalterns from the line, temporarily detailed for such service.

"Then with regard to the election of officers, with which hallucination we alone are afflicted, it is almost useless to say anything further. The militia officer, or intelligent private, who cannot discover the error, to use the gentlest expression, will never learn it from anything but the hardest experience. That our politicians acknowledge it, although they have not hitherto dared to apply the remedy, is proven by Section 6, Article xi., of our State Constitution, by which the Legislature is invested with the power of abolishing this pernicious regulation—pernicious because the parent of so many other vices and weaknesses—and providing for the appointment of officers.

"Would that the writer's pen could make apparent the chief cause, besides the elective principle, of our Militia's decadence and present inefficiency! It is almost entirely owing to the absence of stern and impartial discipline. What is there so repulsive in the word MUST, from which our people recoil with distrust and mistermed independence? It is only another term for, or application of, that Law which throws its aegis over the citizen and his right, wherever the Anglo-Saxon language is spoken, its institutions honored, and its influence acknowledged. Obedience to God, submission to authority and law, and the fulfilling of individual duty, are, one and all, the offspring of that MUST, known in military parlance as 'discipline,' which is the soul of an army—the very life-blood, whose regular pulsation constitutes its vitality.

"Without discipline an army is worse than a mob,

impotent for good, potent for evil. By the agency of discipline, Greece overthrew the mighty monarchies of Asia, Rome became the mistress of the world, and in her decline maintained her sway despite the waning valor and enervated frames of her soldiery; Sweden emancipated Germany from the shackles of Papal and imperial tyranny, and, although a barren and sparsely populated country, dictated terms to her richer and more powerful neighbors; Spain, with a handful of heroes, subdued the Americans; Prussia, from a poor and second-rate power, took, and has since maintained, her place among the great sovereignties of Europe, and, under her great Frederick, repelled and conquered, with hireling forces, armies sixfold their number; Austria, greatest in defeat, reorganized her armaments, so often destroyed, yet always renewed; France imposed her yoke on a vanquished continent, and only fell when her example had taught the conquered the arts of the conqueror; and England, upheld by England's dauntless heart, rolled back the wave of Bonaparte's ambition, wherever Anglo-Saxon bayonet grated against the steel of Celtic foe.

"Ask the historian for those glorious names who have advanced the art of war, and left the impress of their fame on the chronicles of armies—Alexander, with his massive phalanx, Cæsar with his mobile legion, Hannibal with his Cossacks of the ancient world, and, in modern days, Gustavus the originator, Frederick the adaptor, and Napoleon the perfector—and bid them reveal the secret of their marvellous success. Discipline, the application of the simple 'must.'

"Who is universally admitted to be the most illustrious captain this world has ever known, since the days of Nimrod, 'the mighty hunter,' to the present, the dawning of Peace's gentler triumphs? Napoleon Bonaparte! Look to his banners, blackened with the smoke of a thousand conflicts and rent with missiles from every European mine. What words are inscribed on their glorious folds, so fraught with lessons to the soldier? 'Valor' and 'discipline'—only those two; and they

BOOK PLATE OF JOHN WATTS DE PEYSTER
Showing the de Peyster and Watts Arms

rendered his armies for nineteen years invincible on
every battlefield, from the Pillars of Hercules to the
burning sands of the Lybian and Syrian Deserts, and
frozen wastes of Russia. Discipline is the soul and life
of armies, the first element of military greatness and
success. And yet, our Militia Organization claims to
exist without that vital principle! If the fact must be
told, *we have no real militia!"*

Chapter VI consists of a translation of documents
relating to the organization and duties of the fire
battalion of Paris.

Chapter VII is a treatise upon the fire department of
St. Petersburgh. Its members are not only firemen, but
act as a police force. The department is well organized,
but rarely succeeds in extinguishing fires. The methods
employed are those most calculated to defeat their object,
among them being the demolishing of buildings adjacent
to those in flames, and the breaking of window glasses,
which immediately creates a draught, causing the fire to
spread.

The horses in the fire service are the finest in the city,
having been confiscated by the Government on account
of the accidents caused by their spirit or speed. This,
however, does not prevent such accidents, as the drivers
always increase the speed to escape and avoid confiscation. General de Peyster tells us that the Emperor, on
one occasion, seeing that one of the horses attached to
his sledge had a tendency to run away, drove to the
nearest fire station and delivered it to the firemen.

Chapter VIII presents a description of the fire department of the city of Lyons. Its institution was accomplished by an imperial decree of 22 January, 1808. The
present force was organized 1 September, 1852. It is
under military regulations. A description is given of
the staff of officers, tariff of pay, clothing and armament.

Chapter X contains an account of the Berlin fire
extinguishing establishment. It is municipal in character, but with military organization. Berlin is divided
into eighteen wards, each of which has one engine. They

are connected by a telegraphic system. "When a fire is discovered," says General de Peyster, "it is made known simultaneously at all these stations, and it may be reached from the nearest station in two or three minutes, and from the rest proportionately, according to relative distances. The most remote fires may be arrived at from the central point within a quarter of an hour at the very farthest. * * * When at the scene of action, every proceeding * * * is conducted with all the forms, discipline, and regularity of military movements; it is also evident that great advantage is derived from the system."

He closes with statistics regarding this system, and with supplementary accounts of the London fire brigade and the St. Petersburgh fire department.

"There is a greater field for usefulness in the regeneration of our Fire Department, and correction of its lavish expenditure," he writes, in summing up his recommendations on this subject, "than in any other branch of the State or Municipal service, however great the wants, errors, or abuses of any other branch may be found on examination.

"Fire Corps should become a part of our Militia Organization, and be subjected to rigid military discipline; or else, particularly in large cities, established as a permanent municipal force, dependent in a great measure on the Department of Police, and an Auxiliary to the Police itself."

"An unprejudiced examination of the merits of the Parisian Establishment," he says again, "will prove, to a military and scientific mind, the vast superiority of its elements. That iron discipline which has ever conquered, and will ever conquer man, on the field of battle, and alone has been able to overcome nature, will assuredly triumph, as far as human beings can triumph, over every enemy, even the most ruthless fire.

"I cannot take back a syllable of anything I have said in favor of a Militarily Constituted Paid Fire Department, composed of a comparatively few selected, drilled, capable, and reliable men, subject to the Police Magistrates, auxiliary to the Police itself; for very little over the same sum, the city of New York could have, instead of 4,125 Volunteer Firemen, as at present (the majority of whom alone must invariably perform the majority of the duty), 500 Soldier Firemen—experienced, educated men, capable of resisting fatigue and exposure, Life Preservers, in the true sense of the word, Active Policemen, Model Soldiers, Admirable Gymnasts, Practical Machinists, and, unsullied by that canker of our Municipal Institutions, political intrigue, Exemplary Citizens."

He proposes a complete reorganization of the fire department of the City of New York.

"In order to organize a Fire Department for the City of New York, worthy so great and opulent a community, we should first examine what features are common to the majority of the best European systems, and deserving of imitation. The first is the application of horse power for the transport of the Engines, Fire Train, and even Firemen themselves. The second is the introduction of the Paulin Fire Dress and Fire Escapes, originally adopted in Paris, or better ones, if they can be found, and a suitable, economical uniform, &c.

"Thus, at once, we have a foundation to work upon. The addition of Floating Fire Engines for rivers and river fronts, and Steam Fire Engines for the interior of the city—the first already in use in London, on the Thames, in Berlin, on the Spree, &c.; the second, in Cincinnati; the union in one person, the Chief of Police, of the command of the Police Department Proper and the Superior Control of the Fire and Croton Water Department, which would assimilate his authority and duties to those of the Prefect of Police in Paris; a Fire Telegraph, susceptible of being used for Police purposes, on a similar plan to those which have proved so beneficial in Berlin and Boston; a Gymnasium for the instruction of the Police and Firemen, to prepare them for the discharge of all their arduous duties; the distribution, throughout the city, of Fire stations, or posts amply
19

provided with Personal and Material; would enable the
officers, possessed of such extensive, yet necessary, juris-
dictions and resources, so intimately connected and
mutually dependent, to exert an immediate and concen-
trated authority, capable of coping successfully with any
conflagration which might result from negligence,
accident, or crime."

The essential features in the reformation of the New
York fire department advocated by General de Peyster—
the organization of a paid fire department and the introduction of steam fire engines—were adopted by the city
after his reports were published. The improvements
introduced in New York spread to other cities and chief
towns throughout the country, and to General de Peyster
the credit must be given for the initiation of this great
reform. Long afterward, when the present system had
been in operation for many years, under his pen name
of "Anchor," the General contributed to one of the
papers a brief article in appreciation of the effective
work of the New York firemen. Under the title, "Honor
to our Fire Department," he says:

"The writer served with the old Volunteer dis-
organization and first reported in favor of the new, and
therefore can appreciate the damage of the one with the
salvation of the other. Last night at a friend's in Fifth
Avenue a chimney took fire. The volumes of smoke in
the house and adjoining building were enormous and
foreboded something serious.

"With the first flakes of falling soot the writer went
out to order his vehicle to leave the way clear. No
sooner was it so than there was an engine, hose cart, and
truck on hand. It was marvellous. And then the
courtesy, gentleness, and efficiency of the firemen under
Engineer King. Their conduct was unexceptionable.

"The writer has examined into these services abroad
and elsewhere, and can testify to the superiority of the
forbearance and capability of our own. Nor were the
police patrols behindhand in promptness and conduct.
With such firemen and police as were on hand last night,

our citizens can feel assured of a protection to property and person not enjoyed by any other city where the writer has been present at similar scenes."

CHAPTER XXVIII

ADJUTANT-GENERAL

Colonel William P. Wainwright, of the Twenty-second Regiment, was Acting Brigadier-General of the Ninth Brigade from 30 August, 1851, to 28 May, 1853, while General de Peyster was engaged in making his military tours of inspection in Europe and drawing up his reports. Resuming the active command of his brigade on the last mentioned date, General de Peyster continued in charge of it until his assignment as Adjutant-General, a year and seven months later.

His experiments with guns, with other activities looking to the improvement of the State troops, were continued throughout this period. He was Acting Major-General of the Third Division, New York State Military Force, in August, 1853, during the temporary absence of Major-General John Taylor Cooper.

Leave of absence having been granted to General de Peyster, Colonel Wainwright again became Acting Brigadier-General of the Ninth Brigade, 30 December, 1854. Two days later, Myron H. Clark, upon his inauguration as Governor of New York, issued the following order:

"State of New York,
"Executive Department.
"Albany, 1st January, 1855.

"The Commander-in-Chief hereby appoints the following named persons Members of his Staff, and orders and directs that they shall be obeyed and respected accordingly.

"1 J. Watts de Peyster, of Tivoli, Duchess Co.,
                                    Adjutant-General.

 2 Benjamin F. Bruce, " Lenox, Madison Co.,
                                    Inspector-General.

 3 Joseph J. Chambers, of the City of Albany,
                                    Engineer-in-Chief.

 4 O. Vandenburgh,   " "   "   " Syracuse,
                              Judge Advocate General.

 5 James L. Mitchell,   " ~   "   of Albany,
                              Quarter-Master-General

 6 A. H. Hoff,   " "   "   of Albany,
                                    Surgeon-General.

7	E. E. Hendrick.	of the City of Albany, Paymaster-General.
8	E. H. Schermerhorn,	" " " " New York,
9	I. B. Gale,	" " " " Troy,
10	John Sill,	" " " " Albany, Aids.
11	Samuel C. Thompson,	" " " " New York, Military Secretary.

"Myron H. Clark,"

A copy of General de Peyster's commission as Adjutant-General is here given.

"THE PEOPLE OF THE STATE OF NEW YORK, "BY THE GRACE OF GOD FREE AND INDE-PENDENT

"TO J. WATTS DE PEYSTER, Brigadier-General of the IXth Brigade, N. Y. S. M., Greeting:

"We reposing especial trust and confidence, as well in your patriotism, conduct and loyalty, as in your integrity and readiness to do us good and faithful service, have appointed and constituted, and by these presents do appoint and constitute you, the said J. Watts de Peyster, of Tivoli, County of Duchess, S. N. Y., Brigadier-General of the 9th Brigade, IIId Division, New York State Military Forces, ADJUTANT-GENERAL OF THE STATE OF NEW YORK, with rank from 1st January, 1855.

"You are, therefore, to observe and follow such orders and directions as you shall, from time to time, receive from our Commander-in-Chief of the Military Forces of our said State, in pursuance of the trust reposed in you, and for so doing this shall be your Commission.

"IN WITNESS WHEREOF, We have caused our Seal for Military Commissions to be hereunto affixed.

"Witness, MYRON H. CLARK, Governor of our said State, Commander-in-Chief of the Military and Naval Forces of the same, at our City of Albany, the first day of Janu-"(L.S.)   ary, one thousand eight hundred and fifty-five.   Myron H. Clark.

"Passed the Adjutant-General's Office.

"J. Watts de Peyster,
"Adjutant-General."

The document following was issued at the same time.
"THE PEOPLE OF THE STATE OF NEW YORK,
"TO ALL TO WHOM THESE PRESENTS SHALL
    COME:

"KNOW YE, That pursuant to the Constitution and
Laws of our said State, We have appointed and constituted and by these presents do appoint and constitute J.
WATTS DE PEYSTER, Brigadier-General of the Ninth
Brigade, Third Division, N. Y. S. M., ADJUTANT-
GENERAL of the Militia of our said State, with rank
from the first day of January, one thousand eight hundred and fifty-five, to hold the said office in the manner
specified in and by our said Constitution and Laws.

"IN TESTIMONY WHEREOF, We have
caused our Seal for Military Commissions to
be hereunto affixed. Witness, MYRON
H. CLARK, Governor of our said State, and
Commander-in-Chief of the Military and
Naval Forces of the same, at our City of
Albany, the first day of January, in the year
"(L.S.)   of our Lord one thousand eight hundred and
fifty-five.   "MYRON H. CLARK."

The anticipations which his appointment aroused in
the minds of military men who took a genuine interest
in the militia is well illustrated by a letter of congratu-
lation to General de Peyster from Colonel Duryea, of
the Seventh Regiment, dated 6 January, 1855.

"It affords me much pleasure," he wrote, "to congratu-
late you upon your appointment by the Executive of this
State, our Adjutant-General. I feel fully satisfied from
the interest you have always manifested for the Military
Institutions of our country, that a new life and vigor will
be breathed into this sadly neglected Department. May
success attend all your efforts.

"I am under obligation to you for a copy of the
'Eclaireur,' and I perceive by this number that you have
published two others which I would be pleased to possess,
for they treat of a particular branch of military science
in which I am much interested.

"I have contemplated writing to you for some length of time in relation to publishing a work for the Militia of the United States treating of street firing, and all manœuvres incident to street fighting; such a work is much needed and I hope the suggestion will meet with your hearty approval."

These expectations were doomed to but a partial realization. After remaining in office only a little more than two months, General de Peyster resigned a position which had become impossible to a man of his spirit and exalted sense of duty. He had accepted his appointment with eager enthusiasm, believing that it would give him an opportunity to correct abuses in the militia, and to carry into execution many of the reforms which he had advocated. He soon discovered that "the duties the Governor principally expected of him were to dance attendance at balls and parties."

Moreover, he soon came into violent conflict with corrupt political forces at Albany. He insisted upon the practice of economy, and an honest administration under him, and took the high ground that appointments should be made for merit and for the good of the public service. Governor Clark took alarm from the threats of influential politicians. He feared that by a hearty and loyal support of his Adjutant-General he would make himself a target for attacks and injure his prospects.

This painful situation came to a crisis over the retention of Colonel Jonathan Tarbell as Assistant Adjutant-General, after improper conduct towards his superior. Colonel Tarbell was in close sympathy with the political influences which manifested hostility to General de Peyster's efficient administration of his office. The Assistant Adjutant-General's antagonism finally developed into ungentlemanly conduct and insubordination. General de Peyster proposed to dismiss him summarily from office. He was earnestly solicited by Governor Clark to retain Colonel Tarbell, as the following letter witnesses. It will be noticed that the Governor prefers his request "as a personal favor" to himself.

"STATE OF NEW YORK.
"Head Quarters, N. Y. S. M.,
"Adjutant-General's Office.
"Albany, 28th Feb'y, 1855.

"My dear Gen'l:

"I have consulted some of my particular friends, and have come to the conclusion to ask you, as a personal favor, to retain Col. Tarbell as Assistant Adjutant-General until the first of May. It will gratify me very much if you will do so.

"Very truly yours,
"MYRON H. CLARK.

"Brigadier Gen'l J. Watts de Peyster,
"Adj't-Gen'l."

It must be confessed that the Governor's attitude does not reflect credit upon himself or upon his administration. General de Peyster had relieved Colonel Tarbell as Assistant Adjutant-General on 28 February, probably before the Governor's appeal reached him, and on 2 March following he confirmed his appointment of Lieutenant-Colonel James Mulford as Colonel Tarbell's successor. The General Orders to this effect are here given.

"STATE OF NEW YORK, HEAD-QUARTERS,
"Adjutant-General's Office,
"Albany, March 2, 1855.

"GENERAL ORDERS,
"No. 12.

"James Mulford, Lt.-Col. (22d Regiment) N. Y. S. M., having on the 28th February (in pursuance of section 7, article 1, title 8, of the Militia Law of the State), been appointed Assistant Adjutant-General vice Jonathan Tarbell, he will be obeyed and respected accordingly.

By order of the Commander-in-Chief.
"J. WATTS DE PEYSTER, Adj't-Gen'l."

On the same day, 2 March, 1855, the Governor evidently prevailed upon his Adjutant-General to reinstate Colonel Tarbell. The latter's misconduct the Governor refers to in a statement, over his own signature, which he gave to General de Peyster at the time, which also states the grounds upon which General de Peyster finally agreed to re-appoint Tarbell to office. A copy of this document follows.

"Albany, 2 March, 1855.

"Col. Tarbell admitted in my presence that he had behaved in an ungentlemanly and unjustifiable manner towards General de Peyster; that he acknowledged that General de Peyster had, prior to such conduct, treated him with courtesy and kindness, even anticipating his wishes in granting unasked leaves of absence; and that he would resign in writing to General de Peyster, such resignation to take effect on the 1st May.

"General de Peyster at the interview gave him distinctly to understand that he yielded in re-appointing him solely from a desire to please his commanding officer, His Excellency, the Governor, and save him from the unauthorized and unmanly attacks made upon him, the Governor, by interested politicians.

"MYRON H. CLARK."

On the same day Governor Clark addressed the following letter to his Adjutant-General:

"Albany, 2 March, 1855.

"Brig. Gen. J. Watts de Peyster,
"Adjutant-General, S. N. Y.

"General:

"At my solicitation, for the harmony of the Administration, you have re-appointed Jonathan Tarbell as Assistant Adjutant-General, from the 5th inst., to the 1st of May, when he has pledged himself to resign.

"Viewing the fact, the conduct he has evinced towards you a satisfactory reason for not wishing to remain in the office with one, retained for political reasons alone, you are hereafter relieved, at your request, from all responsibilities of the duties of Adjutant-General, except of such as you see fit to discharge, and rest assured I will not permit your military credit or personal honor to suffer by thus yielding to oblige me contrary to your feelings.

"You have always discharged the duties of the office to my satisfaction, and labored faithfully for the benefit of the service, and I deeply regret that circumstances, no fault of yours, have obliged me to make this request.

"Respectfully,
"MYRON H. CLARK."

This letter makes it clear that General de Peyster had refused to work in conjunction with Colonel Tarbell. The Governor weakly hoped to save the situation by relieving General de Peyster from active responsibility as Adjutant-General; but such a situation was intolerable to a gentleman of honor. Upon the following day, 3 March, Governor Clark gave his Adjutant-General discretionary powers in any case of riot throughout the State, as will be seen from the following:

"State of New York, Executive Department.

"Albany, March 3, 1855.

"Brigadier-General J. Watts de Peyster,

"Adjutant-General:

"Sir:

"Relying on your discretion and experience, I hereby authorize you to issue such orders to the military, and take such measures in case of riot in any city of our State as will maintain the laws, protect life and property, and sustain order.

"MYRON H. CLARK."

On the same day, however, General de Peyster tendered his resignation as Adjutant-General. Copies of this, and of the Governor's acceptance of it, are given.

"STATE OF NEW YORK, ADJ.-GENERAL'S OFFICE.

"Albany, March 3d, 1855.

"His Excellency, Myron H. Clark, Commander-in-Chief:

"Sir:—I hereby resign the office of Adjutant-General of the State of New York, to take effect at such time as my successor shall be appointed and qualified.

"J. WATTS DE PEYSTER."

"The Commander-in-Chief hereby accepts the resignation of Brig-Gen'l J. Watts de Peyster, as Adjutant-

General of the N. Y. S. M., and he will forthwith resume
the command of the 9th Brigade, and General Orders,
No. 339, bearing date Dec'r 30th, 1854, granting him
leave of absence from such command to enable him to
perform the duties of Adjutant-General and assigning
the command of said Brigade to Col. W. P. Wainwright
during the absence of Gen'l de Peyster, are hereby
countermanded.

"MYRON H. CLARK."

On the same date, 3 March, Governor Clark addressed
a note to General de Peyster in which he said: "In
accepting your resignation I feel that the course you
have adopted reflects honor upon your character and I
have no hesitation in adding you have won from me
confidence in your soldierly reputation. In accordance
with the understanding between us, Colonel J. Tarbell
shall not be appointed your successor and I will make it
a verbal stipulation with your successor that he shall not
be appointed Assistant Adjutant-General."

Still another letter from the Governor, of the same
date, accepts the Adjutant-General's resignation with
eloquent expressions of regret and many a flowery compliment. Evidently it was intended for public use. We
give it here.

"State of New York,
"Executive Department,
"Albany, March 3d, 1885.

"My dear General:

"Your resignation of the office of Adjutant-General has
been received, and it was with great regret that I read
the announcement of your determination to deprive me
of your valuable services in that Department.

"On ascertaining that I had been called upon by the
People to fill the office of Governor, my mind naturally
turned towards you as the man best fitted to be at the
head of the Military of the State. The reputation which
you had acquired by the very able Reports made to my
predecessor since your return from Europe, and the great
interest you had taken in the improvement of the Militia,

induced me to tender you the appointment. Your
management of the affairs of the Department proved that
I was right in the selection that I made. The records
of the office bear witness to the fidelity with which its
duties have been discharged; and the many valuable
reforms which you have suggested, furnish the evidences
of your industry as well as the interest you have taken in
our Military Organization.

"Nothing but your earnest wish would induce me to
accept your resignation, and thus sever our official connection; and, believe me, that in your retirement you will
carry with you the highest respect and esteem, both as an
officer and as a man, of

"Your friend,
"And ob't serv't,
"MYRON H. CLARK.

"To Brigadier-General
        "J. Watts de Peyster,
            "Tivoli."

The resignation was to take effect upon the appointment and qualification for office of General de Peyster's
successor. This occurred on 5 March, 1855, on which
date General de Peyster resumed the active command of
the Ninth Brigade, Robert H. Pruyn succeeding him as
Adjutant-General.* The following letter, from Colonel
Abraham Van Vechten to General de Peyster, written
6 March, 1855, the day after the latter's retirement from
the   Adjutant-General's   office,   is   interesting   and
significant.

"As the papers have informed you, Robert H. Pruyn
is Ad't Gen'l. He has not appointed any Assistant.
You may rest assured that I shall do everything in my
power to prevent the appointment of Tarbell. I do not
think there is any danger to be apprehended.

"The fact that you have certain papers in your
possession with the signature of the Governor has been

---

*General de Peyster was permitted to name his successor, and
named Mr. Pruyn, at one time United States Minister to Japan, as
"one whose astuteness in politics fitted him to grapple with the
noxious elements which environed the Governor."

bruited about. The Governor himself has mentioned it. Some of the outside 'busy-bodies', have said that I might have prevented that act. The proposition has been made to me to endeavor to get those papers. This I have declined, and have said that it was perfectly idle for me to attempt it.

"In the strictest confidence, let me say to you that Pruyn does not want them to be given up—he wants that excuse for not appointing Tarbell. The truth is he wants to bestow the place upon a friend of his own. In order to strengthen him in not appointing T., he desires me to write you requesting you to consent to it. He says this will draw out from you a reply protesting against it, in which your reasons will be strongly set forth, and he will be justified in acceding to your wishes.

"I have refused to be a party to this transaction, and shall not resort to it unless driven to it to defeat Tarbell. If you should receive such a letter from me you will understand it.

"There is a good deal more connected with this matter which the limits of a letter will not permit me to explain. When we meet you shall know it all, and if your admission behind the curtain which conceals the acts of politicians does not disgust you with them, I am much mistaken.

"You will pardon me, my dear General, but for your own sake I am really glad that you are removed beyond the poisonous atmosphere which hangs about this capital. Before you again attempt to 'live and breathe' in it your whole nature must be changed. Learn to lie and deceive. Learn to do it without letting the blush of shame mantle your cheek with one drop of blood. Forget that you have such a thing as a conscience. Forget that there is any hereafter, or that you will ever be called to account for the 'deeds done in the body.' When you can greet friend and foe with the same smile, and forget what honor is— when you have unlearned and forgotten all this—then, and not till then, accept a political office.

"But a truce, my dear General, to all this. I am true

as steel to the friends I love, and among them all, none occupies a higher place in my estimation than 'you and yours'."

In spite of the shortness of his term as Adjutant-General, General de Peyster succeeded in introducing many important improvements. "Among these," wrote the late General William P. Wainwright, "were the publication of revised regulations for the government of State Troops; the reorganization and permanent settlement of the Adjutant-General's Department; the consociating, so to speak, of the regiments of one arm, by giving them one uniform; the introduction of appropriate artillery; and the preparation of every branch of the State service for emergencies. He also insisted upon the responsibility and accountability of those who presided over the collection and disbursements of the military revenue; perhaps, after all, the most unpalatable of all his 'isms'—as his efforts at reform were sarcastically termed by those whose interest it was to defeat them, by the use of any means."

While Adjutant-General, General de Peyster inaugurated the publication of the "Official Military Circular," of which Volume I, Number I, for January and February, 1855—sixteen pages—was issued during his administration. By General Orders Number 7, dated 13 January, and General Orders 8, dated 18 January, 1855, four military officers of the State had been ordered by Adjutant-General de Peyster to report at his office on 1 February to form a Board, with the Adjutant-General as its President, to present to the commander-in-chief (the Governor) regulations desirable in order to carry into effect certain provisions of the military law of 17 April, 1854. The report of this Board, recommending the publication of the Circular, was as follows:

"STATE OF NEW YORK,
"Adjutant-General's Office.
"Albany, 6th February, 1855.
"To His Excellency, Myron H. Clark, Governor, Commander-in-Chief of the Military Forces of the State of New York:

"We, the undersigned, constituting a Board for the consideration of Rules and Regulations, Forms and Precedents, convened at Albany in pursuance of General Orders Nos. 7 and 8, do respectfully recommend that an Official Military Circular containing:

"1st. All orders, general and special, of importance, emanating from head-quarters.

"2d. All appointments, promotions, resignations and sentences of court-martial.

"3d. Such correspondence of the Adjutant-General's department as may be of general interest.

"4th. Such military instruction and intelligence as the Commander-in-Chief may see fit to communicate for the improvement of the discipline of the state military forces

be

published monthly, bi-monthly

or quarterly, by order of the Commander-in-Chief of the military forces of the State of New York, by the

"Adjutant-General.

"J. Watts de Peyster, Brigr. Gen'l. 9th Brigade, Adjutant-General, President of the Board.

"W. S. Fullerton, Brigr. Genl. 27th Brigade.

"H. B. Duryea, Brigr. Gen. 5th Brigade.

"Z. T. Bentley, Brigr. Genl. 19th Brigade.

"R. B. Van Valkenburgh, Col. Comdg. 60th Regt.

"Approved 6th February, 1855.

"MYRON H. CLARK,

"Governor, Commander-in-Chief of the Military
"Forces of the State of New York."

Adjutant-General de Peyster also compiled and published a complete digest of revised regulations for the government of the troops of the State, under the title, "Rules and Regulations Relative to the Adjutant-General, his Department, Duties, &c.," thirty-six pages. It is drawn up in the technical form of a legislative act, divided into titles, articles, and sections, with foot-note references attached to each section giving the authority upon which its provisions are based. The principal

authorities referred to are the Act of Congress of 8 May,
1792; the Act of Congress of 18 April, 1814; General
Regulations of the United States Army, edition of 1847;
the Military Law of the State of New York of 17 April,
1854; and various General Orders, promulgated by
General de Peyster himself, as Adjutant-General.

Adjutant-General Robert H. Pruyn, General de
Peyster's successor in office, wrote the latter as follows:

"I feel, my dear General, that with your military
enthusiasm and knowledge, you are in many respects
vastly more fitted for this office than I am. I fear I
shall not accomplish as much. My experience has shown
me that it is, if not dangerous, at all events, far from
pleasant to undertake too many reforms. I should as
soon think of partitioning a hornet's nest as of attempt-
ing many things you would have had the boldness to
execute."

Brigadier-General Frederick Townsend, while holding
the office of Adjutant-General, in 1857, wrote to General
de Peyster in a similar strain.

"Permit me, General," he says, in the course of his
letter, "to avail myself of this opportunity to express to
you regret, generally entertained among military men
connected with the militia, that you did not longer
remain at the head of the Adjutant-General's department,
even though at a sacrifice of your own private feelings.
Having traced up much that you did while in the department, and perceiving the direction of the work which
you had laid out for yourself, I must individually bear
testimony of the loss the service sustained on your
resigning the commission of Adjutant-General."

After his retirement as Adjutant-General, General de
Peyster resumed for a time the active command of his
Brigade. In the summer of 1856 he continued his work
of investigation of military conditions, addressing
himself to the situation in other States. The following
from Governor Clark, granting him leave of absence for
this purpose, comments approvingly upon his service to
New York.

"STATE OF NEW YORK,
"EXECUTIVE DEPARTMENT.

"Albany, July 21, 1856.

"Brigadier-General J. Watts de Peyster, Commandant of the Ninth Brigade District, S. N. Y., having applied for leave of absence, to enable him to visit several of the adjacent States, we do hereby commend him to the favorable consideration of the civil and military authorities of the State throughout which he may travel, and earnestly desire that he may receive therefrom all proper aid in acquiring whatever information he may deem important in connection with the military organization, etc., thereof.

"Sent out to Europe on a military mission, 1851-3, by our predecessor, Washington Hunt, General de Peyster brought back a very large amount of extremely valuable information which was embodied in two copious and elaborate reports, which speak for themselves with regard to his capability and energy.

"For the last ten years General de Peyster has devoted a large amount of time, labor and means to promote the efficiency and improve the organization, etc., of the military forces of the State of New York, and he has proved himself one of the most useful and accomplished officers we have.

"Immediately upon the confirmation of our election as Governor of the State of New York, our mind turned upon him as the man best fitted to be at the head of the military system and force of our State, and as the Chief of my Staff (Adjutant-General) he discharged his duties with unsurpassed ability, fidelity and efficiency.

"In testimony of our appreciation of General de Peyster, and our earnest recommendation of him to the good offices of the authorities of the States he may visit,

"We have caused our Privy Seal to be hereunto affixed.
"MYRON H. CLARK."

In September, 1856, General de Peyster resigned the command of the Ninth Brigade. Governor Clark's acceptance of the resignation, dated 1 October, 1856, and sealed with "the Great Seal of the State of New York," contains a summary of the retiring officer's services.

"In pursuance of the power vested in him by Section 36, Title 2, of the Militia Law of the State of New York," runs the document, "the Commander-in-Chief hereby accepts and authorizes the resignation of the Command of his District by Brigadier-General J. Watts de Peyster, Commandant of the 9th Brigade of the Military Forces of the State of New York—such Resignation of command, but not of his commission, to take effect on the 26th December, 1856, who having faithfully discharged the duties of Colonel of the Militia and General of the Military Forces of our said State, in the most efficient and exemplary manner, is entitled to all the privileges and exemptions from Military duty conferred by the different Acts under which he has served.

"In addition to the Military Privileges conferred by his service, he is hereby exempted from serving upon any Grand or Petit Jury within this State in pursuance of Section 75, Title 10, Chapter 10, Part I, Revised Statutes, Third Edition, whose provisions, previously confined to the City and County of New York, were extended throughout the State by Section 13 of the Act, making further provision for the Organization of the Military, etc., etc., passed April 10th, 1849, under the first Section of which Colonel J. Watts de Peyster was assigned to the Command of the 22nd Regimental District on the 3rd of September, 1849, counting from which date his term of service expires on the 3rd of September, 1856, during which time he has discharged his duty with a laborious fidelity, unexceeded, if equalled by any other officer in the State service.

"In accepting the resignation of his command by General de Peyster the Commander-in-Chief is happy to bear testimony to the important suggestions and improvements made by him, in Armament, Equipment and Discipline.

"Previous to the adoption of the Mountain Howitzer on the Prairie Carriage for the use of the United States

Army, Colonel de Peyster suggested and delineated a carriage for a Mountain or a similar light Howitzer, almost identical with that subsequently approved by the U. S. Ordnance Officers.

"He also had a Mountain Howitzer cast at his own expense in order, by practice therewith, to demonstrate its value as an Arm for the Militia, which through his exertions led to its adoption by the Military Authorities of our State.

"He also suggested and delineated a Siege Gun Carriage very similar to the pattern adopted by the Russians for the Armament of their Seacoast defences, and somewhat upon the same principle with the admirable light Howitzer Carriage, for which so much credit is due to Lieutenant John A. Dahlgren, now Commander U. S. Navy.

"He was the first officer in this country to recommend the Tunic or Frock Coat and Light Cap as the Uniform of the N. Y. Militia, afterwards adopted in every European Army, as well as that of the United States likewise.

"The Bayonet Fence, New System (Bersaglieri Chasseurs de Vincennes, Cacciatori Austriaci) of Rifle Tactics, subsequently introduced by the U. S. Military authorities, in accordance with the Tactics compiled and perfected by Brevet Lt.-Col. W. J. Hardee.

"He was also instrumental in the passage of several wise provisions for the better government of the Military Forces of this our State, and the author of many important suggestions with regard to the simplification of Tactics, Military Policy, Armament, Rules and Regulations, Methods of Designating Rank, &c., &c., some of which have been since adopted into the U. S. Cavalry Armament and strongly endorsed by Hon. Jefferson Davis, Secretary of War.

"Sent out to Europe on a Military Mission by our predecessor, Washington Hunt, he fulfilled the duties assigned to him with laborious fidelity, and returned bringing with him samples of valuable and improved

20

Arms, Books, Maps, Plans and engravings, many of which he presented to, and are now in, the State Library and Arsenal, &c., besides a mass of valuable information embodied in two long and elaborate reports.

"Selected by us to fill the post of Adjutant-General, he was untiring in his application to business and has left important mementoes of his determination, capacity and untiring energy and attention to the necessities and business of that Department, besides the preparation of a new Commission as beautiful as appropriate.

"The Commander-in-Chief feels that this testimonial is due to General de Peyster and while he accedes to his relinquishment of his command, regrets a step prejudicial to the interests of the whole Service which continued ill health and other cogent reasons compel him to take."

A little later, 13 November, 1856, the Governor authorized General de Peyster to wear his uniform on all occasions. A portion of the document bearing on this point follows:

"As a testimonial of my satisfaction with him as an officer, and as an acknowledgment of his services, I do hereby authorize him henceforward to wear on all occasions the uniform worn by him on the 11th of November, 1856, when I reviewed his Brigade, with such alterations for Undress, etc., as may have been already, or may be, determined and prescribed by himself."

The officers of the Ninth Brigade expressed great regret in connection with General de Peyster's resignation. In a letter, dated 11 November, 1856, in spite of his state of health, and the probability that he would be unable at times to take the field or assume command, they suggested that he remain at their head.

"We, the Company, Staff and Field Officers of the 9th Brigade, 3d Division, N. Y. S. M. F.," they wrote, "hearing that you and Col. William P. Wainwright are about to resign your command of the 9th Brigade and 22d Regiment, feel that the interests of the Service would suffer so much by such action on your part, that we earnestly request you to reconsider your determination, and suggest that, if Col. Wainwright does not wish to remain at the head of a Regiment, he might be willing to assume the Brigade-Major and Inspector's office, for which he is so eminently fitted as a Military Instructor.

"Perfectly aware that the state of your health is such that you could not take the field in case of active service or assume the command on many occasions, when the Brigade might, but it is not at all likely to, be called out we would be perfectly willing to abide by your feelings on all occasions, considering, that you are the best judge as to when and where you do not consider yourself well enough to turn out; and knowing from past experience, that, sick or well, you have never neglected a duty, we would be content to have you remain at our head for the welfare of the whole."

CHAPTER XXIX

BREVET MAJOR-GENERAL

The subsequent period of about nine years, from his resignation of the command of the Ninth Brigade to the end of the Civil War, was devoted by General de Peyster to the writing and publication of military and historical works. A separate section has been devoted to his literary work, and his activities during this period will be noticed there. At the close of the War of Secession a movement was inaugurated to secure official recognition, by the State of New York, of the important services which had been rendered to that State and to the Union by General de Peyster. The following letter was written to Governor Reuben E. Fenton by Major-General W. S. Rosecrans, 5 January, 1866.

"I am sure you will pardon the liberty I take in submitting to you whether it would not befit the honor of the State, that a gentleman, a citizen of the State, who has devoted so much time and spent his money so freely as has General J. Watts de Peyster to acquire real and accurate knowledge of Military science and art, and who keeps himself so well informed on those subjects, should receive from the Government of his State some recognition thereof. It seems to me it would have a beneficial effect as an example of public appreciation, and would stimulate other gentlemen of education and leisure to devote their time to studies so useful and necessary, and yet so apt to be neglected.

"Again, if you could have conferred on him a brevet or real rank of Major-General there may be public occasions when that might enable the State usefully to avail itself of his services on boards and in organizing your Militia.

"You will, I hope, pardon these suggestions, prompted

310

JOHN WATTS DE PEYSTER
About 1860

by the, to me, gratifying and rare occurrence of finding a gentleman of leisure who is so well learned in all that pertains to the art of war, and so truly an honor to the State."

Endorsements of the letter of General Rosecrans were forwarded to the Governor from Major-General Daniel Butterfield, Chief of Staff to Generals Hooker and Meade, Commander of a division under Sherman, and Commander of the Army of the Potomac; from Major-General G. K. Warren, Chief Topographical Engineer of the Army of the Potomac, and afterward Commander of the Fifth Army Corps; from Brigadier-General T. W. Sweeney, Secretary of War; from Brevet Major-General Charles K. Graham, the re-opener of the James River in May, 1864, and by various others who had been prominent as military commanders or in civil positions. Major-General Joseph Hooker wrote 13 January, 1866, as follows:

"I cheerfully unite with Major-General Rosecrans in recommending General J. Watts de Peyster to the most favorable consideration of your Excellency.

"Gen'l de Peyster was first introduced to me in May, 1861, by his cousin, the late Gen'l Philip Kearny, and I know the high estimate set upon his military ability by that distinguished officer. I too can bear testimony to the accuracy of his judgment in military matters.

"Believing that his studies and ideas, and his practical method of applying them, have been of great value to the State military organization, I take great pleasure in recommending him for a Brevet, as a reward for past services, or for a commission which will enable him to be of further service."

John T. Hoffman, Mayor of New York, wrote concurring with General Hooker. Three ex-Governors, Washington Hunt, Horatio Seymour, and John A. King, forwarded letters of recommendation. "General de Peyster rendered important military service to the State during my administration," wrote Washington Hunt. "He is fully worthy of the favor and recognition recom-

mended by General Rosecrans." "The report made by
General de Peyster, with regard to military science and
organization, was a valuable work," said ex-Governor
Seymour. "It treated of subjects but little understood
and cared for at that time. Late events have shown
their value. I should be happy to learn that some
suitable mark of public appreciation is made by the
Governor or Legislature."

The letter of Brevet Major-General S. W. Crawford,
who participated in thirty battles during the war, was
as follows: "While so many persons in various sections
of the country have been and are receiving from the
General or State Governments a recognition of their
services, civil or military, I would respectfully call the
attention of your Excellency to the case of Brigadier-
General J. Watts de Peyster, N. Y. S. M. I would urge
upon your Excellency that this officer be promoted to
the rank of Major-General, either in full or by brevet.

"The exceedingly valuable contributions to the Militia
organization of the State, as well as the activity and zeal
at all times shown by General de Peyster in promoting
the efficiency and elevating the standard of the citizen
soldier, as well as also in inducing and maintaining
among a large influential class an active interest in
military subjects, should be met by a suitable reward
from his State. There is no one more deserving, no one
more devotedly patriotic, no one who has done so much,
and I would respectfully recommend to your Excellency
the immediate promotion of this officer as eminently due
him. State military affairs have become of the highest
importance, and it is but just that this prominent citizen
of New York should be placed by rank in a position
where, when his services may be necessary, they may be
most efficiently and justly rendered."

We also quote from the letter of George W. Matsell,
ex-Chief of the New York Police, under whom the City,
afterward known as the Metropolitan Police, was organized and rendered effective. "I have been acquainted
with General de Peyster for many years," he wrote.

"While I was Chief of Police he was always busy doing all he could to assist in a thorough organization of the protective forces, especially in regard to systems in connection with the Fire Department and Fire Escapes. The result of one of his Reports and experiments, in connection, a beautiful Fire Escape, he had constructed at his own expense and presented to the Police Headquarters. It was tested by me, and approved. His views were always practical and useful."

The letters of the two Wainwrights, who had served as militia officers under General de Peyster, and afterwards distinguished themselves in the service of the Union, are of especial interest. Brevet Brigadier-General C. S. Wainwright wrote, in part, as follows:

"During the seven years—from 1849 to 1856—I was intimately connected with General de Peyster in the Militia, and know that he gave almost his whole time during that period, and expended several thousand dollars of his own property, in his endeavors to improve and place upon a proper footing the Militia of our own district (Duchess and Columbia Counties), as also of the whole State. As an organizer, I have met with but few men who are General de Peyster's equal.

"His extended reading and laborious research on military subjects have enabled him to accumulate an amount of information such as I have seldom found in an extended acquaintance among the highest military men of our country. While his thorough acquaintance with the National Guard organizations of Europe, acquired during a visit to those countries for the express purpose of examining into those systems, fits him, perhaps better than any other man in the State, to advise and superintend the placing of our own National Guard on such a basis as will make it really efficient and an honor to the State."

The letter of Colonel William P. Wainwright was addressed to General de Peyster. "Understanding that your friends propose making application for some acknowledgment of your services in forming our soldiers for the late war," he writes, "I am desirous of making what little effort I can toward procuring you so well deserved an honor, and therefore forward this for such use as your friends may think fit to make of it.

"No one knows better, or perhaps so well as I, what you have attempted and what you have done for the Militia. Your report on the Militia Systems of Europe will long be a mine of information for those who endeavor to really benefit our own. These reports were grounded on observations and inquiries made in Europe during a tour, which, although undertaken by the authority of the Governor of New York, was conducted at your own expense, and which was apparently devoted almost solely to obtaining material for them.

"For several years you edited and supported a periodical devoted entirely to military subjects, and distributed it gratis, with the sole object of improving the Militia. There was no one perhaps better qualified to judge of the merit of your labors than our lamented friend, General Philip Kearny. I know that he esteemed them highly. I remember his sending an orderly several miles to me in order to borrow a copy of the *Eclaireur,* for the purpose, as he wrote, of consulting one of your articles.

"Your labors in your own Militia command (a Brigade in Duchess and Columbia Counties) were for years incessant. In connection with it, you maintained and horsed a section of artillery, the practice of which, both in manœuvring and firing, was more real than any I had seen out of the Regular Army, before the war actually began. At the same time, your drills of all kinds were devoid of fatigue for show, but gave the men a true, even if unpleasant, idea of what was necessary to prepare them for the field. Many who then complained would probably now acknowledge that yours was the way to form soldiers.

"To the above claims for some token of appreciation may be added your little pamphlet on 'Winter Campaigns,' which, when viewed in the light of what has been done since its publication, might well have been,

if it was not, among the influences which brought about
a more determined conduct of the war.

"I have always regretted that your health prevented
your beginning at those lower commissions which were
the only stepping stones for your obtaining a position
in which you might have been of service in the field."

Colonel W. C. Church wrote to Governor Fenton from
the office of the United States Army and Navy Journal.
"I have read letters from Generals Rosecrans, Hooker
and Warren commending to your notice the service General J. Watts de Peyster has rendered in diffusing correct
military information," he said, "and I take great pleasure
in endorsing what they say in that regard. General de
Peyster has contributed many articles to this journal
during the past two years, and I know they have been
esteemed of great value for the correct military principles
they have presented. He is a gentleman whose information on military subjects is remarkably accurate, as well
as extensive, and whose zeal in the pursuit of military
studies has been active and constant. I do not need to
refer you to the service General de Peyster has done the
State, in the official position of Adjutant-General, as well
as by his published reports and other works. With this
you are undoubtedly familiar, and are aware of the
evidence it affords of careful study and thorough appreciation of the subjects relating to our military
establishment."

"I have known General de Peyster for over sixteen
years," wrote Captain W. W. Tompkins. "I first taught
him artillery tactics and always considered him one of
my best pupils. Previously he had given his attention
solely to infantry. No officer in the Militia was superior
to him in military knowledge. He wrote a great deal
for my paper—the *United Service Journal*—in 1850.
Since then I have known the efforts he made for the
improvement of the organization of our State troops,
and how much New York owes to him. As one of the
most experienced instructors of military exercises in the
country, I feel satisfied that General de Peyster will do

credit and justice to a Major-General's commission, and
a Division command, or any office connected with military
organization or government."

The letter of Captain Frederic Lahrbush to Governor
Fenton, of peculiar interest because of the advanced age
of the writer, bears tribute to the critical knowledge of
campaigns, in which the writer had participated, possessed
by General de Peyster. "On the 9th of March I will be
one hundred years old," he begins. "Seventy-three years
ago I was a soldier in active service in Holland. The
Duke of Wellington was a Major in the same army. I
afterwards served under him when he was Commander-
in-Chief in Spain. I won his honorary mention for
Busaco, and won a medal or cross for Talavara, inscribed
also for Vimiera and Busaco. I served likewise under
the able Lord Cornwallis in Ireland. I have drank
healths with Blucher, and also knew many Russian, Prussian and French military celebrities. I was at Jena
with the Prussian Court, where Napoleon won his greatest
tactical victory. I stood on the shore and saw Napoleon at
the height of his power and glory on the Raft, in the
Niemen, when he dictated laws to Europe; and I guarded
him in the depth of his abasement on the Island of St.
Helena, in the Atlantic, when Europe made laws for his
hourly government, as their captive.

"My memory is perfect, and the details of military
history in which I was an actor are as familiar to me
as those of the past few years.

"I have known General de Peyster for several years.
We have critically discussed the campaigns in which I
was present, and I have often remarked to others that
he was as intimately acquainted with those campaigns,
their battles and the movements of the opposite armies,
and the cause of their successes and defeats, as if he
had been present in the engagement we were discussing.

"As an officer of the highest theoretical strategical
ability, I would consider him fit for any position demand-
ing research and the application of the great rules and
principles of war."

We also give two letters written at the time by General
de Peyster to Captain Bullard, subsequently Major.   In
the first he says: "As you are aware, some of my friends
have suggested that there should be some recognition of
my military labors by the State; after urging, by their
advice I have collected the necessary papers to establish
the facts.   The continued ill-health of a near relative
precludes any chance of my leaving the city, and, therefore, I am compelled to leave the matter to you and
accept your kind offer of attending to it.

"I hand you herewith a collection of letters, for each
one of which, I think, I could furnish a score of equal
value if I had time to have them copied.   That my labors
are not better known or more apparent to the public
arises from the fact that they were almost entirely office-
work, or experiments not open to the public.   A large
portion of my work was done abroad, and I am willing
to base my claim upon my printed works, especially my
Reports and military biographies.   Medals from the King
of Sweden, a long, critical pamphlet and notice in
Holland, my election as member of one of the first
scientific societies of Europe, and numerous letters, speak
sufficiently for themselves in my favor.

"Lieutenant-General Cust, one of the best military
historians living, pays the highest compliment to my
work on the Thirty Years' War.   I have furnished more
contributions to the military papers published in New
York than any other person that I know of, and, as yet,
my positions have never been assailed with success.   In
arms, armament, uniforms, etc., I was years ahead of
the time, and I have lived to see almost every suggestion
I made carried into effect.   The last adoption, whose
suggestion I made, was a paid Fire Department with
steam fire-engines.   Sickness prevented my forcing the
Government to give me a position in the field, during
the past war, but I begged for any position which my
health would permit me to fill.   This I can prove, if
necessary.

"Perhaps it might be well to state that for over twenty

years my health has been such as to render the utmost
care necessary, and it is only within the past six months
that I have been able to use the stimulants necessary to
enable me to work—not when I wish, but at appropriate
times.

"The officer who knew me best and was cognizant of
my labors was my cousin, Major-General Kearny. Were
he alive it would be scarcely necessary to do more than
to refer to him.

"In Europe, the officer with whom I came most in
contact and who afforded me the greatest facilities was
Lieutenant-General La Mọrmora, who perished in the
Crimea.

"There are many officers in this State, who estimated
my work, to whom I would refer were additional proof
necessary. There are others again, with sounding titles,
who never did anything themselves, and never could
appreciate anything useful which others did.

"To my printed works, to my communications to the
papers, to my Reports, to my letters, I would refer His
Excellency, the Governor, and if I could expect anyone
to examine so many publications, my best witness would
be the results.

"The execution done by the Napoleon guns upon the
Rebels is one of the loudest and best witnesses I have had,
for I am not aware that anyone in this country translated
the work upon these guns or printed it before I did.

"This information, as well as much more, was printed
and distributed at my own expense.

"My only offence, if such be an offence, was being in
advance of the time, and I experienced the same fate as
many abler men in Europe to whom the military institutions and organizations which now rule and flourish can
be traced.

"My sole desire was to build up efficient systems, not
popular ones. Efficiency and popularity seldom go
together, and our people have scarcely learned from this
war the vast significance of *must,* and the force of discipline and economy. Had my views been carried out, in

JOHN WATTS DE PEYSTER
In 1863